AP® U.S. GOVERNMENT & POLITICS

2014

Kaplan offers resources and options to help you prepare for the PSAT, SAT, ACT, AP exams, and other high-stakes exams. Go to www.kaptest.com or scan this code below with your phone (you will need to download a QR code reader) for free events and promotions.

snap.vu/m87n

AP® U.S. GOVERNMENT & POLITICS

2014

Ulrich Kleinschmidt

William L. Brown Jr.

KAPLAN

PUBLISHING

New York

© 2013 by Kaplan, Inc.

Published by Kaplan Publishing, a division of Kaplan, Inc.

395 Hudson Street

New York, NY 10014

Printed in the United States of America

10 9 8 7 6 5 4 3 2

ISBN 13: 978-1-61865-252-2

TABLE OF CONTENTS

PART THREE: AP U.S. GOVERNMENT & POLITICS REVIEW

PART FOUR: PRACTICE TESTS

PART FIVE: AP U.S. GOVERNMENT & POLITICS RESOURCES

ABOUT THE AUTHORS

Ulrich Kleinschmidt has been teaching AP U.S. Government & Politics since the early 1990s. He also teaches AP Economics and is the Social Studies Department Chairperson at I. H. Kempner High School in Sugar Land, Texas, a suburb in the greater Houston area. He has been a national grader of the AP U.S. Government & Politics examination since 1999. He also has presented economics seminars for the College Board and has become a national trainer for the AP program.

William L. Brown Jr. began teaching AP U.S. Government & Politics in 1990. He also taught American history and sociology at Eureka High School in Eureka, Missouri, a suburb of St. Louis. He has been a national grader of the AP U.S. Government & Politics examination since 1995 and a table leader since 1999.

KAPLAN PANEL OF AP EXPERTS

Congratulations—you have chosen Kaplan to help you get a top score on your AP exam.

Kaplan understands your goals and what you're up against—achieving college credit and conquering a tough test—while participating in everything else that high school has to offer.

You expect realistic practice; authoritative advice; and accurate, up-to-the-minute information on the test. And that's exactly what you'll find in this book, as well as every other in the AP series. To help you (and us!) reach these goals, we have sought out leaders in the AP community. Allow us to introduce our experts.

AP U.S. GOVERNMENT & POLITICS EXPERTS

Chuck Brownson teaches AP U.S. Government and Politics and AP Economics at Stephen F. Austin High School in Sugar Land, Texas. He is currently a graduate student working on his master's degree in education at the University of Lamar. He has been teaching AP U.S. Government and Politics and AP Economics classes since 2004. He was a reader for the AP U.S. Government exam in 2007.

Melissa Janecek started teaching AP U.S. Government & Politics in 2002 and has taught at High School in Navasota, Texas, and George Bush High School in Richmond, Texas. She has taught at East Bernard High School in East Bernard, Texas, since 2008 and has been an adjunct professor teaching U.S. Government and Politics for Wharton County Junior College since 2009. She has also taught U.S. Government & Politics at North Harris Montgomery County College District. She served as a reader for the AP U.S. Government and Politics exam from 2003 until 2006.

Anthony "Tony" Jones has taught AP courses for the past 10 years, including AP U.S. History, AP European History, and AP World History. He has taught at Houston County High in Warner Robins, Georgia, and Rutland High School in Macon, Georgia. He is a member of the World History Association and the National Council for Social Studies. He is a table leader and reader for the AP World History exam. Additionally, he has been a presenter on integrating technology into the social studies and AP classroom at several conferences.

Part One

THE BASICS

CHAPTER 1: INSIDE THE AP U.S. GOVERNMENT & POLITICS EXAM

This chapter will introduce the basics of the AP U.S. Government & Politics exam format: topics covered on the exam, patterns of previous tests, how your exam will be scored, and registration issues. This guide will help you get started on your approach to study and will help you decide which basic themes to target.

OVERVIEW OF THE TEST STRUCTURE

Most universities use students' scores on the AP U.S. Government & Politics exam to give credit for a freshman-level, three-credit, introductory course. It is considered the equivalent of a university course final examination.

The College Board's test has two major parts: a multiple-choice section and a free-response section. Each section is worth 50 percent of your total score.

Section	Number of Questions	Time Allowed
1	60 (five choices: A to E)	45 minutes (¾ of a minute per question)
2	4 (each a free-response)	1 hour, 40 minutes (25 minutes per question)

The time constraints of this exam are a challenge. Successful students are prepared to recognize key terms and meanings quickly. National graders often note some test-taker fatigue by the time the third and fourth free-response questions are addressed. If you gain a comfort level with the subject vocabulary and train yourself to save time on the free-response questions, you will be ahead of the game.

TOPICS COVERED ON THE AP U.S. GOVERNMENT & POLITICS EXAM

The current structure of the multiple-choice topics can be used as a general guide for study of the different course units. The number of questions per topic are set about two years before the exam is administered, so the 2010 exam was assembled between 2007 and 2008. Percentage guides given by College Board are approximates only. At the time of this publication, the 2010 course guide was the most recent version available. The College Board has not announced any significant changes in this year's exam.

Basic Topics	General Areas within the Topics	Percent of Exam	Approximate # of Questions
1. Constitutional Underpinnings	A. Formulation and Adoption B. Adoption C. Federalism D. Democratic Government	5–15%	3 to 9 questions
2. Political Beliefs and Behaviors	A. Citizens' Beliefs B. Citizens' Learning C. Public Opinion D. Voting and Political Participation E. Differences in Beliefs and Behaviors	10–20%	6 to 12 questions
3. Political Parties, Interest Groups, and the Mass Media	A. Parties and Elections: Functions, Organization, Development, Effects, Electoral Laws and Systems B. Interest Groups and PACs: Interests Represented, Activities, Effects, Characteristics, and Roles C. The Mass Media: Functions and Structure, Impacts	10–20%	6 to 12 questions
4. Institutions: Congress, Presidency, Bureaucracy, Federal Courts	A. Major Formal and Informal Powers B. Relationships Among and Balances of Power C. Linkages: Public Opinions and Voters, Interest Groups, Political Parties, Media, and Subnational Governments	35–45%	21 to 27 questions
5. Public Policy	A. Policy Making in the Federal System B. Formation of Agendas C. Role of Institutions in Enactment D. Role of Bureaucracy and Courts in Policy Implementation E. Linkages: Institutions and Federalism, Political Parties, Interest Groups, Public Opinion, Elections, and Policy Networks	5–15%	3 to 9 questions
6. Civil Rights and Civil Liberties	A. Development of Rights and Liberties by Judicial Interpretation B. Substantive Rights and Liberties C. Impact of the 14th Amendment	5–15%	3 to 6 questions

FREE-RESPONSE QUESTIONS: TOPICS AND EXPECTATIONS

The test structure was revised in 1998 to include four free-response questions. Students are asked to answer all four of the questions, unlike earlier tests that allowed students to select questions from several choices. The following table shows what topics have been selected since 1998.

1998: 1	Primaries and Conventions	Four effects of change: primaries and conventions
1998: 2	Bill of Rights and the 14th Amendment	Incorporation cases: *Gitlow* or *Wolf* or *Gideon*
1998: 3	War Powers, Impoundment	Describe and evaluate the two acts
1998: 4	Low Voter Turnout	Demographics, three institutional obstacles
1999: 1	Candidates and the Media	Two ways that the media affects candidates, ways media are used
1999: 2	Interest Groups and Policy	ID groups, group resources, characteristics
1999: 3	Oversight of Bureaucracy	Two methods of oversight, oversight explanations
1999: 4	Charts: Federal Budget	Mandatory, discretionary, entitlement, changes
2000: 1	Constitution versus Articles	Three problems of articles, policy tensions
2000: 2	Court "Above Politics"?	Three nominee characteristics, two ways of influence
2000: 3	Map: 1992, 1996 Votes	Regions for Dems or GOP, explain factors
2000: 4	Campaign Finance Reform?	Obstacles: select *Buckley*, soft money, incumbency
2001: 1	Formal and Informal Changes	Identify two formal and two informal, state why the changes were made
2001: 2	Chart: Incumbent Reelection	Patterns of elections, factors, consequences
2001: 3	Ratification of 14th Amendment	Significance in cases, due process
2001: 4	Enact Public Policy	Difficult: divided government, weak parties
2002: 1	Divided Government	Problems, ways the president can overcome this
2002: 2	Chart: Benefits for Children and Seniors	Changes in help, relevant factors, effects
2002: 3	Institutions and Minorities	Federalism, parties, electoral system
2002: 4	Lower Voter Turnout	Two factors in turnout, why is turnout higher in presidential elections?
2003: 1	Presidential Approval Ratings	Two factors (positive or negative) in approval of president and why
2003: 2	Nonvoting Participation	Two forms of participation in government other than voting, their advantages

(continued on next page)

2003: 3	Graph of Federal and State Employment	Trends, block grants, mandates
2003: 4	Leaders and Committees	Specialization, reciprocity, logrolling, parties
2004: 1	Presidential Powers: Formal and Informal	Two formal powers and two informal, advantages
2004: 2	Interest Group Techniques	Litigation, contributions, grassroots, groups
2004: 3	Minor Parties	Obstacles to third parties, contributions of third parties
2004: 4	Decline: Confidence in Government	Divided government and decline in confidence in government, the costs, and why it occurs
2005: 1	Independent Courts	Two ways in which the courts are insulated, two ways in which they are not
2005: 2	Change: Federal Government versus the States	Tax and spend, elastic clause, commerce, acts
2005: 3	Federal Protection from States	Selective incorporation, cases that show federal protection
2005: 4	Campaign Finance Reform	Soft money, independent spending, limits on money
2006: 1	Interest Groups, Political Parties: Goals and Support Connections	Define goals of two groups, describe two ways interest groups support parties, describe two ways interest groups are helped
2006: 2	Social Security Receipts, Spending, Reserves Chart	Define entitlements, source of Social Security, threats to Social Security, demographic trends
2006: 3	Congress, President, Agency Powers to Make Policy	Why did Congress give agencies power to execute laws? Select agency and identify policy-making powers. Congress's checks?
2006: 4	Bicameral Legislature of House and Senate	Why two chambers? Unique powers of House and Senate, explain
2007: 1	Electoral College	Explain winner-take-all system
2007: 2	First Amendment, Freedom of Religion	Select a case, describe Supreme Court's decision
2007: 3	War Powers Resolution	Describe two provisions of War Powers Resolution, powers that Congress has
2007: 4	Federal System	Define federalism, how it has increased power of state and federal government

2008: 1	Congressional Reappointment, Redistricting	Define and explain; two goals of gerrymandering; Supreme Court limits on redistricting
2008: 2	Domestic Policymaking	Powers and limits of the president on domestic policymaking
2008: 3	Fiscal Policy, Monetary Policy	Define, describe how set by branches, explain Federal Reserve Board
2008: 4	Fifteenth Amendment	Explain increase in African American voter turnout since 1960s
2009: 1	Majority Rule	Explain how U.S. Government limits majority rule and how the U.S. has become a more democratic system
2009: 2	Voter Turnout	Demographics; requirements that impede voting; links beyond voting
2009: 3	Majority Party	Advantages of majority party and its effect on lawmaking
2009: 4	Media and Agenda Setting	Policy agenda, media coverage, advantages of president over Congress, implications
2010: 1	Interest Groups	Explain rights and limits of interest groups, how they operate
2010: 2	Federal Bureaucracy	Merit system, bureaucratic independence, Congressional limitations
2010: 3	Southern State Partisanship	Identify, explain partisan shift in the South since 1940; explain partisan shifts in three other groups
2010: 4	Limited Government	National executive, Bill of Rights limitations, states' rights
2011: 1	Supreme Court	Judicial review, writ of certiorari, state decisis, judicial
2011: 2	Public Opinion Polls	Valid polls, influences of polls, factors limiting public
2011: 3	National Conventions	Primaries, caucuses winner-take-all, superdelegates, nomination strategy versus election strategy
2011: 4	Balance of Power	How presidential powers are affected by Congress and vice versa

As noted, all major topics of the government course are represented in recent free-response selections. The questions require that students understand how the U.S. government balances the needs of many different groups: how it changes, how citizens participate, and how power is shared. As will be discussed in much greater detail later, the free-response section also includes the key instructions to "describe" and "explain" each section of each question. This is where well-prepared students will gain critical exam points.

HOW THE EXAM IS SCORED

Because section 1 has 60 questions and 60 possible points, the free-response questions are also converted to a possible 60 points, making each section worth 50 percent of the final score.

MULTIPLE-CHOICE SCORING RULES

Scores are based on the number of questions answered correctly. **There is no penalty for incorrect answers.** No points are awarded for unanswered questions. Therefore, you should answer every question, even if you have to guess.

FREE-RESPONSE SCORING RULES

Each of the four questions is graded using a "rubric" point system. Each question may be worth a different number of possible rubric points. Recent free-response questions have been worth 6 to 7 points each. It is usually very easy to determine the number of rubric points that a question is worth by examining the structure of the question and the number of points that need to be addressed in the answer. Questions are written with this in mind. An example would be a question with two parts, listed A and B. In part A, the student would be asked to "identify" and "explain" a particular item. In part B, the instructions to "identify" and "explain" might be repeated. The student and the grader will immediately look for 4 points in the answer, one for the identification and one for the explanation of each A and B. The total score for the question would depend on how many of the points asked in the question have been adequately addressed in the response. In this example, the student could score up to 4 rubric points for his or her response.

Regardless of the individual points set for each free-response question, the four questions are converted to a total of 60 points, or 50 percent of the test.

COMPOSITE SCORING RULES

The most important scoring issue to note is that each year's test scores are "relative" to national results of that year. There is no set number of points that results in a passing score. The College Board gives each student a final score of 1 through 5, with 5 being the highest. The national office uses careful sets of statistics to ensure that the appropriate number of students receive scores that correctly identify the levels of mastery appropriate for the universities. If a test is particularly difficult in a given year and overall raw scores are down, the number of 5s, etc., continues to be similar to that of past years.

SCORING RESULTS, 2009

Number of Students (Total = 160,315)	Exam's Final Score (College Board Description)	Percent of Total
19,486	5 (Extremely Well Qualified)	12.2
25,964	4 (Well Qualified)	16.2
40,085	3 (Qualified)	25.0
40,170	2 (Possibly Qualified)	25.1
34,610	1 (No Recommendation)	21.6

Fifty percent of students who took the exam in 2009 received at least a 3. Many universities will extend some sort of class credit for scores of 3 and above. Almost all universities accept scores of 4 and 5, and about 25 percent of all students qualify in that range.

Many students and teachers ask what kind of raw score will result in a desirable final score. Each year's scores differ based on the relative difficulty of the questions. Usually, a raw score of over 70 percent will translate into a 5. A composite score above 60 percent is within the usual range of 4s. The test is challenging but manageable. A high final score can be achieved through preparation.

RECEIVING SCORES

AP Grade Reports are sent to students' homes, high schools, and requested universities in July. Students may also call for scores, but there is a fee for this service. Check the College Board website for test dates and fee information.

REGISTRATION AND FEES

To register for the exam, contact your guidance counselor or AP Coordinator. If your school does not administer the AP exam, contact the College Board for a listing of schools that do. Registration occurs in the spring; most schools complete the paperwork in March. At the time of this printing, the fee for an exam is $89 within the United States, and $117 at schools and testing centers outside of the United States. Many possible deductions are available. For those qualified with acute financial need, the College Board offers a $28 credit. In addition, most states offer exam subsidies to cover all or part of the remaining cost for eligible students. To learn about other sources of financial aid, contact your AP Coordinator.

ADDITIONAL RESOURCES

For more information on the AP Program and the U.S. Government & Politics exam, contact the following:

AP Services
P.O. Box 6671
Princeton, NJ 08541-6671
Phone: 609-771-7300 or 888-225-5427
Email: apexams@info.collegeboard.org
Website: collegeboard.com/apc/Controller.jpf

CHAPTER 2: STRATEGIES FOR SUCCESS: IT'S NOT ALWAYS HOW MUCH YOU KNOW

INTRODUCTION

As noted in the first chapter, the AP U.S. Government & Politics exam is divided into two major parts of equal value: the multiple-choice section of 60 questions and the free-response section of 4 questions. Each correct multiple-choice question earns a point toward the maximum of 60 raw score points for that section. Each correct free-response question is worth 12.5 percent of the total score but is graded on a rubric unique to each question.

The College Board keeps statistics on the relationship between high and low scores on the multiple-choice questions and free-response sections. It is often reported that there is a strong correlation between the two parts of the exam. A student who earns high scores on the multiple-choice part often tends to earn a larger number of free-response points as well. On the other hand, it is unusual that a student who does a poor job on the multiple-choice section rescues his or her total score with superior free-response answers.

What does this mean for you? You need to balance your study time and preparation skills. The same strengths that will help you with the first part of the exam will serve you well in the second. What strengths do successful students bring to the AP U.S. Government & Politics exam? For this test, the keys are vocabulary, the ability to make connections, and an understanding of the test expectations.

GENERAL TEST-TAKING STRATEGIES

Most students who take this exam are taking the AP class at their school. Many are also signed up for several other AP courses and may be taking multiple exams in May. Be realistic with your choices and your time. These are university-level exams on which you can do very well, but you'll need extra preparation. Attend any study sessions that your teachers provide. Use this manual as much as possible. Focus on the unique language of the subject. Watch for extensions of logic and questions that

CLEAR YOUR HEAD

Avoid interference from other subjects by making U.S. Government the one you study right before you go to sleep.

go beyond simple identifications. Divide your time into manageable units and don't burn out. Be sure to rest before the exam.

HOW THIS BOOK CAN HELP

Kaplan's *AP U.S. Government & Politics* contains precisely the information you will need to do well on the test. There's nothing extra in here to waste your time: no pointless review of material you won't be tested on, no rah-rah speeches—just the most effective test preparation tools available.

1. **Test strategies geared specifically to the AP U.S. Government & Politics exam.** Many books give the same talk about process of elimination that's been used for every standardized test given in the past 20 years. We're going to talk about process of elimination as it applies to the AP U.S. Government & Politics exam and only to the AP U.S. Government & Politics exam. There are several skills and general strategies that work for this particular test, and these will be covered in the next two sections.

2. **A well-crafted review of all the relevant subjects.** The best test-taking strategies alone won't get you a good score. As its core, this AP exam covers a wide range of topics, and learning these topics is necessary. However, chances are good you're already familiar with these subjects, so an exhaustive review is not needed. In fact, it would be a waste of your time. No one wants that, so we've tailored our review section to focus on how the relevant topics typically appear on the exam and what you need to know to answer the questions correctly. If a topic doesn't come up on the AP U.S. Government & Politics exam, we don't cover it. If it appears on the test, we'll provide you with the facts you need to navigate the problem safely.

3. **Two full-length practice tests to help you identify your strengths and weaknesses.** Few things are better than experience when it comes to standardized testing. Taking these practice AP exams gives you an idea of what it's like to answer government and politics questions under test conditions. Granted, that may not be a fun experience, but it is a helpful one. Practice exams give you the opportunity to find out what areas are your strongest and what topics you should spend some additional time studying. And the best part is that it doesn't count! Mistakes you make on our practice exams are mistakes you won't make on the real test.

These three points describe the general outline of this book: strategies, review, and then practice. This chapter will help you learn some specific skills you can use on the AP U.S. Government & Politics exam.

HOW TO APPROACH THE MULTIPLE-CHOICE QUESTIONS

Remember, there will always be five answer choices, and you have only 45 minutes to complete 60 questions. It is critical to recognize quickly any key words or terms in the question. Don't rush your reading of the question, because one important word may be the key to a correct response.

The following table is a list of such words from recently released multiple-choice questions.

In the released test, there were 10 questions (16.7 percent) with the key word *best* in the question. There were another 10 questions (16.7 percent) with a phrase including the word *most*. A third of the multiple-choice test section was on recognizing trends. There were also six charts, graphs, or cartoons that required students to interpret, statistics, or trends.

KEY MULTIPLE-CHOICE WORDS

Terms Used	Meaning/Hints
best	This is used in the general instructions and hints that some answer choices may be close to correct but are not the "most" correct.
best describes *or* best illustrates *or* best supports *or* best explains	You should know historic patterns or watch for significant data.
most *or* most likely *or* most important *or* most substantially	Same as above.
clear evidence	Watch for specific patterns and overwhelming evidence.
generally true	Watch out for choices that are not always, but are generally, true.
NOT *or* EXCEPT	A negative question is often used, also with the term *least* or the phrase *least likely*.
usually	These questions will be similar in style to "best" questions.
never, always, none, all	Extreme words; watch out for absolute terms.

TIME MANAGEMENT AND SCORING

The multiple-choice section of the test is no longer penalty scored. Incorrect answers are no longer deducted from your score, so you will benefit from guessing. Every correct answer adds to your score. No points are awarded for unanswered questions. Therefore, you should answer every question, even if you have to guess. As with other multiple-choice tests, you'll increase your chances of guessing correctly if you can eliminate a few wrong choices.

CHANGE IS GOOD

Don't be afraid to change your answer to a multiple-choice question. If you don't feel confident about your answer, trust your instincts and go back to it if time allows.

PICK YOUR BATTLES

If a question deals with a topic you *know* is one of your weak spots, don't waste valuable time reviewing the question more than twice. Make a guess and move on.

Pace yourself. You have 45 minutes to complete 60 questions. You should spend no more than 45 seconds on any single question. As you're reading a question try to predict the answer, keeping in mind any key words such as "least likely" or "best." Then try to eliminate at least two answer choices that are out of the scope of the question and take your best guess anyway. If you have no idea what the answer is and cannot eliminate any of the answer choices, guess anyway. The no-penalty scoring makes this a wise decision. Go through the easy questions first, answer as many of them as possible, and get all the easy points quickly. Don't get caught running out of time before answering the easy questions. After going through all of the easier questions first, go back during the remaining time and tackle the questions about which you have the most doubts.

HOW TO APPROACH THE FREE-RESPONSE QUESTIONS

As national graders, we've noticed that students make the same kinds of mistakes year after year. We've also observed the ways successful students earn points. One of the biggest issues is the number of questions answered. Even though students have equal amounts of time available for the four free-response questions, they tend to make one of two mistakes: Either they spend too much time on one question, or they get tired after three good answers and essentially skip a final answer. The students who are high scorers are careful to give equal time and effort to all of the questions. These students do so with a simple strategy. First, they make a brief outline of each question that focuses on the number of rubric points suggested by the question. Successful students also label their outlines to match the rubric. They include key words and phrases in the outline that reflect the question. Once they've done this for all four questions, they use these outlines to create responses that include well-written sentences and clear explanations.

Remember, this section is called a "free-response" section. Many students immediately focus on writing a five-paragraph essay, with introduction, body, and conclusion. This is not needed, or even desired, on this exam. Well-written sentences and clear explanations will help the grader recognize that you have mastered the material. However, introductions that do not address the question or that merely restate the question are simply a waste of your time. You gain no points for these and only lose time. Concluding paragraphs that rephrase all of the points already made are equally useless.

Perhaps the most egregious error is the response that summarizes the topic of the question but never directly answers the question. Wonderfully written essays have been produced that hint all around the topic but never get to the specific content needed to score points. Remember, the questions are graded on a rubric point system, and graders can only give points if the student provides the information for which the question specifically asks. For an example, see the sample question described later in this section.

The answers to free-response questions must identify, describe, or explain what the question asks. If the question requires one or two examples, only give the number requested. If the question requires that a link between sections be made, make that link.

The following list restates the approach to free-response questions previously described. This strategy is important enough, and successful enough, to warrant repetition.

STEPS TO ANSWERING THE FREE-RESPONSE QUESTIONS

1. Make an outline for each section of each question. (See the following sample.)

2. Fill in all the key words and concepts you immediately remember for all parts of your outline. Do this for all four questions.

3. Answer each question, in well-presented but concise sentences, using the key terms and topics.

4. Check to see if you not only "listed" and "identified" but also "described" and "explained" as needed.

5. Don't waste time rephrasing the question in an introduction.

6. Don't waste time presenting a conclusion paragraph that restates the items you have already completed. Use the time to be thorough on all four questions.

SAMPLE QUESTION AND STRATEGIES

The following question appears on the College Board website as a released question from 2006.

> Question #1:
>
> While interest groups and political parties each play a significant role in the United States political system, they differ in their fundamental goals.
>
> (A) Identify the fundamental goal of interest groups in the political process.
>
> (B) Identify the fundamental goal of major political parties in the political process.
>
> (C) Describe two different ways by which interest groups support the fundamental goal of **political parties** in the political process.
>
> (D) For one of the forms of support you described in (C), explain two different ways in which that form of support helps **interest groups** to achieve their fundamental goal in the political process.

Note that the question asks for three levels of answers: identify, describe, and explain. A description must go beyond a mere listing, and the question is specific in the ways the interest groups and parties must be connected. An explanation must go to the level of showing "how and why."

You must first decipher the number of points expected. An outline approach would address this quickly and help the grader immensely in finding your points. Here is a sample of a possible outline:

(A) 1 point: Give the fundamental goal of interest groups. Give only one goal. *Note: Students who listed more than one fundamental goal lost this point.*

(B) 1 point: Give the fundamental goal of political parties. Give only one goal. *Note: Students who listed more than one fundamental goal also lost this point.*

(C) 2 points: Describe how interest groups support the party goal in two ways. Make sure the interest groups' support you describe actually supports the "fundamental" goal of political parties you gave in (B).

(D) 2 points: Select one of the goals you described in (C) and explain how interest groups support the fundamental goal of political parties that you identified in part (B). Be sure that the two ways you describe actually support the fundamental goal you identified. *Note: One point is earned for each way interest groups support the political party fundamental goal. No additional points are given for additional ways. Make sure that you focus on one of your descriptions from (C). Students who used both methods from (C) and gave one explanation for each did not receive the second point.*

Without tackling all the possible correct answers, a plan has been formed for receiving maximum credit. You now know what to answer and how to structure the answer with the correct connections to include. This outline also shows that the rubric will include 6 points. The command to "explain" in part (D) is very important; it is the key to achieving a high score. If you start with such an outline, you will not forget to answer any section, you will organize your thoughts, you will find the key connections, and you will have time to fully answer the question.

STRESS MANAGEMENT

You can beat anxiety the same way you can beat the AP U.S. Government & Politics exam—by knowing what to expect beforehand and developing strategies to deal with it.

DON'T STRESS

Remember, if you write good responses and get ¾ of the multiple-choice questions, you will get a high score on the exam. Don't worry about missing a few multiple-choice questions along the way.

SOURCES OF STRESS

In the space provided, write down your sources of test-related stress. The idea is to pin down any sources of anxiety so you can deal with them one by one. We have provided common examples—feel free to use them and any others that apply to you.

- I always freeze up on tests.

- I'm nervous about the domestic policy development section (and/or the legislative branch section, the political beliefs and behaviors section, etc.).

- I need a good/great score to get into my first-choice college.

- My older brother/sister/best friend/girlfriend/boyfriend did really well. I must match that score or do better.

- My parents, who are paying for school, will be disappointed if I don't do well.

- I'm afraid of losing my focus and concentration.

- I'm afraid I'm not spending enough time preparing.

- I study like crazy, but nothing seems to stick in my mind.

- I always run out of time and get panicky.

MY SOURCES OF STRESS

_____

_____

_____

_____

_____

Read through the list you made. Cross out things or add things. Now rewrite the list in order of most stressful to least stressful.

My Sources of Stress, in Order

_____

_____

_____

_____

_____

_____

Chances are, the top of the list is a fairly accurate description of exactly how you react to test anxiety, both physically and mentally. The later items usually describe your fears (disappointing Mom and Dad, looking bad, etc.). Taking care of the major items from the top of the list should go a long way toward relieving overall test anxiety. That's what we'll do next.

STRENGTHS AND WEAKNESSES

Take 60 seconds to list the topics of U.S. government and politics of which you have strong knowledge. They can be general (foreign policy) or specific (the Bill of Rights). Put down as many as you can think of and, if possible, time yourself. Write for the entire time; don't stop writing until you've reached the one-minute stopping point. Go.

Strong Test Subjects

_____

_____

_____

_____

_____

Now take one minute to list topics of this subject at which you're not so good, just plain bad, have failed, or keep failing. Again, keep it to one minute and continue writing until you reach the cutoff. Go.

WEAK TEST SUBJECTS

_____

_____

_____

_____

_____

_____

Taking stock of your assets and liabilities lets you know which areas you don't have to worry about and which ones will demand extra attention and effort. It helps a lot to find out where you need to spend extra effort. We mostly fear what we don't know and are probably afraid to face. You can feel more confident when you know you're actively strengthening your chances of earning a higher score.

Now, go back to the list of your strengths and expand on it for two minutes. Take the general items on that first list and make them more specific; take the specific items and expand them into more general conclusions. Naturally, if anything new comes to mind, jot it down. Focus all of your attention and effort on your strengths. Don't underestimate yourself or your abilities. Give yourself full credit. At the same time, don't list strengths you don't really have; you'll only be fooling yourself.

Expanding from general to specific might go as follows. If you listed "domestic policy" as a broad topic in which you feel strong, you would then narrow your focus to include areas of this subject about which you are particularly knowledgeable. Your areas of strength might include regulatory policies, grant programs, and so on. Whatever topics you know well go on your expanded strengths list. OK. Check your starting time. Go.

STRONG TEST SUBJECTS: AN EXPANDED LIST

_____

_____

_____

_____

_____

After you stop, check your time. Did you find yourself going beyond the two minutes allotted? Did you write down more things than you thought you knew? Is it possible you know more than you've given yourself credit for?

You just took an active step toward helping yourself. Enjoy your increased feelings of confidence and use them when you take the AP U.S. Government & Politics exam.

VISUALIZE

This next group of activities is a follow-up to the listing of your strengths and weaknesses. Sit in a comfortable chair in a quiet setting. If you wear glasses, take them off. Close your eyes and breathe in a deep, satisfying breath of air. Really fill your lungs until your rib cage is fully expanded and you can't take in any more. Then, exhale the air completely. Imagine you're blowing out a candle with your last little puff of air. Do this two or three more times, filling your lungs to their maximum capacity and emptying them totally. Keep your eyes closed, comfortably but not tightly. Let your body sink deeply into the chair as you become even more comfortable.

With your eyes shut, you can notice something very interesting. You're no longer dealing with the worrisome stuff going on in the world around you. Now you can concentrate on what happens inside of you. The more you recognize your own physical reactions to stress and anxiety, the more you can control them. You may not realize it, but you've begun to gain a sense of being in control.

Imagine there are TV screens on the insides of your eyelids. Let images begin to form on those screens. Allow the images to come easily and naturally; don't force them. Visualize a relaxing situation. It might be a special place you've visited before or one you've read about. It can be a fictional location that you create in your imagination, but a real-life memory of a place or situation you know is usually better. Make it as detailed as possible and notice as much as you can.

Stay focused on the images as you sink further into your chair. Breathe easily and naturally. You might have the sensation of stress or tension draining from your muscles and flowing downward, out your feet and away from you.

Take a moment to check how you're feeling. Notice how comfortable you've become. Imagine how much easier it would be if you could take the test feeling this relaxed. You've coupled the images of your special place with sensations of comfort and relaxation. You've also found a way to become relaxed simply by visualizing your own safe, special place.

Next, close your eyes and start remembering a real-life situation in which you did well on a test. If you can't come up with one, remember a situation in which you did something that you were really proud of—a genuine accomplishment. Make the memory as detailed as possible. Think about the sights, the sounds, the smells, even the tastes associated with this experience. Remember how confident you felt as you accomplished your goal. Now start thinking about the AP U.S. Government & Politics exam. Keep your thoughts and feelings in line with that previous, successful experience. Don't make comparisons between them. Just imagine taking the upcoming test with the same feelings of confidence and relaxed control.

This exercise is a great way to bring the test down to earth. You should practice this exercise often, especially when you feel burned out on test preparation. The more you practice it, the more effective the exercise will be for you.

EXERCISE

Whether you enjoy running, walking, biking, aerobics, push-ups, or a pickup basketball game, physical exercise is a very effective way to stimulate both your mind and body and to improve your ability to think and concentrate. Also, sedentary people get less oxygen to their blood and, hence, to their brains than active people. You can watch TV with a little less oxygen; you just can't think as well. Lots of students get out of the habit of regular exercise when they're preparing for the exam.

Any big test is a bit like a race. Finishing the race strongly is just as important as being quick early on. If you can't sustain your energy level for the last sections of the exam, you could blow it. Along with a good diet and adequate sleep, exercise is an important part of keeping yourself ready and thinking clearly for the long haul.

There's another thing that happens when students don't make exercise an integral part of their test preparation. Like any organism in nature, you operate best if all your "systems" are in balance. Studying uses a lot of energy, but it's all mental. When you take a study break, do something active. Take a 5- to 10-minute exercise break for every 50 or 60 minutes that you study. The physical exertion helps keep your mind and body in sync. This way, when you finish studying for the night and go to bed, you won't lie there unable to sleep because your head is tired while your body is still energized.

One warning about exercise: It's not a good idea to exercise vigorously right before you go to bed. This could easily cause sleep-onset problems. For the same reason, it's also not a good idea to study right up to bedtime. Make time for a buffer period before you go to bed. Take 30 to 60 minutes to take a long hot shower, meditate, or watch TV.

ISOMETRICS

Here's another natural route to promote relaxation and invigoration. You can do it whenever you get stressed out, including during the test. Close your eyes. Starting with your eyes—without holding your breath—gradually tighten every muscle in your body (but not to the point of pain) in the following sequence:

- Close your eyes tightly.
- Squeeze your nose and mouth together so that your whole face is scrunched up.
  (If it makes you self-conscious to do this in the test room, skip the face-scrunching part.)
- Pull your chin into your chest and pull your shoulders together.

- Tighten your arms to your body and then clench your fists.

- Pull in your stomach.

- Squeeze your thighs and buttocks together and tighten your calves.

- Stretch your feet, then curl your toes (watch out for cramping during this part).

At this point, every muscle in your body should be tightened. Now, relax your body, one part at a time, in reverse order, starting with your toes. Let the tension release from each muscle. The entire process might take five minutes from start to finish (you can shorten it to a couple of minutes during the test). This clenching and unclenching exercise might feel silly at first, but if you get good at it, you will feel very relaxed.

COUNTDOWN TO THE TEST

The following table is just one suggestion of a logical approach to test preparation. The earlier in the year you are able to commit some study time, the easier the exam will become.

Starting Early: (Several months before the exam)	• Take a diagnostic test to determine your strengths and weaknesses. Once or twice a week, spend about an hour reading a review chapter and tackling a few multiple-choice questions.
	• Take notes on the terms/topics you don't understand and ask your teacher about them. Read your text sections.
	• As the test date approaches, take a full practice test. Score yourself on the multiple-choice section and have your teacher, or a peer, grade the free-response section.
	• Before the test, review vocabulary, case names, political units, etc.
If You Start Nearer the Exam Date: (A couple of weeks before)	• Take a diagnostic test to determine your strengths and your weaknesses.
	• Be efficient with your study hours. Skim review chapters and focus on the vocabulary. Take one of the practice tests in its entirety and adhere to time constraints. Focus on the areas you don't know as well.
	• Work with peers and help teach one another topics you don't know.
	• Just before the exam, make a list of terms you have had the most trouble learning and concentrate on those.

STUDY SCHEDULE

The schedule presented here is the ideal. Compress the schedule if needed to fit your needs. Do keep in mind, though, that research in cognitive psychology has shown that the best way to acquire a great deal of information about a topic is to prepare over a long period of time. Because you may have several months to prepare for this exam, it makes sense for you to use all of that time to your advantage. This book, along with your text, should be invaluable in helping you prepare for this test.

If you have two semesters to prepare, use the following schedule:

September:

Take the diagnostic test in this book and identify areas in which you need help. The diagnostic will serve to familiarize you with the type of material you will be asked about on the AP exam. Begin reading your textbook along with the class outline.

October through February:

Continue reading this book and use the summaries at the end of each chapter to help guide you to the most salient information for the exam.

March and April:

Take the two practice tests and get an idea of your score. Also, identify the areas in which you need to brush up. Then go back and review those topics in both this book and your U.S. government and politics textbook.

May:

Do a final review and take the exam.

If you only have one semester to prepare, you'll need a more compact schedule:

January:

Take the diagnostic test in this book.

February through April:

Begin reading this book and identify your areas of strengths and weaknesses.

Late April:

Take the two practice tests and use your results to guide you in your preparation.

May:

Do a final review and take the exam.

THREE DAYS BEFORE THE TEST

It's almost over. Eat an energy bar, drink some soda—do whatever it takes to keep going (but watch the caffeine). Here are Kaplan's strategies for the three days leading up to the test.

Take a full-length practice test under timed conditions. Use the techniques and strategies you've learned in this book. Approach the test strategically, actively, and confidently.

WARNING: *Do not* take a full-length practice test if you have fewer than 48 hours left before the test. Doing so will probably exhaust you and hurt your score on the actual test. You wouldn't run a practice marathon the day before the real thing.

TWO DAYS BEFORE THE TEST

Go over the results of your practice test. Don't worry too much about your score or about whether you got a specific question right or wrong. The practice test doesn't count. But do examine your performance on specific questions with an eye as to how you might get through each one faster and better on the actual test.

THE NIGHT BEFORE THE TEST

DO NOT STAY UP LATE STUDYING. Get together your AP supplies containing the following items:

- A watch (with alarm sounds turned off)
- A few No. 2 pencils
- Black or blue pens for the free-response section. Do not write the free-response answers in pencil.

(Please be ready to write legibly. Undecipherable writing may result in significant loss of free-response points.)

- An eraser
- Your photo ID card
- Your admissions ticket

Know exactly where you're going, exactly how you're getting there, and exactly how long it takes to get there. It's probably a good idea to visit your test center sometime before the day of the test so that you know what to expect—what the rooms are like, how the desks are set up, and so on.

Relax the night before the test. Practice the relaxation and visualization techniques. Read a book, take a long hot shower, or watch something on TV. Get a good night's sleep. Go to bed early and leave yourself extra time in the morning.

The Morning of the Test

First, wake up. After that...

- Eat breakfast. Make it something substantial but not anything too heavy or greasy.

- Don't drink a lot of coffee if you're not used to it. Bathroom breaks cut into your time, and too much caffeine is a bad idea.

- Dress in layers so that you can adjust to the temperature of the test room.

- Read something. Warm up your brain with a newspaper or a magazine. You shouldn't let the exam be the first thing you read that day.

- Be sure to get there early. Allow yourself extra time for traffic, mass transit delays, or detours.

During the Test

Don't be shaken. If you find your confidence slipping, remind yourself how well you've prepared. You know the structure of the test; you know the instructions; you've had practice with—and have learned strategies for—every question type.

If something goes wrong, don't panic. If the test booklet is defective—two pages are stuck together or the ink has run—raise your hand and tell the proctor you need a new book. If you accidentally misgrid your answer page or put the answers in the wrong section, raise your hand and tell the proctor. He or she might be able to arrange for you to regrid your test after it's over, when it won't cost you any time.

After the Test

You might walk out of the AP U.S. Government & Politics exam thinking that you blew it. This is a normal reaction. Lots of people—even the highest scorers—feel that way. You tend to remember the questions that stumped you, not the ones that you knew. We're positive that you will have performed well and scored your best on the exam because you followed the Kaplan strategies outlined in this book. Be confident in your preparation and celebrate the fact that the AP U.S. Government & Politics exam is soon to be a distant memory.

Now that you have a strategy for your preparation, continue your exam prep by taking the diagnostic test that follows this chapter. This short test will give you an idea of the format of the actual exam, and it will reflect the scope of topics covered. After the diagnostic test, you'll find answers with detailed explanations. Be sure to read these explanations carefully, even if you got the answer correct, because you can pick up additional bits of knowledge from them. Use your score to learn which topics you need to review more carefully. Of course, all the strategies in the world can't save you if you don't know anything about U.S. government and politics. The chapters following the diagnostic test will help you review the key concepts and facts that you will encounter on the AP U.S. Government & Politics exam.

Part Two

DIAGNOSTIC TEST

HOW TO CALCULATE YOUR SCORE

This diagnostic test is a brief multiple-choice exam to help you identify your strengths and weaknesses in the area of AP U.S. government and politics. The goal is to help you determine the areas that you should focus on while studying. The questions are drawn from all areas covered on the actual AP U.S. Government & Politics exam.

DIAGNOSTIC TEST ANSWER GRID

1. Ⓐ Ⓑ Ⓒ Ⓓ Ⓔ
2. Ⓐ Ⓑ Ⓒ Ⓓ Ⓔ
3. Ⓐ Ⓑ Ⓒ Ⓓ Ⓔ
4. Ⓐ Ⓑ Ⓒ Ⓓ Ⓔ
5. Ⓐ Ⓑ Ⓒ Ⓓ Ⓔ
6. Ⓐ Ⓑ Ⓒ Ⓓ Ⓔ
7. Ⓐ Ⓑ Ⓒ Ⓓ Ⓔ

8. Ⓐ Ⓑ Ⓒ Ⓓ Ⓔ
9. Ⓐ Ⓑ Ⓒ Ⓓ Ⓔ
10. Ⓐ Ⓑ Ⓒ Ⓓ Ⓔ
11. Ⓐ Ⓑ Ⓒ Ⓓ Ⓔ
12. Ⓐ Ⓑ Ⓒ Ⓓ Ⓔ
13. Ⓐ Ⓑ Ⓒ Ⓓ Ⓔ
14. Ⓐ Ⓑ Ⓒ Ⓓ Ⓔ

15. Ⓐ Ⓑ Ⓒ Ⓓ Ⓔ
16. Ⓐ Ⓑ Ⓒ Ⓓ Ⓔ
17. Ⓐ Ⓑ Ⓒ Ⓓ Ⓔ
18. Ⓐ Ⓑ Ⓒ Ⓓ Ⓔ
19. Ⓐ Ⓑ Ⓒ Ⓓ Ⓔ
20. Ⓐ Ⓑ Ⓒ Ⓓ Ⓔ

Section I: Multiple-Choice Questions

Time: 15 Minutes, 20 Questions

Directions: Select the answer choice that best answers the question or completes the statement.

1. Which of the following statements concerning the attitudes of the founding fathers is **TRUE**?

   (A) They were a cross section of that era's citizens—both rich and poor—who were proportionately represented.

   (B) They were really not all that concerned with establishing a system that provided for the separation of powers.

   (C) They were a group that was motivated by a commitment to the public good, with little desire to advance their own agendas.

   (D) The founders had competing definitions of federalism.

   (E) The founders were innovative because what they created was original and was not borrowed from earlier governmental concepts.

2. Which of the following descriptions concerning the *Federalist Papers* is **NOT** correct?

   (A) Alexander Hamilton, John Jay, and James Madison used the pen name "Publius."

   (B) The names of the authors of the *Federalist Papers* were a secret at the time of their publication.

   (C) The *Federalist Papers* probably played only a small role in securing ratification of the constitution.

   (D) These essays have had a long-lasting value as an authoritative and profound explanation of the Constitution.

   (E) The *Federalist Papers* were almost exclusively printed in the Philadelphia newspapers.

3. Which of the following statements **BEST** describes the term *silent majority*?

   (A) The silent majority consists of those people who advocate traditional values no matter what their economic status, especially in face of the counterculture of the 1960s.

   (B) The silent majority refers to a group of mostly liberal, progressive thinkers of the 1950s.

   (C) *Silent majority* was a term utilized by the founding fathers to describe the people they believed they were representing.

   (D) The silent majority was a political group that founded the "Bull Moose Party," one of the most successful third parties in American politics.

   (E) The silent majority was first used to describe those citizens opposed to the Supreme Court's ruling in *Roe v. Wade*.

4. Which of the following statements concerning political participation in the United States is **NOT** correct?

   (A) The motor-voter bill was designed to make it easier to register to vote.

   (B) In the United States, the entire burden of registering to vote falls on the individual voters.

   (C) The difficulty Americans have in registering to vote leads to low levels of political participation in the United States.

   (D) In the United States, a majority of the voting-age population is registered to vote.

   (E) The majority of registered American voters do not vote in elections.

GO ON TO THE NEXT PAGE ⟹

5. In the United States, voter turnout is highest for presidential elections among which of the following groups?

   (A) Unionized workers motivated by the union leadership

   (B) Eighteen- to 25-year-olds enthused about voting for the first time

   (C) Citizens of lower socioeconomic status who are dissatisfied with government

   (D) Those U.S. citizens with college educations, no matter their ethnic or social standing

   (E) Women, who are motivated by gender-centered issues

6. Most research shows that voters primarily base their decisions on how they are going to vote in presidential elections upon which of the following factors?

   (A) Party platforms created at the conventions

   (B) The competence of the candidate's chosen running mate

   (C) Party identification or single issues on which the voter tends to perceive one party more favorably

   (D) Effective television advertising developed by advertising professionals

   (E) The effectiveness of a candidate during televised debates

7. Which of the following statements BEST describes the role of today's party conventions?

   (A) They are important gatherings where decisions are made for long-term party goals.

   (B) They allow for important fund-raising by selling the television rights to networks.

   (C) Delegates perform an important function by establishing important party policies for the election at hand.

   (D) They are mostly symbolic pep rallies used to give their candidates a popularity boost.

   (E) They are the presidential candidate's forum for considering and choosing his or her running mate.

8. Which statement is **NOT** true concerning political parties in the United States?

   (A) The founding fathers of our country generally disliked the concept of parties, considering them to be motivated by ambition and self-interest.

   (B) The first two American political parties were the Republicans and Federalists.

   (C) The party system as reorganized during the Jacksonian period was organized from bottom to top, rather than from the top down.

   (D) U.S. democracy was always intended to be a two-party system, and this concept is established in the Constitution.

   (E) The development of the convention system was in part a reform allowing for some local control of the nominating process.

9. Political parties have been declining in influence for which of the following reasons?

   (A) Candidates and voters are more independently minded today.

   (B) Sponsorship of the parties under the Constitution has been reduced in the past 50 years.

   (C) Candidates in the last half of the 20th century were mostly self-funded.

   (D) Because candidates try to take popular stances, there really is very little difference between the two parties.

   (E) Parties have lost the ability to raise funds because of changes in the regulation of "soft money."

GO ON TO THE NEXT PAGE

10. Which statement is **MOST** correct concerning third parties?

    (A) Third parties are encouraged by our election system today because they act as important outlets for voter participation.

    (B) Their existence is protected under the Bill of Rights.

    (C) The emergence of third parties has led to a rise in straight-ticket voting as a response to their influence.

    (D) They benefit equally as much as the two major parties under federal campaign financing laws.

    (E) They have occasionally changed the outcome of presidential elections.

11. Which of the following is **NOT** correct concerning the House of Representatives?

    (A) Unlike the Senate, it contains a very powerful rules committee.

    (B) House members are not limited in the length of debate on bills.

    (C) It is known as a noncontinuous body.

    (D) The length of a representative's term is shorter than that of a senator.

    (E) The House resulted from the Virginia Plan at the Constitutional Convention.

12. Which of the following is **TRUE** concerning congressional redistricting?

    (A) The process of redistricting takes place every 20 years according to the Constitution.

    (B) Redistricting is usually based upon the voter turnout in the previous elections.

    (C) Partisan politics never plays a role in the redistricting process.

    (D) Redistricting is handled by the legislatures in each of the states.

    (E) The process can only add seats in the House and can never reduce the number of representatives.

13. The system of checks and balances between Congress and the executive branch is illustrated in all **EXCEPT** which of the following?

    (A) The House and Senate overriding a presidential veto

    (B) The Senate confirming a president's Supreme Court justice nominee

    (C) The Senate using its power of cloture to consider a bill

    (D) Congress voting on a declaration of war requested by the president

    (E) The Senate confirming a presidential nominee to the cabinet

14. Which of the following terms concerning Congress is incorrectly described?

    (A) Members of Congress enjoy a *franking privilege* that allows them to keep their constituents informed by using the U.S. mail system free of charge.

    (B) The *filibuster* is a process that often hinders legislation in the House of Representatives.

    (C) The term *pork-barrel legislation* refers to bills passed that give tangible benefits to constituents in hopes of winning voters.

    (D) *Gerrymandering* is a process of drawing a House district in an erratic manner to favor one party over another.

    (E) A *rider* is a provision added to a piece of legislation that is not consistent with the bill's purpose.

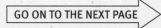
GO ON TO THE NEXT PAGE

15. Which of the following statements concerning the presidency is correct?

  (A) Presidential vetoes are overridden in the vast majority of instances.

  (B) The inauguration date for presidents was changed from March to January.

  (C) Presidential succession always provided for the vice president to assume the presidency upon the death of a president.

  (D) Presidential term limitations were addressed in the Bill of Rights.

  (E) The president is no longer required to be a native-born American; naturalized citizens are also eligible.

16. Which of the following Supreme Court decisions dealt with the rights of an accused criminal in the United States?

  I.   *Gideon v. Wainwright*
  II. *Mapp v. Ohio*
  III. *Korematsu v. United States*
  IV. *Miranda v. Arizona*

  (A) I only
  (B) I and IV only
  (C) I, II, and IV only
  (D) II, III, and IV only
  (E) I, II, and III only

17. Often specific interest groups benefit from policies that are paid for by the general public. This type of politics is known as

  (A) majoritarian politics.
  (B) client politics.
  (C) entrepreneurial politics.
  (D) interest group politics.
  (E) progressive politics.

18. The economic theory that maintains that variations in the money supply have major influences on the health of the economy goes by which of the following labels?

  (A) Supply-side economics
  (B) Communism
  (C) Keynesian economics
  (D) Monetarism
  (E) Gold standard

GO ON TO THE NEXT PAGE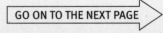

Use the chart provided to answer questions 19 and 20.

Supreme Court Losing Favor: Favorable Opinion of Supreme Court	Jan 2001 %	June 2005 %	Change
Total	68	57	−11
Republican	80	64	−16
Democrat	61	51	−10
Independent	69	62	−7
Conservative Republican	78	59	−19
Moderate-Liberal Republican	84	72	−12
Conservative-Moderate Democrat	66	52	−14
Liberal Democrat	54	51	−3
White Protestant	71	57	−14
Evangelical	73	51	−22
Mainline	69	63	−6
White Catholic	74	64	−10
Secular	58	52	−6

Source: Pew Research Center for Religion and Public Life.

19. According to the chart, which of the following groups showed the **LEAST** amount of change in its favorable opinion of the Supreme Court?

(A) Conservative Republicans
(B) Moderate-liberal Republicans
(C) Conservative-moderate Democrats
(D) Liberal Democrats
(E) None of the above

20. According to the chart, which of the following statements is **NOT** correct?

(A) In January 2001, moderate-liberal Republicans had the most favorable view of the Supreme Court.

(B) In June 2005, the favorable opinion of the Supreme Court held by white Catholics had decreased 10 percent from January of 2001.

(C) The white Protestant evangelical group showed the greatest amount of change in its opinion of the Supreme Court during the period surveyed.

(D) Overall favorable opinion of the Supreme Court is lower in the Democratic Party than the Republican Party.

(E) Only mainline white Protestants showed an increase in their favorable opinion of the Supreme Court.

STOP

ANSWER KEY

1.	D	11.	B
2.	E	12.	D
3.	A	13.	C
4.	E	14.	B
5.	D	15.	B
6.	C	16.	C
7.	D	17.	B
8.	D	18.	D
9.	A	19.	D
10.	E	20.	E

DIAGNOSTIC TEST: ASSESS YOUR STRENGTHS

The following tables show how the diagnostic is broken down by topic, the same as it would be on the official AP U.S. Government and Politics exam. If you need help with the free-response section, refer back to Chapter 2: Strategies for Success.

Topics	Question	If You Missed These Questions, Study*:
Constitutional Underpinnings of U.S. Government	1, 2	Ch 1, 2
Political Beliefs and Behaviors	3, 4, 5, 6	Ch 6
Political Parties, Interest Groups, and Mass Media	7, 8, 9, 10	Ch 8, 10, 11
Institutions of National Government: The Congress, the Presidency, the Bureaucracy, and the Federal Courts	11, 12, 13, 14, 15, 19, 20	Ch 12, 13, 14, 15
Public Policy	17, 18	Ch 17, 18
Civil Rights and Civil Liberties	16	Ch 15

* Although topics do not exactly coincide with the chapters in this book, they should be used as a general guideline of where you need to focus your studies.

Topics	Number of Questions	Answered Correctly
Constitutional Underpinnings of United States Government	2	
Political Beliefs and Behaviors	4	
Political Parties, Interest Groups, and Mass Media	4	
Institutions of National Government: The Congress, the Presidency, the Bureaucracy, and the Federal Courts	7	
Public Policy	2	
Civil Rights and Civil Liberties	1	

ANSWERS AND EXPLANATIONS

1. D
The founding fathers themselves were in some disagreement over what the term *federalism* meant. This caused some of the best-known names of that period either to oppose or at the very least to have considerable reservations about their new form of government.

2. E
The role of the *Federalist Papers* is believed to have been relatively small as far as ratification was concerned. Their value has been in explaining the deeper meanings of the Constitution as interpreted by the three men who wrote the *Federalist Papers*—Alexander Hamilton, James Madison, and John Jay. The *Federalist Papers* were printed in New York papers, not in Philadelphia papers, because New York was a pivotal state for ratification purposes.

3. A
The *silent majority* was a phrase popularized by the Nixon administration to describe the diverse group that it believed supported a more conservative social agenda than that of the counterculture.

4. E
Statistics show that the vast majority of registered voters do vote in American elections. The debate has been about the difficulty of registering individuals so that they are eligible to vote.

5. D
The greatest factor in voter participation is level of education. Higher-educated Americans are the most likely to vote.

6. C
Party identification continues to be the strongest factor in determining voter habits. Single issues about which voters care deeply have also gained in importance in recent years. Despite the media circus surrounding them, research has shown that the televised debates are not as critical to voters'

decisions. Party platforms, running mates, and television advertising have been shown to have minimal impact as well.

7. D
It is widely agreed that today's conventions are little more than symbolic pep rallies that are used to "spike" the approval ratings of the candidates. Networks do not pay parties for television rights, and this has led to less network television coverage of recent conventions compared to those of the 1950s and 1960s.

8. D
It is not true that U.S. democracy was always intended to be a two-party system and that this concept was established in the Constitution. There is no sanctioning of parties in the Constitution. The evolution of a two-party system is something that happened completely by circumstance. While today's election statutes favor a two-party system, third parties can still make a significant impact on U.S. elections.

9. A
Parties are declining in influence because candidates and voters act more independently today. Straight-ticket voting is almost unheard of, and "coattail effects" are minimal at best. Voters in many states vote for one party for president but elect governors, senators, and representatives from the other party.

10. E
Third parties have definitely changed the outcome of some presidential elections. Theodore Roosevelt, Ross Perot, and Ralph Nader were all third-party candidates who had an impact on a presidential election.

11. B
Because of the logistics and practicality of the issue, House members are limited in the length of their debate on bills. The length of debate on a particular

issue is something that is decided by the extremely important Rules Committee.

12. D

Congressional redistricting is handled by the various state legislatures every 10 years after a census is conducted. While there are guidelines for this process, the final decisions are left up to those in state legislatures, and it has always been a partisan, highly contested issue.

13. C

The power of cloture has nothing to do with the system of checks and balances between the legislative and executive branches. Overriding vetoes, confirming judicial and cabinet appointments, and declarations of war are all considered a legislative check on the executive branch.

14. B

The filibuster does not hinder legislation in the House of Representatives. In fact, members of the House of Representatives do not possess the ability to filibuster; the Senate exclusively holds this ability.

15. B

The 20th Amendment to the U.S. Constitution changed the presidential inauguration date from March to January. This was done, in part, as a result of the time lag following the 1932 presidential election, which many believed deepened the Depression.

16. C

Korematsu v. United States was a case concerning the internment of Japanese-Americans during World War II. The other three cases all dealt with various rights of the accused. These include the right to a lawyer (*Gideon v. Wainwright*), the freedom from unreasonable search and seizure (*Mapp v. Ohio*), and the right to have your rights read to you at the time of your arrest (*Miranda v. Arizona*).

17. B

Client politics is policy making in which some specific group receives the benefits of the policy and the public at large bears the costs.

18. D

Monetarism is an economic theory that proposes that government should promote the steady, predictable increase in the money supply at a rate about equal to the growth in an economy's productivity.

19. D

The chart shows that the change in the favorable opinion toward the Supreme Court among liberal Democrats fell only 3 percent. This is only half as much as the next lowest change.

20. E

The chart shows that from January 2001 to June 2005, the favorable opinion of the Supreme Court fell for every group surveyed.

HOW TO MAKE THIS BOOK WORK FOR YOU BASED ON THE RESULTS OF YOUR DIAGNOSTIC TEST

If you have completed the 20-question diagnostic test, you should now consider the results. What have you learned about the question structures? What have you gained from experiencing the kinds of topics covered on the AP exam?

Note that this sample was constructed with the course description in mind. The questions are arranged in the same sequence as the College Board's suggested outline. Questions 1 and 2 cover topic 1 (Constitutional Underpinnings), questions 3 and 4 cover topic 2 (Political Beliefs and Behaviors), and so on. Key terms and phrases were chosen, such as asking you to find the answer that is "not correct" or the one that is "most correct." Focus on those key instructions, and you will have a much better level of understanding the demands of the multiple-choice section.

CONVERTING A RAW SCORE TO THE AP SYSTEM

The diagnostic test is only one-third of the length of the full test and, therefore, of limited use in predicting your final score. If you take this sample after you have completed the school course, your expectations should have been high. But because there is no set number of points that guarantee certain scores in any given year, you cannot directly match the percentage you got correct on the diagnostic with the AP scoring system. However, the diagnostic test will give you a general idea about your strengths and weaknesses, which will enable you to organize your study time for maximum effectiveness.

Number of Diagnostic Questions Answered Correctly	Percent That Represents	Comments
15 to 20	75% and higher	You are well on the way to earning a 4 or 5 if you do this well on the actual test. Keep up the same level of success on the free-response questions!
10 to 14	50% to 70%	Focus on vocabulary. Watch for the ways questions are phrased. You will need to score well on the free-response questions.
0 to 9	Up to 45%	Study and review time is here! Focus on the topics that gave you the most trouble. Develop a mastery of terms and concepts of government.

Part Three

AP U.S. GOVERNMENT & POLITICS REVIEW

CHAPTER 3: THE DEVELOPMENT OF THE U.S. FEDERAL SYSTEM

IF YOU LEARN ONLY SIX THINGS IN THIS CHAPTER . . .

1. The Declaration of Independence identified freedoms and rights that the U.S. government continues to further and protect.

2. Many features of the U.S. Constitution were designed to correct of flaws in government found under the Articles of Confederation.

3. The Constitutional Convention of 1787 was in part a contest between political groups favoring federal power and political groups favoring state power. It was also a contest between states with large populations and those with small populations.

4. The ratification debate created a need for a federal Bill of Rights. It also led to the *Federalist Papers*, a collection of essays explaining our system of government.

5. The two-party system developed quickly after the Constitution was adopted, with political parties forming in response to Hamilton's calls for a strong central government and Jefferson's advocacy of State controls.

6. These two early parties began the tradition of U.S. political parties having competing visions of American government.

STEPS FROM THE DECLARATION OF INDEPENDENCE TO THE CONSTITUTION

The creation of the current system of government for the United States was innovative and daring yet based on established political ideals and real cultural problems. The result of the Convention of 1787 was a new form of federal republic, but the Constitution of 1787 was vague in its descriptions of the powers and functions of the government. There were intense debates in several key states over ratification, especially in New York and Virginia, where opponents to the new plan held early leads. Even after ratification, the nation continued to debate various interpretations of the appropriate level of federal powers. These debates continue into the 21st century.

We can begin our discussion of the development of the U.S. Constitution by discussing the goals of government presented by the Declaration of Independence of 1776. Thomas Jefferson and a committee of delegates to the second Continental Congress agreed on a statement that explained a need for independence from Britain. However, the list of charges leveled against King George III also had a significant impact on the goals of the Articles of Confederation and then on the Constitution itself. The Declaration of Independence lists many abuses brought about by bad leadership. Using the philosophical arguments of John Locke and others, this list is a blueprint of what government should not be allowed to do. It enumerates what freedoms government must provide for citizens and how citizens should control the government. Using Locke's "Second Treatise of Civil Government" (1690) as a model, Jefferson argued that government is a form of social contract between citizens and leaders. Locke wrote that government exists to provide liberties and freedoms for those who agree to abide by its rules and limits. He also wrote that people have natural rights that cannot be taken away by any government. Jefferson used Locke's phrase "life, liberty, and pursuit of property" to emphasize the fundamental goals of the country's governmental structure. The Declaration of Independence remains a key guide to the rights promoted by American government.

When the United States gained independence in 1781, a plan for government—the Articles of Confederation—had already been debated and accepted. The Articles of Confederation included many features aimed at allowing the goals of the Declaration of Independence to be achieved. Drafted by a committee headed by John Dickinson, the Articles of Confederation allowed for the supremacy of state power, the control of taxes at the regional level, and a loose union of states. This government could not effectively deal with threats from foreign nations, disagreements between states, or the resulting financial chaos. The national leadership would then attempt to balance the need for a more powerful central government with the memories of British rule.

SPECIFIC WEAKNESSES OF THE ARTICLES OF CONFEDERATION

Under the Articles of Confederation, no national executive branch was established, nor was there any separate judiciary. The central government could not collect taxes, but states were expected to volunteer "extra funds." A final, major flaw was the inability to make any needed amendments without the unanimous approval of all states. Alexander Hamilton predicted that the Articles of Confederation would fail and called for a new plan for government almost every year of the Articles' existence. The shock of European banks refusing to accept U.S. credit applications and the chaos caused by Shay's Rebellion finally goaded other leaders into action. As a result of these weaknesses, the years of 1781 to 1787 saw very few advances. The passage of the Northwest Ordinance helped establish some expansion plans, but states continued to feud over commerce, the English continued to take advantage of our weaknesses, and regional disputes between merchants and planters deepened.

Continuing Importance of the Declaration of Independence and Articles of Confederation

The goals of the Declaration of Independence and the faults of the Articles of Confederation were key influences on the debates over the creation of the Constitution. Many of the structures and provisions missing from the Articles of Confederation were added in the new plan. Many who later objected to the Constitution made sure that the basic freedoms listed in the Declaration of Independence were secured with the addition of a federal Bill of Rights.

Key items missing from the Articles of Confederation were the following:

- No separate executive branch was established.

- No methods for the central government to collect taxes were present.

- No federal judiciary was created to settle interstate disputes.

- No amendments could be added without unanimous state approval. (None ever were.)

As a result...

- Only two major pieces of legislation were passed under the articles—the Land Ordinance of 1785 and the Northwest Ordinance of 1787.

- Disputes over trade and taxes raged between states, and no central authority could settle these problems.

- Veterans from the Revolutionary War were not paid for their military service, except through credit certificates.

- The central government had no funds.

- State governments were often bankrupt and had no place to turn for help.

- National credit in European banks collapsed.

- There were no agreements on tariffs, trade negotiations, or key issues such as support from France or the United Kingdom.

- Growing disputes began between northern and southern states.

- Shay's Rebellion panicked enough leaders to call for a convention to confront the growing economic and political crisis.

(Memorization of all of the problems of the Articles of Confederation years is not needed for the AP test. However, knowing how the Constitution addressed these issues will give a fuller understanding of the structure and powers of the new government.)

THE DIFFICULT CONVENTION

It is important to remember how difficult the creation of the Constitution turned out to be and how close the debates came to collapsing. Several important leaders, such as Patrick Henry, refused to participate. Rhode Island refused to allow any representatives to attend. Delaware warned other states that it would not participate in a treasonous "coup." The main leaders who did attend were Alexander Hamilton, James Madison, Benjamin Franklin, George Washington, Governor Morris, and James Wilson. Summer heat made the meetings difficult. The New York delegation was so divided that all three members left in disgust and two (John Lansing and Robert Yates) would try to defeat the ratification effort. Governor Edmund Randolph of Virginia, another key state, refused to sign the document and also campaigned against it. Both New York's and Virginia's legislatures would struggle for long periods before ratification.

FORMATION OF CONGRESS

> The biggest debate at the convention was over the issue of representation in Congress. States with large populations were determined to have greater representation than those with smaller populations. Under the Articles of Confederation, each state had an equal vote, no matter what its population. But smaller states refused to create a system where they could be dominated by more populous states. The final compromise, which created the current House of Representatives and Senate, took weeks to settle. These competing plans were later named for the states that sponsored them.

The larger, more populated states were led by Virginia and Pennsylvania and advocated the Virginia Plan. Drafted by Madison and presented by Governor Randolph at the very beginning of the convention, this plan based representation in Congress on the relative populations of the states. This plan, which was approved quickly, also included a Senate selected by members of the House, a "president" selected by Congress (a parliamentary system), and a federal court selected by Congress.

Only the ability to call for multiple votes allowed the smaller states to keep asking for reconsideration of this plan and then led them to produce the New Jersey Plan. Drafted by William Paterson, this plan called for a single-chamber congress (unicameral), where each state would have the same number of representatives. This return to the legislative representation of the Articles of Confederation was not acceptable to the more populated states. After weeks of heated debate and several rejections, the Connecticut Plan, or "Great Compromise," was passed. This plan, crafted by Roger Sherman, established a House of Representatives with representation based on each state's population and a Senate with every state having an equal number of representatives.

Other sticking points included the creation of a single executive elected by special "electors." This alone had to be put to a vote about 60 times. Other issues were often defined by those who favored a more centralized power versus those who supported state authority. "Nationalists" and "localists" were the forerunners of the coming split between Federalists and Anti-Federalists. This would be the central division between the first party leaders, Hamilton and Jefferson. The delegates also deadlocked on whether or not enslaved African Americans would be counted in the populations of the southern states. The compromise that was reached would count three-fifths of a state's slaves in apportioning representatives, presidential electors, and direct taxes in exchange for ending the Atlantic slave trade in 20 years.

Some Federalist arguments for ratifying the new Constitution included the following:

- Time for action had run out, and the country was collapsing.

- The Articles of Confederation did not provide for the following:

  - Federal taxes to fund the operation of government

  - Federal courts to stop interstate disputes

  - Federal powers to execute federal laws

  - Fair balance of power between large and small states

  - Federal powers to deal with foreign threats

- The Constitution would appropriately balance state and central powers.

- There were sufficient checks and balances, and separations of power, to keep the federal government in line.

- Citizens controlled the House of Representatives, and states controlled the Senate.

- Limits to legislative powers were included and carefully listed.

- The new, single executive held powers that were shared or checked at almost every level.

Some Anti-Federalist arguments against the new Constitution included these:

- The new plan gave too many controls to a "distant" and centralized government.

- The new executive was too powerful and "kinglike."

- The federal power to tax was a dangerous control over citizens and states.

- The legislative powers were long and detailed. Where was the list of limits?

- What were the basic civil freedoms that the federal government could not remove? States had created such "Bills of Rights"; why didn't the Constitution?

RATIFICATION ISSUES

When state legislatures began to debate the new plan, the arguments in favor of adoption were supported by the need for immediate economic reforms and by some concerns about growing international threats. However, opponents focused on the need for more structure in defining the rights of citizens. Only with the promise of a federal Bill of Rights did many agree to the Constitution. The approval of only 9 of the 13 states was required for ratification, and 9 states completed this by the summer of 1788. However, opponents had held up the process in New York and Virginia. The nation understood that if either of these key states rejected the Constitution, the other nine votes would be relatively meaningless. Proponents called for giving the new system a trial, knowing that time for further discussions was being eliminated by foreign threats.

Opponents were stuck with making warnings about the reduction of state powers and creating a distant dictatorship, but they admitted that crises were at hand. During the months of state legislature meetings concerning the ratification the new Constitution, many essays were written in newspapers that defended or attacked the plan. New York became the key area, with hundreds of articles printed. The most famous were written by Madison and Hamilton and were later collected as a book under the title the *Federalist Papers*. Historians note that the readership of the *Federalist Papers* was relatively limited at the time of its original publication. Often, these essays were aimed only at those who had already decided to support or oppose ratification. However, the *Federalist Papers* became more valuable later. To attract undecided readers, the writers did not use their own names. They collectively used "Publius," a reference to Roman debates about good government.

The *Federalist Papers* stand as great explanations of how the U.S. government balances power, protects different political factions, settles disputes, and runs a diverse nation. Madison's essay "Number 10" is regarded as a definitive analysis of regional political divisions. This essay addresses how and why to guard against the rise of "factions" and predicted the rise of interest groups and partisan politics. Essay "Number 51, " probably written by Madison, is known as the great advocacy of the checks and balances and separations of power within this new plan. Hamilton's "Number 78" explained and justified the structure of the proposed judicial branch.

Anti-Federalists had points to make about the dangers of an executive leader, the excessive powers to tax, and the lack of a list of limits to federal power. Even though at that time each state had a "Bill of Rights" in its state constitution, Anti-Federalists successfully forced Federalists to agree to add federal guarantees of rights as amendments. When the first Congress convened in 1789, Representative James Madison led the effort to create 12 proposals, and 10 were adopted as the new Bill of Rights.

THE DEVELOPMENT OF PARTIES UNDER THE CONSTITUTION

The early republic saw the creation of political parties under the leadership of Hamilton and Jefferson. Both worked in Washington's administrations and were temporarily initially wary of such organizations, yet they could not stop from advocating opposing approaches to government. The political coalitions that eventually formed under the names "Federalist" and "Democratic-Republican" were not created in a historical vacuum. Federalists held views similar to the Tories of England. They wanted stronger leadership, especially economically and militarily. The English Tories developed in response to the memories of the chaos of the English Civil War, and the American Federalists formed in response to weaknesses of the Articles of Confederation. The Democratic-Republicans developed their approach to government in response to experiences under British colonial rule.

THE LIBERAL DEMOCRATIC-REPUBLICANS

> Democratic-Republicans reflected the beliefs of early liberals, for whom tolerance, freedom, and independent action were primary. Jefferson wanted to reinforce the values of the American Revolution and create the freest government in the world.

Hamilton wanted a strong central government. Jefferson supported states' rights and a decentralized approach to government. Jefferson would prevail on Madison to embrace his approach, and both men would lead the dominant Democratic-Republican Party of the early 1800s.

The Federalist Party would not be successful nationally after 1800, but its centralized approach to stability endures. In fact, both of these basic approaches to government still dominate the two-party system of the modern United States. The modern-day Democratic Party advocates centralized authority to promote social and economic equality, while the present-day Republican Party advocates a decentralized approach to government to promote these same ideals.

EARLY DEVELOPMENT OF POLITICAL PARTIES

The first major step toward the creation of a two-party system in the United States came during the Washington administration.

The first great ideological split was between Jefferson and Hamilton. Jefferson became the leader of the "liberal/radical" opposition, and Hamilton became the main spokesperson of the "conservative" Federalist government. Adams took on Federalist leadership during his presidency.

Washington tried to remain above partisan politics during his terms. Madison started as a great advocate of the centralized approach but ended as a supporter of Jefferson's approach, favoring weaker government.

The election of 1800 is considered the first major transition of American political power. The Federalists, under Adam's leadership, gave up power without a struggle to the Democratic-Republicans under Jefferson's leadership. Federalists would not wield major power again.

EARLY POLITICAL DIVISIONS IN THE UNITED STATES

General Time Period	Groups that favored federal power: Stability, safety through good government, and centralization (more conservative at the time the Constitution was being drafted):	Groups that favored state power: Liberty, choices, and limited government (more liberal at the time the Constitution was being drafted):
Colonial Development	• Anglican church Leaders • Monarchists • Tories	• Other Protestant church Leaders • Parliamentarians • Whigs
The Early U.S. Republic	• Federalists • Centralists • Federalist Party (Hamilton, Adams, Washington)	• Anti-Federalists • States' Rights • Jefferson's Republicans • Jefferson's Democrats • Democratic-Republican Party (Jefferson, Madison, Monroe)
Early to Mid-1800s	• Federalists (remnants) • Whigs • Republican Party	• Jacksonian Democrats • Democratic Party

REVIEW QUESTIONS

MULTIPLE-CHOICE QUESTIONS

1. The Constitutional Convention of 1787 included all of the following issues **EXCEPT**

   (A) those who wanted a significantly stronger federal government argued with those who wanted to retain the Articles of Confederation.

   (B) leaders from states with large populations argued with representatives from states with small populations over representation in Congress.

   (C) leaders from Rhode Island refused to attend.

   (D) advocates of states' rights feared the creation of a dictatorship.

   (E) Virginia's leaders initially wanted a parliamentary system.

2. The *Federalist Papers* were

   (A) aimed at convincing readers that the Constitution would properly limit the powers of the new federal government.

   (B) aimed at convincing the public that Jefferson and Adams would support the Constitution once they returned from Europe.

   (C) not successful in keeping opponents from demanding a Bill of Rights.

   (D) key in ensuring ratification in Virginia and New York.

   (E) critical of the new plan for government.

3. The development of political parties in the early republic

   (A) can be traced to the leadership of Washington.

   (B) was resisted by early American politicians.

   (C) was dominated by the ideological conflict between Adams and Hamilton.

   (D) was rooted in English traditions of political views.

   (E) gave the Federalists a long period of dominance.

4. Madison's role in the early political development of the United States included all of the following **EXCEPT**

   (A) drafting the bulk of the Constitution.

   (B) leading the debates supporting the new plan.

   (C) staying loyal to the Federalist program.

   (D) helping create the goals of Jeffersonian Democratic-Republicans.

   (E) writing an important essay on the powers of the central government.

5. Federalists supported _____.
   Democratic-Republicans supported _____.

   (A) a conservative agenda; a liberal agenda

   (B) Jefferson; Hamilton

   (C) Washington; Adams

   (D) a liberal agenda; a conservative agenda

   (E) trade with our ally, France; trade with England

FREE-RESPONSE QUESTIONS

1. The government under the Articles of Confederation was ineffective, yet some political leaders still feared a new form of republic.

    (A) Identify and describe two reasons some leaders feared the new plan.

    (B) Give two specific examples of how the fears you identified in part (A) were alleviated in the compromises reached at the Constitutional Convention.

2. The two-party system became entrenched in the early years of the United States.

    (A) Identify the two major approaches to government and one label used to identify both of these groups.

    (B) Explain how this early split into two political camps shaped any two of the compromises that were reached during the writing of the Constitution.

ANSWERS AND EXPLANATIONS

MULTIPLE-CHOICE ANSWERS

1. A

Almost immediately, it was agreed that the Articles of Confederation were beyond revision. The Constitutional Convention of 1787 included disagreements between leaders from states with large populations and states with smaller populations over Congressional representation; leaders from Rhode Island who refused to attend; states' righters who feared the creation of a dictatorship; and Virginia's leaders, who initially wanted a parliamentary system. However, none of the delegates advocated retaining the Articles of Confederation.

2. C

In many states, supporters demanded a federal Bill of Rights. Choice (A) is not the best answer because the papers focused on how the new government would function well and not necessarily be limited. Although Adams and Jefferson were both in Europe at the time, choice (B) is not true because the *Federalist Papers* were not aimed at convincing the public that Jefferson and Adams would support the Constitution once they returned. Choice (D) is incorrect because the essays probably did not sway votes in Virginia and New York; Hamilton seems to have gained needed support in New York, and Madison's pleas for a new system helped in Virginia's convention. Choice (E) is incorrect because the *Federalist Papers* were not criticisms of how the government was organized.

3. D

The development of political parties in the early republic was rooted in English political traditions of liberal and conservative views. English traditions of Whigs and Tories influenced our leaders greatly. Washington did not trust party conflicts; Hamilton opposed Jefferson, not Adams; and the Federalists lasted only two presidential administrations.

4. C

Madison's role in the early political development of the United States included drafting the bulk of the Constitution, leading debates supporting the new plan, helping to create the goals of Jeffersonian Democratic-Republicans, and writing an important essay on the powers of the central government. Choice (C) is the best answer because during the Jefferson presidency, Madison left the Federalist Party; he did not stay loyal to the Federalist program.

5. A

Federalists supported a conservative agenda. Democratic-Republicans supported a liberal agenda. These were the labels given at the time.

FREE-RESPONSE ANSWERS

1. **4-point Rubric**

   2 points in part (A): (any two reasons)

   - Fear of a loss of state authority
   - Fear of a loss of tax authority
   - Fear of a too-powerful executive
   - Fear of a loss of many basic civil rights guaranteed by state constitutions
   - Fear of national control of military powers
   - Fear that the goals of the Declaration of Independence would be abandoned

   2 points in part (B): (any two from the Constitution)

   - Specific mentions of state powers in sections such as Article IV
   - Restrictions on tax legislation, with it only being originated in the publicly elected House
   - Many checks on the executive, such as congressional override of a presidential veto
   - The limits of power listed in Article I (protections of writs of habeas corpus)
   - Promises of a Bill of Rights
   - Control of the military by the House and Senate (selected by states)

2. **5-point Rubric**

   3 points in part (A): (identify two, label one)

   - A desire for better central government versus an emphasis on states' rights
   - Whigs or Tories
   - Nationalists or Localists
   - Federalists or Anti-Federalists
   - Federalists or Jeffersonian Democratic-Republicans

   2 points in part (B): (explain the two sides shaping the Constitution)

   - More central powers to tax
   - More central powers to control interstate trade
   - More central powers over a military
   - More central powers with a federal court system
   - Retained local powers of states
   - Retained local control of selecting the Senate
   - Retained local controls over selecting the executive

CHAPTER 4: THE FEDERAL CONSTITUTION OF 1787 AND THE AMENDMENTS

IF YOU LEARN ONLY SIX THINGS IN THIS CHAPTER . . .

1. "Federalism" as a political concept has changed dramatically since its inception. The Civil War, the Great Depression, and World War II were major events that led to these changes.

2. The U.S. Constitution is short, focuses mostly on Congress, and was designed to guide the development of the national government. The writers did not intend to describe all possible powers and interpretations.

3. The Preamble lists the six basic goals of the new government.

4. Article I contains the most details and descriptions, covering the organization and powers of Congress. Critical powers are established in the Commerce Clause and the Elastic Clause sections.

5. Almost all executive powers listed in Article II are vague and checked by Congress. The remaining descriptions of judicial and state powers are even less detailed.

6. Since the Bill of Rights was ratified in 1791, only 17 additions have been made. Many are governmental procedures, and only a handful of important expansions of civil liberties have been added in over 200 years.

BASICS OF FEDERALISM

The definition of *federalism* has changed over the centuries, beginning with its use by supporters and opponents of the Constitution. Prior to the Constitutional Convention of 1787, many in the country used the word to describe a government where states had power, with interstate problems being settled by a central authority. Supporters of the Constitution used the word for describing their political ideal in which the federal and state governments would share power, but federal power would be supreme. Changes to federalism were extensive during the 20th century, especially after the Great Depression and World War II, both of which led to new demands for controls by the national government. Federalism has come to mean both economic leadership from the national capital and, more recently, the reduction of the size and responsibilities of the federal government and a return of power to the states.

FEDERALISM

Federalism did come to stand for a stronger central government, yet early leaders such as Jefferson made sure that state controls remained intact. This was most clearly reflected in judicial questions, where the Bill of Rights was defined as applying only to federal laws. State laws, and their inclusion of civil liberties, could differ from federal laws. The most glaring example of this was the right of states to allow holding "citizens in bondage" (slavery).

THE CONSTITUTION OF 1787

The original Constitution contained eight basic parts: an introductory sentence explaining its goals and seven articles defining the powers of the new government. Most of the document concerns the legislature, which was considered the primary branch of government by the founders. Evidence from the Constitutional Convention shows that the most time was spent designing this branch. Almost half of the document is concerned with Congress. Almost all details of specific governmental powers are about Congress. Congressional officers, such as the Speaker of the House and President of the Senate, are specifically listed. Congress is given a list of 17 duties, including items such as interstate commerce, regulating money, creating courts, declaring war, taking care of roads, awarding patents, preventing counterfeiting, and making rules for the military.

Although the president can veto legislation, the Congress can vote to override the president's veto.

The Constitution also placed specific limits on the powers of Congress. Congress cannot suspend certain rights without declaring emergencies, cannot tax exports, and cannot grant titles of nobility.

THE EXECUTIVE BRANCH

> As a point of comparison, most of the description of the executive branch covers details about the Electoral College, and much of that has been amended. The job description of the president is minimal; in addition, his or her powers are often directly checked by Congress and somewhat open to interpretation.

Article II outlines the powers and responsibilities of the executive branch. According to these powers, the president oversees the cabinet departments, but no other descriptions or duties are included. The president is commander of the military but must allow Congress to fund and manage the military. The president appoints officials and negotiates treaties, but both powers require congressional approval. Presidents can also be removed from office by Congress if convicted of "treason, bribery, or other high crimes and misdemeanors."

THE JUDICIAL BRANCH

> The section of the Constitution describing the federal judiciary is even less detailed, with minimal descriptions of how courts can be created and what their jurisdiction includes.

Lower courts can be established to help the federal courts' workload, if Congress creates them. Federal judges and justices serve for life, unless they are impeached and removed. Federal courts have jurisdiction over cases involving states suing or being sued. The rest of the article concerning the judicial branch covers the issue of treason, a crime defined very broadly in other nations. In the United States, treason can only exist if someone is "levying War against them [the United States], or in adhering to their Enemies, giving them Aid and Comfort."

Articles IV, V, and VI describe how states relate to other states, describe how amendments can be created, and establish the legal status of the new government. Article IV has states give "Full Faith and Credit" to the laws of the other states. States must return fleeing criminals to other states upon receiving extradition requests from governors. No states can be created from lands inside existing states without the states' permission. Article V lists the ways Congress and the states create possible amendments. Article VI gives the promise that debts from prior times will be honored by the new government. Also, the "supremacy" status of the Constitution is established.

Article VII describes the ratification process, which was completed in 1788.

FIVE BASIC FORMS OF POLITICAL AUTHORITY

The Constitution establishes the five basic forms of political authority that are central to American government: leadership through representatives that serve at the will of the voters (republic), national and local levels of authority (federalism), different areas of authority for different branches of government (separations of powers), limits to power by having branches control each other (checks and balances), and specific freedoms that cannot be taken away from the public (civil liberties). The interpretations of these competing powers make up the basic political debates of our system.

INTERPRETATIONS AND ADJUSTMENTS

THE PREAMBLE

With the first sentence of the Preamble to the Constitution, the authors explained that this new plan was aimed at correcting the problems of the Articles of Confederation. The call for a "more perfect Union" showed that the existing government was a less-than-perfect union. The other goals of "justice," "domestic Tranquility," "defence" (defense), and "general Welfare" were clearly practical issues that were not being addressed during the turmoil of the early 1780s. The final call for securing the "Blessings of Liberty" is a return to the goals of the Declaration of Independence.

ARTICLE I

The original primacy of the legislative branch is demonstrated by the length and care given to this article. Congress is given leaders, organization, and at least 17 duties. Furthermore, Congress is given instructions to "make all Laws which shall be necessary and proper." This sentence has been given the title the "Elastic Clause" and has become one of the most controversial points of constitutional interpretation in the history of the United States. Clearly, the founders anticipated change and new challenges for American government. They did not intend to leave Congress without powers to adapt to changing times. However, the scope of possible adaptations is still debated.

Modern-day conservatives point to two phrases to support their argument that the powers of Congress should be limited. In the first sentence of Article I, Section 1, the words "herein granted" could be interpreted as an indication that the founders felt that Congress must only exercise those powers listed in the Constitution, specifically those listed in Section 8. Also, the Elastic Clause contains the phrase "for carrying into Execution the foregoing Powers," suggesting that Congress can do what is necessary and proper for powers specifically listed but not anything else. Modern liberals emphasize Congress's authority over "Commerce … among the several States" and the phrase "all other Powers vested by this Constitution" to argue for the expansions of governmental power.

Even though the descriptions in Article I are lengthy, many current practices have been created beyond the original framework. Congress has developed the complex committee system to manage their workload. Agencies and their powers are separate inventions. These parts of government were not included in the original plans. Even the portion of Article I that lists some limits to Congress's powers has been at the center of some controversies.

In Section 9, Congress is prohibited from suspending the "*Writ of Habeas Corpus*" rights. Citizens cannot be arrested and held without being able to answer to charges, unless "the public Safety may require it." Under what circumstances should Congress be able to make such a declaration? What happens when Congress needs to make such a declaration and can't or won't? This happened in 1861, and Abraham Lincoln used the powers given in Article IV to suspend such writs. Should this Article I power be available to the executive?

Article II

Much of this article describes the selection process known as the Electoral College. Most of this section was amended by the 12th Amendment. What remains is an outline of a presidential office with significant but limited and checked powers. As will be discussed in detail in Chapter 13, the Constitution allows the president to command the military, deal with foreign nations, and have "Heads of Departments" but gives the office no further powers. The founders did not trust concentrated power. They also did not let presidents be selected directly by the public. The history of the U.S. presidency is, therefore, a history of stretching the limits of constitutional powers. Major events like the War with Mexico, the Civil War, the Great Depression, World War II, and the Cold War have all been steps in the development of a powerful executive leader. During times of crisis, it is often impossible for the country to wait for the political system. Citizens, and the Congress, have given presidents new levels of authority over a vast bureaucracy, the formation of economic policies, and national security.

Article III

Article III states that there will be federal courts, that Congress can create them, and that judges' salaries are guaranteed, and it carefully defines *treason*. These are the basics covered in the article, and little else is present. The power of judicial review was established by the court case of *Marbury v. Madison*. Federal courts do have jurisdiction of cases "under this Constitution," and special cases go directly to the Supreme Court. The development of court powers and its attempts at making public policy have been major points of controversy historically and are at the center of recent struggles between conservatives and liberals.

ARTICLE IV

According to Article IV, states must give the various laws of other states "Full Faith and Credit." Some controversies have arisen over certain laws, such as those permitting gay marriage or those permitting the extradition of criminals to a state to face the death penalty.

The last portion of Article IV has been a source of much controversy. States are guaranteed protection by Congress, but the sentence also contains the directive to presidents to step in if "the Legislature cannot be convened." Presidents since James K. Polk have used this clause to expand powers. Polk ordered troops into disputed areas of Texas, knowing hostilities would begin and that Congress wanted more time for negotiations. Lincoln suspended habeas corpus to protect Maryland under Article IV.

ARTICLE V

According to Article V, amendments may be proposed in two ways, and they may be approved by the states in two ways. Congress can propose amendments with a two-thirds vote by each house, or two-thirds of state legislatures can request that Congress call for a national convention for that purpose. Ratification occurs with either the approval of three-fourths of state legislatures or three-fourths of the states approving through conventions specifically called for that purpose. All amendments except the 21st have been created by Congress proposing and state legislatures approving. The 21st Amendment was passed by Congress proposing it and state conventions being called for ratification. No amendments have been proposed by states requesting a national convention.

ARTICLE VI

The "Supremacy Clause" is the label for this establishment of the constitution as the "supreme Law of the Land." This article also contains the promise to honor prior debts of the nation, which was important for the ratification debate. Government leaders are also protected from having to make religious oaths as part of their duties.

ARTICLE VII

Once 9 of the 13 states ratified the Constitution in 1788, it was in effect. The nation did, however, wait for Virginia and New York to vote for ratification before holding elections for the new Congress and executive. Later, North Carolina reversed itself and ratified, thus making 12 states under the new constitution. Rhode Island, the one state that did not ratify the Constitution in 1789, did so in 1791.

THE BILL OF RIGHTS AND OTHER AMENDMENTS

Anti-Federalists fought the ratification of the Constitution, especially in New York, Virginia, and North Carolina. The major sticking point was the lack of clear limits to federal power. The Federalists agreed to add a series of amendments as soon as the new Congress could form, and this was done in 1789. Madison, then a member of the House of Representatives, led the drafting of the first set of amendments, which became the Bill of Rights. The section on civil liberties in Chapter 15 will further explore the debates surrounding amendments; however, the chart at the end of this chapter provides an overview of the amendments. Note the key legal concepts associated with specific amendments listed in the table.

It is remarkable how little the Constitution has changed since 1791, when the Bill of Rights was added. Only 17 other amendments have been ratified. Seven of these amendments concern civil rights, and the other 10 are about government procedures. The seven rights are as follows:

1. Freedom for enslaved African Americans

2. Due process and equal protection for African Americans

3. Voting rights for all men

4. Senators elected by citizens of states and not state legislatures

5. Voting rights for women

6. Voting rights for African Americans

7. Voting rights for those age 18 to 20

All of the other amendments cover issues of lawsuits against states, changing electoral votes, income tax, prohibition and its repeal, the earlier inauguration date, two-term limits for presidents, electoral votes for the District of Columbia, presidential succession, and congressional pay.

Congress has now established time limits for proposed amendments, especially because the 27th Amendment took 203 years to ratify. In 1917, Congress set a seven-year limit on each proposed amendment, and this limit contributed to the failure of changes like the Equal Rights Amendment.

OUTLINE OF THE CONSTITUTION

BASICS OF THE CONSTITUTION

- Preamble: The goals of this new plan for government
- Articles: Seven major sections that delineate the structures and powers of the federal government, the duties of states, and the ratification process
- Amendments: Changes made

The following are the five basic principles of the Constitution:

1. Popular sovereignty
2. Federalism
3. Separation of powers
4. Checks and balances
5. Limited government

OUTLINE AND KEY TERMS OF THE CONSTITUTION (NOT INCLUDING ITEMS REMOVED/AMENDED)

THE PREAMBLE

The basic goals of the new government of 1787:

- "form a more perfect Union"
- "establish Justice"
- "insure domestic Tranquility"
- "provide for the common defence"
- "promote the general Welfare"
- "secure the Blessings of Liberty"

ARTICLE I: LEGISLATIVE BRANCH

Sections 1, 2, 3: The Organization of House and Senate

- There is a bicameral legislature (two bodies: House and Senate).

- House members serve for 2 years, must be 25 years old and citizens for 7 years, and reside in their states.

- The Speaker is the leader of the House.

- New apportionment or reapportionment of districts and seats occurs after every 10-year census.

- The House has the power to impeach the president.

- Senate members serve for 6 years, must be 30 years old, and citizens for 9 years, and must reside in their state.

- The President of the Senate is the vice president of the United States.

- The President *"Pro Tempore"* (*pro tem*) serves if the vice president is not available.

- The Senate has the power to try those impeached by the House.

Sections 4, 5, 6, 7: Workings of the Congress

- An annual session of Congress is required.

- Congress has power over members, attendance, and qualifications.

- Congress must keep a journal of its proceedings (*The Congressional Record*).

- Congress sets its own salary (limited by the 27th Amendment).

- Members are immune from arrest during a session.

- Members may not hold double political offices.

- Revenue bills must initiate in the House.

- Removal powers require a two-thirds vote.

- Congress can override a presidential veto with a two-thirds vote.

Section 8: The Powers of Congress "Delegated," "Enumerated," "Implied," "Necessary and Proper"

- There are 18 clauses that give specific lists of federal powers.

- Key examples:

  - Clause 2: "To borrow Money ..."

  - Clause 3: "To regulate Commerce ..." (the Commerce Clause)

  - Clause 9: "To constitute Tribunals ..." (create lower federal courts)

  - Clause 11: "To declare war ..."

  - Clause 18: "To make all Laws which shall be necessary and proper ..." (the Elastic Clause)

Section 9: "Powers Denied to Congress"

- *Writ of Habeus Corpus* may not be suspended unless "the public Safety may require it."

- No "Bills of Attainder" may be created.

- No "*ex post facto*" laws may be created.

- No tax may be levied on exports from states.

- No titles of nobility can be given.

ARTICLE II: THE EXECUTIVE BRANCH AND THE ELECTORAL COLLEGE

Section 1

- The president's term is four years, and the Electoral College will select the president.

- The president must be 35 years old, a U.S. resident for 14 years, and a "natural" (native-born) citizen.

- Electors will be "equal to the whole Number of Senators and Representatives to which the State may be entitled."

- Presidents will receive salaries set by Congress.

- *Note*: Much of this section has been amended by the 12th and 25th Amendments.

Sections 2, 3: Powers and Duties of the President

- Is commander in chief of the armed forces.

- Makes/negotiates treaties.

- Nominates ambassadors and judges.

- Works with "Heads of Departments" (Cabinet).

- Fills "Recess" appointments, lasting until the end of Congress's next session.

- Gives the "State of the Union" message.

- May adjourn Congress if they can't agree on a time.

- Receives foreign ambassadors.

- Takes "Care that the Laws be faithfully executed."

- Commissions "all Officers" of the military.

Section 4: Removal of the President, Vice President, or "all civil Officers of the United States"

- Impeachment (House)

- Trial (Senate)

- Removal upon "Conviction of, Treason, Bribery, or other high Crimes and Misdemeanors"

ARTICLE III: JUDICIAL BRANCH

Section 1, 2: The Federal Courts

- There will be one Supreme Court, and there will be inferior courts if created by Congress.

- There will be life terms for federal judges, whose salaries are set by Congress.

- The jurisdiction of the Supreme Court will be cases under the Constitution.

- The Supreme Court has original jurisdiction in certain cases and appellate jurisdiction in cases from lower courts.

Section 3: Treason

- Treason "shall consist only in levying War against them (United States), adhering to their Enemies, giving them Aid and Comfort."

- Two witnesses are required in open court.

- Congress can set the punishment if convicted.

- No punishment will be extended to families (no "Corruption of Blood").

ARTICLE IV: STATES

Sections 1, 2, 3, 4: Relations among the States

- There is "Full Faith and Credit," meaning states recognize laws from other states that might be different from their own laws.

- Provides for extradition of criminals back to another state.

- New states can be created by Congress.

- Congress remains in charge of federal properties.

- All states are guaranteed a "Republican Form of Government" and protection provided by Congress or the president.

ARTICLE V: AMENDMENTS

- Congress proposes amendments with a two-thirds vote of each house.

- State legislatures ratify with a three-fourths vote.

  or

- Two-thirds of state legislatures request a national constitutional convention where an amendment is proposed.

- Three-fourths of specifically called state conventions vote to ratify.

ARTICLE VI: STATUS OF THE CONSTITUTION

Supremacy Clause

- The Constitution "shall be the supreme Law of the Land ..."
- Leaders are bound by oath to support the Constitution.
- No religious tests can be given as a condition or qualification for a government office.
- All debts of the United States incurred under the Articles of Confederation will be honored.

ARTICLE VII: RATIFICATION

- Nine of 13 states were needed to ratify the Constitution for it to take effect.
- This was completed in 1788.

AMENDMENTS AND KEY TERMS

Amendment and Topics	Key Issues/Terms (see Chapter 15)	Related Legal Issues/Terms (see Chapter 15)
1. Religion Speech Press Assembly and Petition	Establishment Clause versus Free-Exercise Clause Abridging? Just Speech? Peaceably, Redress	Which to Emphasize? • *Lemon Test* • *Clear-and-Present-Danger Test* • *Pure Speech* • *Symbolic Speech* • *Community Standards* • *Incitement* • *Prior Restraint* • *Libel and Slander*
2. Right to Bear Arms	Regulated Militia versus Rights of the People	Which to Emphasize?
3. Quartering of Troops		
4. Search and Seizure	Unreasonable Search versus Probable Cause	*Exclusionary Rule, Good Faith Exception,* Privacy? Reasonable?
5. Indictments, Double Jeopardy, Just Compensation	Compelled, Due Process	*Self-Incrimination, Eminent Domain*
6. Speedy and Public Trial, Confront Witness, Counsel	Speedy, Impartial Jury	What Levels of Courts?
7. Jury in Civil Trials		
8. Excessive Bail, Cruel and Unusual Punishments		Death Penalty?
9. Rights Retained by the People		Privacy and How Much?

10. Rights to States	Reserved Powers	How Broad? When in Conflict with the 14th?
11. Rules for Lawsuits against States		One State Cannot Be Sued in Another State
12. Separate Votes for President and Vice President	Reforms of the Electoral College	Corrections for the Elections of 1796 and 1800
13. Abolition of Slavery		
14. Citizenship, Due Process, Equal Protection (See Chapter 15 for further details.)	Application to States	*Incorporation* "Congress shall have the power to enforce, by appropriate legislation.…"
15. Voting Rights and Race	No Denial on Account of Race, Color…	
16. Federal Income Tax		
17. Direct Election of Senators		
18. Prohibition		In Effect From 1920 to 1933
19. Women's Vote		Suffrage
20. New Start for Federal Terms	Congress = January 3 President = January 20	
21. Repeal of Prohibition		Local Control
22. Two-Term Limit for the President	Two Full Terms or Maximum of 10 Years	
23. Number of Votes for president for Washington, D.C.	No Fewer Electoral Votes than the Least Populated State (= 3)	
24. No Poll Tax		Jim Crow Laws
25. Succession	If the President Dies or Becomes Incapacitated, the Vice President Must Assume the Presidency; If There Is No Vice President, Then the President Must Appoint One and Congress Must Confirm the Appointment.	Procedures for Succession? What Constitutes the State Where the President Can No Longer Serve?
26. Voting Age Lowered to Age 18		
27. Congressional Pay Raises	Congress Should Wait Until after the Next Election.	Did Congress Avoid This by Tying Their Pay Increases to Social Security COLAs? Cost-of-Living Adjustments

MAJOR CONSTITUTIONAL "CLAUSES"

Major Examples/Common Names

ASC = Article, Section, Clause (Paragraph):

Name	ASC Location	Meaning
Admissions Clause	A4S3C1	Congress admits new states. If parts of an existing state are involved, the state must give permission.
Advice and Consent Clause	A2S2C2	Treaties and nominations: President starts, Senate approves with two-thirds vote.
Appointments Clause	A2S2C2	Congress can give permission for "inferior" officers to be set without the Senate's approval.
Arisings Clause	A3S2C1	"The judicial Power shall extend to all Cases, in Law and Equity, arising under this Constitution…."
Comity Clause	A4S1	Congress can determine the "effect thereof" of state laws if they conflict with laws of other states.
Commerce Clause	A1S8C3	Congress can "regulate Commerce with Foreign Nations, and among the several States…."
Compact Clause	A1S10C3	"No state shall, without Consent of Congress … enter into any Agreement or Compact with another State…."
Contract Clause	A1S10C1	No state may "pass any … Law impairing the Obligation of Contracts…."
Elastic Clause	A1S8C18	(Congress) "To make all Laws which shall be necessary and proper for carrying into Execution…."
Exceptions Clause	A3S2C2	Supreme Court has appellate jurisdiction in cases "with such Exceptions … as Congress shall make."
Full Faith and Credit Clause	A4S1	States must give different laws and rules of other states the "Full Faith…."
Guarantee Clause	A4S4	Each state shall be guaranteed a republican form of government by Congress or the president.
Origination Clause	A1S7C1	Bills raising revenues (taxes) must originate in the House of Representatives.
Presentment Clause	A1S7C2	Bills must be presented to the executive for final processing or veto.
Subscription Clause	After A7	The list of the original signers of the Constitution (39 of the 55 delegates in Philadelphia; 3 refused to sign)
Supremacy Clause	A6S2	The Constitution, laws of the United States, and treaties: "shall be the supreme Law of the Land…."

REVIEW QUESTIONS

MULTIPLE-CHOICE QUESTIONS

1. *Federalism* originally meant that

    (A) the national government would protect civil rights in states.

    (B) state governments would have power equal to the federal government.

    (C) the national and state governments would protect the same rights.

    (D) political power is shared and divided between national and state governments.

    (E) states would join the union only if they ratified the Constitution.

2. All of the following are evidence of the original dominance of Congress **EXCEPT**

    (A) presidential veto powers.

    (B) the length and detail of Article I.

    (C) checks on presidential appointments.

    (D) presidential "recess appointment" powers.

    (E) All are examples of congressional dominance.

3. Which power was **NOT** included in the Constitution?

    (A) The vice president's role in two federal branches

    (B) Congress's power to declare the punishment for treason

    (C) The Senate's power to filibuster bills

    (D) Congress's power to suspend *writs of habeas corpus*

    (E) Congress's ability to tax exports

4. A dispute between presidents and Congress centers on

    (A) presidents assuming powers given to Congress in Article I.

    (B) presidents acting without actual constitutional authority.

    (C) Congress's unwillingness to allow presidents to be a true "commander in chief."

    (D) Congress giving presidents power to control rules of the military.

    (E) Congress's refusal to protect the states in times of crisis.

5. Congress has all of the following powers **EXCEPT**

    (A) the right to set salaries for its members.

    (B) the right to remove members of Congress.

    (C) the right to create a national debt.

    (D) the power for its members to serve temporarily as members of the Electoral College.

    (E) the right not to pay military personnel.

FREE-RESPONSE QUESTIONS

1. Federalism is the layering of governmental powers.

   (A) Identify two ways in which federalism developed in the United States.

   (B) Explain how these changes occurred.

2. The Preamble of the Constitution identifies the goals of government.

   (A) Identify any two of these goals.

   (B) Identify and explain where and how these goals are addressed in the Constitution.

ANSWERS AND EXPLANATIONS

MULTIPLE-CHOICE ANSWERS

1. D

Federalism originally meant that layers of political power are shared and divided between national and state governments. The national government would ensure "republican" governments in states, but not all rights. States could, and did, have vastly different sets of citizens' rights. Approval by only 9 of the original 13 states was needed for ratification of the Constitution.

2. E

Presidential veto powers, the length and detail of Article I, checks on presidential appointments, and presidential "recess" appointments are all evidence of the powers of Congress. If the president vetoes, Congress can still override. "Recess appointments" must be approved after a year.

3. C

The Senate's power to filibuster bills to death is tradition. Choice (A) is incorrect because the vice president is also president of the Senate. Choice (B) is incorrect because the Constitution clearly states Congress's power to declare the punishment for treason. Choice (D) is incorrect because, according to the Constitution, Congress can suspend *writs of habeas corpus* in emergencies. (Congress can also declare national emergencies.) Choice (E) is incorrect because Congress can't tax exports.

4. A

A major dispute between presidents and Congress comes from presidents assuming powers that were granted to Congress in Article I. President Lincoln started this trend when he got away with suspending *writs of habeas corpus* in 1861. He claimed that Congress could not act, thus allowing him to take on Article I powers. Congress has never questioned the president's role as civilian commander.

5. D

Members of Congress do not have the right to serve temporarily as members of the Electoral College. All of the other rights listed are granted by the Constitution except this dual role. Members of the Electoral College may not hold elected office.

FREE-RESPONSE ANSWERS

1. **4-point Rubric**

   2 points in part (A): (identify any two forms)

   - States and federal government are separate and relatively equal.
   - State rules apply to states; federal rules and the Constitution apply to federal areas/jurisdiction only.
   - National laws come to dominance.
   - National rules and rights apply to states.
   - The Bill of Rights applies to states.

   2 points in part (B): (explain the change)

   - Supreme Court makes interpretations of federal authority.
   - Great Depression changes demand for federal authority.
   - WWII changes demand for federal authority.
   - Civil rights movement and Cold War make demands (discussed in later chapters).
   - Reagan Revolution

2. **6-point Rubric**

   2 points in part (A): (identify any two goals)

   - A more perfect union
   - Justice
   - Domestic tranquility
   - Common defense
   - General welfare
   - Blessings of liberty

   4 points in part (B): (2 for identifying in the Constitution, 2 for explanations)

   - Stronger central powers, such as federal tax powers, courts, and chief executive, make a more perfect union.
   - Some limits on Congress and state powers in Articles I and IV, along with federal courts, give justice.
   - *Writs of habeas corpus,* no bills of attainder, no *ex post facto* laws, no taxes on exports, and guarantees of republican governments would create domestic tranquility.
   - Congress's power to regulate the military and the president's powers to be commander in chief would provide defense.
   - Congress's powers to regulate trade and commerce and the court's ability to mediate conflicts would promote the general welfare.
   - The inclusion of a Bill of Rights secured the blessings of liberty.

CHAPTER 5: FEDERALISM AND THE U.S. GOVERNMENT

IF YOU LEARN ONLY SIX THINGS IN THIS CHAPTER . . .

1. Federal powers are listed in the Constitution or directly implied by the Constitution. All powers not listed in the Constitution are considered to be reserved to the states.

2. Federalism has shifted in meaning from a sharing of power between federal and state authority to the preponderance of governmental power being in the hands of the federal government. The unwillingness of states to protect basic rights has contributed to this shift.

3. Federal powers are limited by the separation of powers and checks and balances.

4. Judicial review was not listed in the Constitution but was established by the Supreme Court decision in *Marbury v. Madison*.

5. Control of federal funds has been a major way the federal government has extended its power.

6. The scope of federal powers has increased and decreased over the history of the United States.

BASIC STRUCTURE OF THE FEDERAL SYSTEM

Federalism is a basic principle of American government. Dividing powers among national and state governments is a complex task and the source of many debates, but the constitutional framework of the U.S. federal system is relatively simple. The powers of the national and state governments are divided into four basic categories.

1. The first category is the powers of the national government, which are divided into three subcategories. **Delegated powers**, or expressed powers, are those that are written in

the Constitution. **Implied powers** may be "reasonably inferred" from the Constitution through the **Elastic Clause**. **Inherent powers** do not rely on specific clauses of the Constitution; usually they are in the area of foreign affairs and grow out of the very existence of the national government (e.g., the power to recognize foreign states).

2. **Reserved powers** are those powers that are not delegated to the federal government or denied to the states. These powers are not expressly listed but are guaranteed to the states by the 10th Amendment. Generally, these powers enable state governments to regulate their internal affairs.

3. **Concurrent powers** are those held by both the federal and state governments. These are the powers that the Constitution does not give exclusively to the national government or denies to the states. These powers include those to levy and collect taxes, make laws, and provide for the health and welfare of citizens.

4. **Prohibited powers**, also known as restricted powers, are denied to the federal government, the state governments, or both. The taxing of exports is an example of a prohibited power.

THE "SUPREMACY CLAUSE"

Article VI of the Constitution states that the document is "the supreme Law of the Land." All officials of the country must give oaths to support the Constitution. States cannot override the national powers.

THE ORIGINAL SCOPE OF FEDERALISM

The original interpretation of federalism, called **dual federalism**, was prevalent until the Civil War. Dual federalism interpreted the Constitution as having given limited powers to the national government and having left most power in the hands of the states. Both of these levels of government were viewed as being able to dominate their own spheres of influence, with the Supreme Court acting as a referee when disputes arose between the two. Dual federalism was criticized for being inadequate for dealing with states that denied freedom (e.g., slavery) and civil rights (e.g., Jim Crow laws) to their inhabitants, as well as for being unable to handle the economic and social changes that were taking place in the United States.

CHANGES IN U.S. FEDERALISM

One of the most fundamental and important changes in American government has been the gradual, but significant, evolution of federalism. The territorial expansion of the country, the upheaval of the Civil War, America's development into an industrial and international power, the collapse of world economies in the mid-20th century, the struggles of two world wars, and threats of expanding communism have all significantly changed the public's expectations of central powers. Congress uses the Commerce and Elastic clauses to deal with interstate trade and civil rights issues.

The abolition of the institution of slavery as a result of the Civil War changed the scope of federalism as it applied to the rights of citizenship and was the springboard for applying other federal rights to the states. The Great Depression led to an increased acceptance of a strong role for the national government in promoting the economic health of the nation.

As the federal government has expanded its responsibilities, revenue distribution has become a central feature of its power. When the federal government distributes tax dollars to the states, it attaches rules and regulations to those monies. States are left to decide whether they want to accept the needed funds and adhere to federal rules or whether they would prefer to attempt to do without the funds and determine their own policies. Even conservative administrations, such as that of George W. Bush, use such tactics to pressure states to follow their guidelines on policies such as the "No Child Left Behind" education standards. This modern interpretation of federalism is called "**fiscal federalism**."

Any discussion of federalism must include the courts. Supreme Court rulings concerning federalism have been made since the early 1800s. The Supreme Court has expanded federal power to enable creation of a national banking system, control of the economy, and the building of a vast transportation and communication networks. Details of such rulings will be covered in Chapter 15.

COOPERATIVE FEDERALISM

Cooperative federalism views federalism as a system that helps to provide goods and services to citizens. This providing of various goods and services requires a good deal of cooperation among federal and state governments. This interpretation of federalism is a variation of the dual federalism that was prevalent for the first hundred years after the American Revolution.

EXAMPLES OF U.S. FEDERALISM: SEPARATIONS OF POWERS

Congress has the authority to create legislation for the federal government. The executive branch can establish priorities and attempt to veto, but Congress can ignore the priorities and override vetoes. The Supreme Court might declare legislative acts of Congress unconstitutional but only if constitutional challenges are made, work their way up to the Supreme Court, and are accepted by the Supreme Court. Even then, Congress can propose amendments that will change the way the Court can rule on such challenges in the future. If states ratify such amendments, Congress's powers are reestablished.

The president and his or her administration are in charge of executing the laws created by the Congress. The executive branch has been given extensive powers to create bureaucracies to execute these laws. These agencies have some judicial powers to restrict citizens' rights under their rules and regulations.

EXAMPLES OF U.S. FEDERALISM: CHECKS AND BALANCES

The main purpose of the legislative branch is to create laws. The president can veto such proposed legislation; however, Congress can override a presidential veto with two-thirds of votes from each chamber. The president can kill legislation that is delayed until there are fewer than 10 days left in a session. This **pocket veto** is a significant power over Congress.

The president appoints justices to the Supreme Court. Congress must approve these appointments. These events are relatively rare and widely debated. The nation understands the importance of these lifetime appointments and their potential impact on the nation's laws.

The president creates the very important federal budget. Congress reacts to this budget, creating its own version, but still faces the threat of veto. The ultimate responsibility for finalizing the budget belongs to Congress. Two mid-1990s attempts by Congress to blame President Bill Clinton for budget problems backfired, because the public understood where the final responsibility rested.

Congress can impeach and remove the president or members of the Supreme Court. The House may charge (impeach), and the Senate may try the case. The potential punishment from Congress is limited by the Constitution to stripping the guilty persons from office, blocking them from future government positions, and not paying their pensions. Even when the House goes to the extraordinary effort to impeach, the Senate may choose to leave the offender in office. In the famous cases of Andrew Johnson and Clinton, the House did impeach, but the Senate fell short of votes required for removal. Both presidents finished their terms.

The Supreme Court can interpret laws created by Congress and declare them unconstitutional. This is known as *judicial review* and was established by the court case of *Marbury v. Madison* in 1803. Judicial review was not part of the original Constitution but was included in Hamilton's arguments in the *Federalist Papers*. Judicial review has been practiced for over two centuries.

EXAMPLES OF U.S. FEDERALISM: FISCAL FEDERALISM

When the international economy collapsed in the 1930s, many reforms that were enacted in the Progressive Era were expanded and made central components of the duties of the U.S. government. The core of many of these new programs was the distribution of funds to build dams, build roads, provide energy sources, and fund job programs. States are often unable to address these areas, especially for minority groups. The federal government has become a major source of financial support, and with this support, federal powers over the states have been expanded. All levels of government must cooperate to address some of the ills of the nation, such as persistent poverty, natural disasters, or states in need of budget bailouts from the federal government. However, presidential administrations and Congresses have attached strings to many of these funds. State and local governments must follow federal rules about discrimination, equality, affirmative action, and other guidelines to be eligible for federal funds.

EXAMPLES OF NATIONAL AND STATE POWERS IN MODERN FEDERALISM

BASIC NATIONAL POWERS

- Delegated, implied, and inherent in the Constitution. These are mostly found in the Preamble, Article I Section 8, Article II, Article III, Article IV Section 4, and Article VI. Examples include the following:

  - Taxation

  - Raise and maintain an army

  - Declare war

  - Regulate commerce

- Rulings by the Supreme Court; for example, *Marbury v. Madison,* 1803, and *McCulloch v. Maryland,* 1819

- Rights incorporated from the 14th Amendment. *Incorporation* is the concept of federal rights being applied to the states. The key phrases used in most of such cases are the 14th Amendment requirements that states may not "deprive any person of life, liberty, or property, without due process of law; nor...the equal protection of the laws."

- Acts made federal offenses by acts of Congress. Examples include the following:

  - Kidnapping

  - Crossing state lines with intent to commit crimes

  - Threatening or attacking federal officials

  - Violating the civil rights of citizens

BASIC STATE POWERS

- Reserved to the states: conduct elections, select local officials, and select electors

- Rights held under the 10th Amendment

- Traditional rights held by states. Examples include the following:

  - Business licenses

  - Marriage licenses

  - Legal practice licenses

  - Professional licenses

  - Civil laws not involving federal issues

  - Criminal laws not made federal

  - Education rules

MAJOR EVENTS IN FEDERALISM

1789 to the Civil War	Dual federalism is dominant. States can define full citizenship. Specific court cases are used to define federal authority over trade, interstate commerce, and banking.
Civil War Amendments (1860s)	The 13th, 14th, and 15th Amendments take from the states the rights to allow slavery, define levels of citizenship, and stop African American men from voting.
Post-Reconstruction (1876 to early 1900s)	States regain authority over status of citizens in areas of voting and segregation, formalized in the case of *Plessy v. Ferguson*, 1896.
New Deal and World War II (1930s and 1940s)	Federal authority over commerce is expanded during the New Deal and legislation after WWII. The Employment Act of 1946 is a key example.
Civil Rights Era (1950s to the 1970s)	With *Brown v. Board of Education*, the Civil Rights Act of 1964, and the Great Society programs, federal authority over civil liberties and public welfare is expanded.
Devolution Era (New Federalism) (1980s to the present)	With the election of Ronald Reagan in 1980 and the Republican majorities in Congress in 1994, efforts have grown to limit the size and scope of the federal government. More power is given to states. More emphasis is being placed on privatization.

REVIEW QUESTIONS

MULTIPLE-CHOICE QUESTIONS

1. Federalism is the idea that our two levels of government

   (A) share power.

   (B) have equal power.

   (C) are sovereign.

   (D) are checked and balanced.

   (E) are democratic.

2. In the early days of the republic, federalism was meant to

   (A) allow for strong local governments.

   (B) guarantee equality.

   (C) protect civil liberties.

   (D) encourage voting by all eligible voters.

   (E) strengthen the power of the national government.

3. One major goal of recent Republican administrations and congressional majorities has been to

   (A) give control of federal funds to states.

   (B) return more control of civil rights to the states.

   (C) return power to the states.

   (D) return more tax authority to the states.

   (E) All of the above

4. Major shifts in the conception of federalism were caused by

   (A) states failing to protect civil rights.

   (B) the inability of capitalist economies to avoid major collapses.

   (C) conflicts between republics and totalitarian nations.

   (D) changes in attitudes about the rights of minority groups.

   (E) All of the above

5. After the Great Depression and the civil rights era, the interstate commerce powers of Congress came to include

   (A) the regulation of goods and services across state lines.

   (B) the regulation of goods but not of laborers.

   (C) the general movement of goods anywhere within the United States.

   (D) activities related to racial discrimination.

   (E) criminal acts inside states.

FREE-RESPONSE QUESTIONS

1. Federalism in the United States has shifted from a form known as "dual federalism" to a newer "cooperative federalism."

   (A) Define these two kinds of federalism.

   (B) Explain why this newer concept of "cooperative federalism" favors the powers of the central government.

2. Federalism was designed to protect the rights of citizens.

   (A) Identify three ways in which the structure of federalism is used to protect the rights of U.S. residents.

   (B) Explain how the three ways identified in part (A) actually work to protect the rights of citizens.

ANSWERS AND EXPLANATIONS

MULTIPLE-CHOICE ANSWERS

1. A
Federalism is the idea that federal and state governments share power. Choice (B) is incorrect because the preponderance of governmental power has shifted between the federal and state governments over time as federalism has evolved. Choice (C) is incorrect because *sovereign* means that no power is above a government and the federal government has power over the state governments. Choice (D) is incorrect because checks and balances are a basic principle of American government, not a feature of federalism. Choice (E) is incorrect because federalism involves levels of government power, not types of government.

2. C
In the early days of the republic, federalism was meant to protect civil liberties. Layered government was, and is, designed to meet this goal. Choice (A) is incorrect because local governments do not need to be strong or to be equal to the federal government. Choice (B) is incorrect because federalism in the early days of the republic was not meant to guarantee equality. Choices (D) and (E) are incorrect because increasing voting levels and stronger national powers were not aims of early federalism.

3. C
One major goal of recent Republican administrations and congressional majorities has been to return power to the states. New federalism is aimed at allowing states to maintain control of their policies, even if they use federal funding. Choice (A) is incorrect because the goal is not to cut federal control of federal funds. Choice (B) is incorrect because the goal is not to change civil rights. Choice (D) is incorrect because the goal is not to change the ability of the federal government to tax.

4. E
Major shifts in the conception of federalism were caused by all of the factors listed. Choice (A) refers to the changes brought about by the Civil War, choice (B) refers to the changes that resulted from the Great Depression, choice (C) refers to Cold War changes, and choice (D) refers to the changes that came about during the civil rights era.

5. D
After the Great Depression and the civil rights era, interstate commerce powers of Congress came to include activities related to racial discrimination. Choice (A) and choice (B) are incorrect because they represent earlier interpretations of interstate commerce powers. Choice (C) is incorrect because it is not a correct description of the interstate commerce powers of Congress. Choice (E) is incorrect because criminal acts inside states remain under state authority.

FREE-RESPONSE ANSWERS

1. **4-point Rubric**

   2 points in part (A): (define the two types)

   - Dual—state and federal governments are relatively independent but interrelated; judicial rights are separate to their own jurisdictions; separate Bills of Rights; separate definitions of citizenship for individual states.

   - Cooperative—interstate commerce in the federal realm; issues related to interstate commerce (civil rights) also in the federal realm; federal funds help states but imply federal control of the rules; civil rights from the federal Bill of Rights apply to states; citizenship a national issue.

   2 points in part (B): (explain how this favors the federal powers)

   - States need money and must rely on federal help; therefore, federal rules override state choices.

   - All states must follow minimum federal civil rights standards.

   - Interstate commerce can be interpreted very widely, thus applying many federal regulations on businesses and individuals.

2. **6-point Rubric**

   3 points in part (A): (identify three ways the structure is used)

   - Checks of power

   - Separations of power

   - Balances of power

   - Different jurisdictions of power

   - Reserved powers

   - Supremacy Clause

   3 points in part (B): (explain how the three ways protect)

   - No branch can function fully independently without the influence of other branches.

   - Each level of government has only certain powers and no others.

   - At least three levels of powers exist, and each is often distinct (local, state, national).

   - Federal civil rights specifically apply to individuals regardless of the states.

   - If conflicts occur, they can be resolved by national authority, especially if local and state governments abuse rights.

   - Incorporation

CHAPTER 6: POLITICAL BELIEFS AND BEHAVIORS

IF YOU LEARN ONLY SIX THINGS IN THIS CHAPTER . . .

1. Most people in the United States agree fundamental values of freedom, equality of opportunity, and individualism.

2. Labels of "conservative" and "liberal" have changed meaning many times. What has remained stable are differences between those who advocate governmental controls and those who advocate individual choices.

3. Voter turnout levels in the United States are low but stable.

4. The political ideology of the U.S. electorate has always been relatively centrist.

5. Influences on political beliefs are dominated by family background, gender, and level of education.

6. Voting access has historically been restricted in the United States, but recent efforts have opened the process.

TRADITIONS OF CITIZEN BEHAVIOR

Political participation revolves around some key assumptions. People should be active and involved in politics and government. Citizens should be free to participate in government. Citizens should be informed of the policy-making process and decisions, and leaders should answer to the public about the decisions. made Government offices should be for public service rather than for self-aggrandizement.

A two-party system has always dominated American politics, despite many changes in regional populations, economic developments, and changes in the parties themselves. There are several reasons for this, but the primary causes seem to be a structure of government that allows for flexible approaches by politicians and parties, long periods of economic growth and prosperity that kept third parties from flourishing, and the relatively moderate political views of most U.S. voters.

The two major political viewpoints, liberal and conservative, stem from responses to the same sources. The Declaration of Independence's goals, the Article of Confederation's failures, the Constitution's simplicity, and the layered powers of federalism contribute to the beliefs of members of both parties. Political leaders fundamentally agree to support the system of government, the goal of individual liberty, and the general goals outlined in the Constitution's Preamble. What leads to disagreements is the possible ways that the government and citizens can best reach those goals. Should we emphasize control and collectivism, or should we emphasize choices and individualism? Only smaller, more radical groups in the United States call for significantly different forms of basic governmental powers, the elimination of private property, the mixing of church and state, or wholesale changes in the Constitution.

VIEWPOINT ORIGINS

The support for limited government has deep historical roots, so as a result, governmental powers were initially limited. The addition of the Bill of Rights exemplified public support for less government.

EARLY REPUBLIC: CONSERVATIVES VERSUS LIBERALS

In the earliest days of the republic, American liberals and conservatives resembled their European counterparts. Conservatives wanted a more centralized system. Liberals advocated decentralized power. Party labels came and went, but those who wanted a stronger use of the Constitution and generally more centralized government opposed those who wanted states' rights, no national banks, and private enterprise.

By the mid-1800s, the Jeffersonian view of state power had become mainstream, and early Republican calls for increased national power became almost radical. After the Civil War, support of federal power became the mainstream, until both major parties found themselves shocked by a rising tide of calls for help for workers and farmers. The once-radical agendas of the Populists and Progressives are now mainstream, with an eight-hour workday, legal unions, national transportation systems, federally controlled banks, and progressive taxes barely being debated.

The ideological shifts of the 20th century were greatly influenced by the Great Depression and civil rights movements. Liberals became the champions of national controls of economic policies, social welfare, and civil liberties. Conservatives took over the agenda of free enterprise, states' rights, and governmental controls of many social and moral issues. Yet there were further instances in which third-party leaders attacked both parties as being nearly identical in ideology.

PARTICIPATION AND VOTING

Possibly the most discussed issues regarding U.S. political behavior are voter participation and election turnout. Although rampant fraud, "machine" coercion, and fewer eligible voters in the 19th century created higher voter turnouts, the fact that modern-day voter turnout continues to drop is troubling. The greatest concern has been that citizens have grown so indifferent that they have stopped bothering to vote—the 2008 election may contradict this concern as voters turned out, though not in record numbers, to support candidate Barack Obama.

On a more positive note, reforms have started to make voter registration quicker and simpler. Statistical studies indicate that turnouts of those who have registered to vote have been relatively stable. This means that falling percentages are often a symbol of population growth rather than voter apathy. Family influence, education level, age, and socioeconomic status influence who votes, even if these factors do not influence how they vote. The Internet has also become a way for voters to become more involved. With websites, campaign videos, and celebrity endorsements, younger voters are being politically educated and inspired to register and to vote.

PARTICIPATION AND CIVIC RESPONSIBILITY

Civic participation for the common good is a long-standing tradition and practice in the United States. Civic participation is very political in nature because civic groups themselves are considered independent vehicles of change, policy formulation, and party support.

Religious groups provide public assistance and lobby. Education groups exist to give children new opportunities and shape educational policy. Medical groups advocate for many policies concerning public health. Business groups issue policy briefs and lobby extensively. Many groups exist just to give advocacy assistance to those with similar political goals. Environmental groups also play key roles influencing policy decisions. All of these groups are founded on the belief that citizens should try to make a difference in society. Their efforts are made possible by individuals making the choice to participate, the lack of governmental control of such groups, the groups' ability to determine their own causes, and the ability of these groups to influence policy makers.

One of the biggest changes in the way civic groups influence the national political agenda has been the vast expansion of these groups and how they lobby the leadership. More ***single-issue groups*** have emerged with the expansion of legal forms of campaign influence.

In fact, numerous competing causes have emerged. Access to funds and national attention has expanded. More groups can attempt to form political action committees and hire lobbyists. The system has become more money driven. As a result, polls show that citizens have less faith in the power of their individual participation.

THE POLITICAL SPECTRUM

There are numerous approaches to the discussion of political beliefs and groups. This section will focus on the modern uses of ideological terms and how they are represented in the United States, and it will provide a brief description of how they have changed over time.

THE AMERICAN POLITICAL SPECTRUM (FROM LEFT TO RIGHT)

Socialism. This is the idea that the citizens of a republic should control the means of production. Socialists believe that this should be done for the benefit of all. The public education system in the United States is an example of a socialist system. Most adults pay for the system through taxation, and then all families can access the benefits of public schooling. Even those who pay but do not have children in the schools should benefit from a better educated, trained, and skilled citizenry. In many parts of Western Europe, socialist programs of this kind extend to energy production, transportation, housing, and health care services.

Liberalism. Since the Progressive Era, and certainly since the Great Depression, liberals support the government in taking a central role in promoting economic development and social welfare. Since the Cold War, liberals have wanted the government to protect privacy, avoid church and state relations, and promote free speech.

Populism. Modern forms include those that are both liberal and conservative. On the modern political right, leaders such as Pat Buchanan claim a form of "populism." These populists see themselves as more independent than the major parties and more concerned with the needs of the people. On the modern left, Ralph Nader claims a form of "populism." He and his supporters feel that the government is excessively concerned with supporting large corporations at the expense of workers, and they are opposed to government interference in personal choices.

Conservatism. Since the late 1800s, conservatives have supported the ideas of economic competition and free enterprise with minimal government interference. Conservatives are very supportive of capitalism. They usually believe that markets will create improvements and innovations for all. They oppose socialist programs as inefficient, unfair, and controlling. Since the 1960s, conservatives in the United States have supported government control over social issues such as school prayer and gay marriage.

Libertarianism. Libertarians are very supportive of broad economic and social freedoms. Libertarian ideas about leaving the economy alone are popular with many Republicans. Libertarian ideas about social freedoms strike a responsive chord with some Democrats.

OTHER MODERN TERMS AND CONCEPTS OF POLITICAL BELIEFS

Neo-conservatives (neo-cons). These modern, more libertarian conservatives emphasize the need for a strong defense, open competition in economic markets, and free world trade.

Bible Belt conservatives (theo-cons). A product of the civil rights changes in the South, these conservatives tend to be Southern Baptists and more fundamentalist Christians. They dislike central government yet support issues such as prayer in public schools. The name is a reference to the traditional stretch of support that runs across the middle of the Old South. The "Moral Majority" and "Christian Coalition" political groups represent these kinds of voters. These groups have grown rapidly in number and political power and are key to current Republican support. These voters see liberalism as attacking family values and individualism.

Dixiecrats. This is the traditional label given to Southerners who remained conservative but were loyal to the Democratic Party from about 1880 to 1980. As the civil rights era and Vietnam moved the Democratic Party to more liberal stances, Dixiecrats finally forgave the Republican Party for the Civil War and joined their fellow conservatives in the Republican camp. They had always supported more conservative positions on foreign policy, states' rights, and social values, but they had worked within the Democratic Party. Between 1880 and 1980, most Southern states were run by one Democratic Party that had two major wings—conservative and progressive. When national Democratic policies became more liberal, the Southern Democratic conservatives began to defect. The emergence of the Republican Party in Southern states has become a major feature of the "political realignment" that has affected the fortunes of the two parties.

New Deal liberals. This group tends to favor a central role of the government in the economy. They support unions, Social Security as a safety net system, and generally want the government to take a leading role in promoting equality. The original coalition of New Deal liberals was built by the supporters of FDR. Key support groups were union workers in northern cities, residents of rural areas that needed federal economic help, and African Americans.

Greens (feminist liberals, environmentalist liberals, civil rights liberals, etc.). The civil rights struggles, the environmental movement, and reactions to Vietnam and Watergate created groups that wish to have the government promote social equality and establish strict environmental protections. They tend to distrust big business and the major party leaders.

Rust Belt. This region includes the Northeast, mid-Atlantic states, and portions of the eastern Midwest, which was where most of American industry was concentrated until a decline in industrial production began in the 1970s. This decline led this region to earn this nickname. Relatively high levels of unionized workers have made this region a Democratic Party stronghold since the New Deal.

Sun Belt. The South and Southwest are the fastest growing regions of the country; they contain relatively low levels of unionization, have a history of supporting states' rights, and since the 1980s have been a Republican Party stronghold.

Farm Belt. This includes the states of the Midwest that are known for agricultural production and include Iowa, Kansas, Minnesota, Nebraska, North Dakota, and South Dakota. Historically, this region has been known for its conservatism and tends to align itself with the Republican Party in the present day.

West Coast. High levels of immigration, pressing concerns over the environment, and a tradition of liberal lifestyles make the area along the Pacific more liberal.

Southern strategy. Made popular by the Nixon campaigns, Republican strategies aimed to build a powerful and loyal conservative base in the South, denying Democrats one of their traditional core support areas. Critics of this strategy claim that it was designed to play to racial divisions and tensions in the South.

MAJOR SHIFTS IN POLITICAL LABELS IN THE UNITED STATES

The terms *liberal* and *conservative* have long histories. Liberal has been associated with the "left" at least since the French Revolution. The same is true with conservatives and the "right." What have changed, often dramatically, are the goals of party groups associated with these labels. Compare the table of historical changes on the next page with the tables on U.S. political party changes that appear in Chapter 8.

When the Constitution was ratified, national concerns focused on stimulating the economy, strengthening central powers, and increasing trade with a more conservative England. As a result, early American conservatives called for a strong central government and less reliance on state power. Early American liberals called for more emphasis on state power and individual liberties. By the mid-1800s, liberals had become dominant, with conservatives mostly concentrated in the cities of the Northeast.

Modern-day liberals still strive to protect individual rights. However, their belief about what constitutes the appropriate scope of federal powers has changed. This change is best evidenced by the rapid expansion of federal power that occurred during the New Deal. Liberals today favor the use of federal power to promote economic stability as well as individual liberties and social progress.

During the late 19th and early 20th centuries, when the United States experienced rapid industrial development, conservatives began to espouse strong beliefs in the free-enterprise system and individual, especially property, rights. As with their liberal counterparts, modern-day conservatives' beliefs about the appropriate size of government changed dramatically as a result of the New Deal. Conservatives generally opposed New Deal policies and programs, which they believed made people dependent on government and unable to help themselves. Conservatives today advocate for small government, and believe that individuals, their families, and charities should meet human needs, not government programs.

LIBERALISM AND CONSERVATISM

Civil rights reforms expanded the scope of U.S. liberalism, as minority rights campaigns led to the women's rights movement and then the environmental movement. Because many environmental problems are seen as industry and corporation problems, liberals advocate strict regulation of the powerful business sector. Conservatives chafe at national control over some cultural issues, all business decisions, and economic assistance to those in need. The late 1900s saw the rebirth of conservative dominance, when economic expansion strengthened calls for less interference in the economy and smaller government.

LABELS OVER TIME

Time Period	Groups Called "Liberal"	Groups Called "Conservative"
Early 1800s	Jeffersonian Democratic-Republicans Democrats	Federalists Whigs
Civil War Era (1850s to 1870s)	Republicans	States' Rights Democrats
Late 1800s	Populists/Grange/People's Party	Republicans Democrats
Early 1900s	Progressives Teddy Roosevelt Republicans Wilson Democrats	Taft Republicans
Mid-1900s	New Deal Democrats Civil Rights Democrats	Republicans Dixiecrats States' Rights Democrats Goldwater Republicans
Late 1900s	Democrats Greens	Reagan Republicans Christian Republicans

POLITICAL EFFICACY AND POLITICAL PARTICIPATION

Political participation is determined in part by peoples' sense of **political efficacy**, which is the sense that they can make a difference through political participation. There are two types of political efficacy. **Internal efficacy** is the sense that one can understand and therefore participate in politics. **External efficacy** is the belief that one is effective when participating in politics. When voters do not have a sense of political efficacy, they tend to shun political participation. Polls indicate that peoples' sense of political efficacy has declined over time.

INFLUENCES ON POLITICAL BELIEFS

Family	This remains the most influential determinant of political beliefs. Liberal and conservative views are shaped by family influences. People tend to identify with, and vote for, the party their parents supported, but may disagree with their parents on specific economic and social issues.
Religious Affiliation	Religious beliefs can influence political beliefs, especially on economic issues and social issues. For example, some studies have concluded that Catholics tend to be more liberal on economic issues and more conservative on social issues, and that Protestants tend to be more conservative on economic issues and more liberal on social issues.
Gender	While differences in the political beliefs of men and women have been evident since women secured the right to vote in 1920, the political party receiving more female support has changed. Up until the 1950s, women tended to support the Republicans. By the 1960s, they were shifting their allegiance in large numbers to the Democrats.
Education	Traditional studies reported that those with higher levels of schooling tend to be more liberal. Two pieces of information now contradict that view. Those who have higher degrees often also have more wealth than those who don't, which often equates to modern conservatism. Conservatives have also led large-scale attacks on university programs that have radical and liberal biases. More university youth groups emphasize conservative policies. Education clearly makes a difference in voting turnout patterns. Higher-educated voters cast ballots in much higher percentages than less-educated voters.
Race and Ethnicity	In general, African Americans have been consistently liberal in their beliefs, at least since the civil rights movement. Less data are available for Latinos, but studies indicate that Mexican Americans and those with Puerto Rican heritage tend to support the Democrats. Limited research shows wide variations among the political beliefs of Asian Americans.
Economic Status	In general, those with more personal wealth tend toward the conservative end of the spectrum, and those with less are more liberal. This trend is likely due to the conservative belief in lower taxes and more personal financial freedom; those with more money want to keep it, while those with less want to benefit from liberal-backed taxpayer-funded programs. However, in the 2008 presidential election, 52 percent of voters with annual incomes over $250,000 voted for Democrat Barack Obama for president, indicating that economic interests are not necessarily a deciding factor for voters.

FACTORS INFLUENCING VOTING

The greatest predictor of whom people will vote for is party identification. Although voters may follow political contests and the issues presented in them closely, voters tend to rely on party labels when it is time to cast their ballots. Voters are also greatly influenced by candidate appeal. This factor explains why many military heroes as well as other popular and charismatic figures have been elected president. A third major factor that influences voter behavior is their positions, and the candidates', on specific issues. Many studies reveal that the state of the economy is often the most important issue in political campaigns.

The weakest factors in determining how people vote are running mates, media ads, and presidential debates. Even though a vast amount of attention is given to ads and debates, voters who care for political issues stand by their party and its candidates. Voters may complain that their party's candidate is the "lesser of two evils," but usually will stick with their party. Those voters who don't care much about issues will find the candidate's personality or image more important.

U.S. VOTER TURNOUT

Voter turnout in the United States is relatively low, especially in nonpresidential elections. Comparisons between U.S. voter turnout and that of other republics usually show that U.S. levels are much lower. The greatest factors influencing low turnout are political efficacy and the registration process. The registration process has undergone tremendous changes in recent history to increase voter turnout and access to the polls for all registered voters.

NEGATIVE ASPECTS OF LOW VOTER TURNOUTS

When voter turnout is low, political leaders and the policies they advocate and enact do not accurately reflect the will of the majority. Moreover, this situation empowers interest groups to have more control over the political process, thus further weakening American democracy.

POSITIVE ASPECTS OF LOW VOTER TURNOUTS

When the United States is socially and economically stable, voters tend to be complacent. Viewed in this light, low voter turnout can be viewed positively as a sign of economic, political, and social stability. A more cynical analysis posits that low voter turnout keeps the uninformed from casting their ballots and corrupting the political process.

OTHER FACTORS INFLUENCING U.S. VOTER TURNOUT

Crisis/War	Levels of patriotism, reactions to national threats, and domestic crises will bring out voters.
Age	Senior citizens vote more often, have time to vote, and tend to believe in the political system.
Income	Voters with limited income may lack adequate transportation to reach their polling places. Over half of the states require that employers give their employees time off from work to vote, although they may not be paid for this time. There is no federal law requiring that employees be given time to vote. Depending on their location, registered voters may find they simply cannot afford to vote.
Region	Rural voter turnouts tend to be high and conservative, yet they are less important at the national level. Southern states are key to politicians with national ambitions due to pockets of extreme conservatism and trends of higher growth.
Electoral Power	Voters may abstain from national elections if they support the candidate their state is most likely to support. If a majority is clear before the polls open, individuals may feel that their singular vote is less valuable and choose not to vote.
Apathy	When party platforms are similar, races are one-sided, or candidates are bland, turnouts are reduced.

BLOCKS TO VOTING IN THE UNITED STATES (INSTITUTIONAL RESTRICTIONS)

- Some registration processes are very lengthy and require paperwork be completed a month ahead of the election.

- Residency laws might require lengthy periods of residence in the district or state to vote.

- So many offices are being decided that ballots can be very lengthy. Some voters do not have the patience for this and ignore "down-ballot" races. Voters also tend to know less about the candidates or issues for these "down-ballot" choices and thus ignore them.

- State primary systems often limit those who do not register with parties or allow only one-party voting.

- The lack of holiday status for Election Day reduces votes. Some efforts have been made to create a national election holiday to increase voter participation.

- The Electoral College system leaves many less-populated states with little influence over the presidential selection. The winner-take-all system also discourages voting by those who feel that their minority vote will count for nothing in their state.

RECENT EFFORTS TO INCREASE VOTER TURNOUTS

In 1995 the National Voter Registration Act was passed to make voter registration easier. This "motor-voter bill" enables people to register to vote when they apply for driver's licenses and permits registration through the mail as well as at some state offices.

Moreover, some states have made absentee voting more convenient and instituted online registration.

REVIEW QUESTIONS

MULTIPLE-CHOICE QUESTIONS

1. U.S. ideas of liberalism and conservatism are grounded in

   (A) a basic belief in limited government.

   (B) the need for liberty and order.

   (C) ideas concerning political authority.

   (D) support of the constitutional framework.

   (E) All are true for liberalism and conservatism.

2. Civic participation in the United States may be declining for all of the following reasons **EXCEPT**

   (A) growing political control of a few powerful groups.

   (B) lack of belief in civic participation among minority groups.

   (C) the rapid expansion of the number of interest groups.

   (D) declining belief that participating will make a difference.

   (E) voter apathy.

3. The **GREATEST** change in U.S. liberalism has been

   (A) a shift from advocating for state power to advocating for federal power.

   (B) a shift to the Northeastern part of the country.

   (C) the rise of the Populist Party.

   (D) the rejection of Teddy Roosevelt by the Republicans.

   (E) the rise of the women's movement.

4. The **GREATEST** change in U.S. conservatism has been

   (A) the move of Dixiecrats to the Republican party.

   (B) the rejection of Progressivism in the 1920s.

   (C) the change from emphasizing national leadership to local leadership.

   (D) the emergence of religious leadership.

   (E) the rising control of rural and western states.

5. The **GREATEST** change in political behavior of citizens has been

   (A) their willingness to participate in the system.

   (B) their decreased support of leaders and their hopes for reform.

   (C) the lack of civil rights reforms sought.

   (D) increasing voter turnout.

   (E) efforts to amend the Constitution to allow for more voter access.

FREE-RESPONSE QUESTIONS

1. The labels *liberal* and *conservative* have changed dramatically in how they have been applied in U.S. politics.

    (A) Identify three such changes in U.S. political history.

    (B) Explain why these changes occurred.

2. Voter participation can be viewed as a negative for the country but also as a positive piece of evidence about our political system.

    (A) Identify two negatives of low U.S. voter turnout patterns.

    (B) Identify two ways in which low turnout is possibly positive evidence about our political system.

ANSWERS AND EXPLANATIONS

MULTIPLE-CHOICE ANSWERS

1. E
The ideas of liberalism and conservatism are grounded in the basic belief in limited government, the need for liberty and order, notions of political power, and the support for the Constitutional framework.

2. B
Civic participation in the United States is not declining due to a lack of belief in civic participation among minority groups. Minority groups participate in the same way as all other groups. All of the other choices are true.

3. A
The greatest change in U.S. liberalism has been a shift from advocating for state power to advocating for federal power. The other choices are also true but not as central to this change.

4. C
The greatest change in U.S. conservatism has been from emphasizing national leadership to emphasizing local leadership. Again, this is the greatest change from this list; the other events listed occurred but were not as central.

5. B
The greatest change in the political behavior of citizens has been the decreased support that citizens give to leaders and their hopes for reform. Many citizens have lost hope that reforms will be enacted. Choice (A) is incorrect because citizens still participate in the system. Choices (C), (D), and (E) are not true.

FREE-RESPONSE ANSWERS

1. **6-point Rubric**

   3 points in part (A): (identify three changes)

   - Early Republic: Liberal meant state controls; conservative meant federal.

   - Jeffersonian liberals versus Hamiltonian conservatives

   - Civil War: Liberal meant federal power in the economy; conservative meant states' rights.

   - Progressive Era: Liberal meant nationalist; conservative meant laissez-faire.

   - Great Depression/Civil Rights: Liberal meant national support for workers and African Americans; conservative meant pro-business and less government.

   3 points in part (B): (explain)

   - Federalists won under Washington, built a stronger federal government, became dominant; states' righters under Jefferson were liberals.

   - Slavery and states' rights became the status quo; liberals wanted national control of the rights of citizenship.

   - Populism and Progressivism shaped liberalism and its agenda.

   - Great Depression liberals expanded federal power; conservatives wanted local controls and less national government.

2. **4-point Rubric**

   2 points in part (A): (identify two negatives)

   - Less political unity

   - Less support for parties and leaders

   - Less optimism about government

   - Less belief that things can change

   - Less belief in the overall republic (apathy)

   - Less belief that one vote makes a difference

   2 points in part (B): (two ways possibly a form of positive evidence)

   - Trust in the current system

   - Sign of stability

CHAPTER 7: PUBLIC OPINION AND POLLING

IF YOU LEARN ONLY FOUR THINGS IN THIS CHAPTER . . .

1. U.S. citizens are only moderately interested in politics and are more focused on job and money concerns.

2. Collecting data about public opinion is important to executive and legislative leaders when they pursue their agendas.

3. The public values opinion polls, but leaders are often wary of public moods and the public's mastery of the facts.

4. Polls are based on statistical samples and carefully developed questioning techniques.

INTRODUCTION

Political scientists use "public opinion" as a way to determine how citizens evaluate leaders, candidates, issues, or institutions that control the laws and the government. Public opinion is critical to the ability of political leadership to gauge and gain supporters and assess citizens' willingness to follow laws.

Campaigns and parties tend to focus on "pocketbook" issues, sensing that the public raises its level of concern only when money and jobs are involved. Presidential elections certainly turn on such truths. For the entire 20th century, the outcome of about two-thirds of all elections could be predicted on election-year economic conditions. When economic conditions were improving in the year of the election, the incumbent party usually won. When these conditions were worsening, the incumbent party usually lost. This dynamic was proven true in the 2008 election with Democratic candidate Barack Obama defeating Republican party candidate John McCain in a time when a Republican was in the White House and the United States was in an ever-worsening recession.

THE DEVELOPMENT OF OPINIONS

Political loyalties are often created by way of *political socialization*. Research consistently shows that the biggest factor is family; that is, family most significantly affects a person's values, concerns, level of party loyalty, and sense of trust in government.

Another important factor in political socialization is a person's level of education. Those who have college degrees are more likely to be involved than those without degrees. Job status is important as well; for those who may have lost economic standing due to a job change or loss, participation is high. Those who live closer to the poverty level have lower levels of involvement.

OPINION DATA

Modern communications have made gathering opinion data instantaneous. Political groups use data to determine voting patterns, make economic projections, and develop money gathering strategies. Political leaders use these data to test levels of support, determine issue priorities, and watch for potential conflicts. Television and the Internet, in addition to the continued use of the radio, have dramatically changed the nature of political analysis.

Many elements of government use opinion data. Presidential staff constantly monitor the popularity of the president, the influence of the president, and the impact of presidential speeches. Members of Congress monitor the popularity of programs, potential legislation, and their images.

THE NATURE OF PRESIDENTIAL POPULARITY

Presidents face continual assessments of popularity. Right after a president is elected, the public always grants him or her a *honeymoon* period. The president enjoys a great deal of popularity at that time and is expected to take the initiative in forming policy. Congress is aware of the public's desire for change and so often initially cooperates. After about three months, however, the public begins to lose patience, and Congress becomes more independent.

The middle years of second terms are notorious times for low presidential approval ratings. "Lame duck status" sets in, and support for many presidential initiatives is low. Voters also begin blaming the president for problems that have not yet been resolved by their administrations.

POLLS AND POLLING

The business of monitoring public opinion developed after coast-to-coast forms of communication were invented. This process makes careful use of statistics and bias control. *Polling*, as it is now known, is a massive, lucrative, and controversial business used by all parties.

Monitoring public opinion dates back to the Great Depression, with the work of George Gallup. The sciences of demography and statistics advanced greatly during World War II, as did computer science. Radio and television made opinion data easy to disseminate.

With the famous exception of the 1948 election of Harry Truman over predicted winner Thomas Dewey, polling organizations have been overwhelmingly correct in predicting turnouts and election results. Their levels of accuracy have given them power. Parties pay careful attention to what voters want. Candidates change stances on issues and even entire platforms to bend to popular opinion. Leaders adjust legislative priorities based on what is on voters' minds.

There are two negative consequences to such accurate polling. First, campaign funds flow mostly to leaders in political races or to statistically even races. Polls tell us which candidates have a good chance at winning, and because few people want to venture a risk on someone with little chance for victory, unknown candidates end up with little or no access to needed funds. Second, many leaders hesitate to take on unpopular issues and tend to advocate only what is popular. This often means that issues are not addressed.

Both major political parties hire polling companies, and each carefully uses the results that will help its own party's image. Party leaders manage which poll information is released to the media, when it is given, and how it is analyzed. In addition, poll data is used to convince supporters to step up levels of support and to build party morale.

FEATURES OF PUBLIC OPINION AND POLLS

There is a "public" in our system.	Individuals are considered politically important; their opinions have merit; and they form groups based on common beliefs, interests, and regions.
There are values to "opinions."	In our political culture, public opinion influences the actions of leaders.
Polls are useful tools for forming policy.	The opinions collected reflect the overall views of the nation.
Most people are ambivalent about polls.	The vast majority of people value individual opinions and are suspicious of many poll results.
Leaders distrust the public will.	Leaders have never completely trusted public opinion polls. Polls consistently show that the public knows very little about the issues and that people change opinions quickly due to emotional shifts.
Leaders who follow polls too much are criticized as being weak.	Leaders are expected to take charge and make decisions without always having to worry about popularity numbers. At the same time, they may face criticism for not bending to the public will.

ISSUES REGARDING PUBLIC OPINIONS

Distribution	How big a piece of the electorate is concerned about an issue? If a large or critical part of the entire electorate has the same opinion on a particular issue, then that issue tends to be addressed. If the electorate is evenly split, the issue will be addressed at a regional level or left alone.
	If the electorate is deeply divided, the issue is said to be polarized. Polarized issues are often at the heart of party platforms to draw core supporters, but in reality, politicians and courts are reluctant to tackle them. That is because they provoke strong reactions from the opposition.
Intensity	Gun control, gay marriage, public school prayer, and abortion are but a few of the issues that have uncompromising supporters. These issues are often called *litmus test* issues. Core party supporters use them to determine which members are trusted to be "pure" to the cause. Litmus test issues are frequently used when Supreme Court appointees are being questioned by Senate leaders. True to form, the 2009 nomination of Sonia Sotomayor, a Latina judge, led to pointed questions about race and reverse racism.
Latency	Leaders constantly try to understand what will move the public in the future, how they will react to possible changes, and how angry they will be if no change or resolution is attempted.
Salience	Some issues change in importance over time. Union rights caused massive conflicts and violence in the past, but they are rarely seen as critical in most parts of the country.

MAJOR INDEPENDENT POLLING COMPANIES/GROUPS

Gallup	FOX News
Harris	CNN/USA/Gallup
CBS/NY Times	ABC/Washington Post
Reuters/Zogby	Pew Research

Polling must be accurate to be useful.

ISSUES IN POLLING ACCURACY

How many people are being sampled?	Everyone can't be questioned. Therefore, all polls are restricted to specific sample populations. Time and expense limits the size of polls and can cut the level of accuracy.
How was the sample population selected?	Random polling depends on knowing all of the potential population involved. Care must be taken that even seemingly random choices are actually that. The famous case of "random" telephone calls in 1948 failed to take into account that more wealthy families had personal phones at the time so the sample was biased toward upper-class voters.
If samples are taken by request, are the results valid?	Many news outlets and businesses invite responses that might be tainted by those who only listen to that outlet or are strongly opinionated.
How biased are the questions?	No form of poll question is completely neutral to all respondents. Polling groups have demonstrated this many times by getting opposite responses when a few key words of questions are changed.
How close to the election is the poll taken?	More mistakes can be made when polls are rushed, because some participants will fake answers to alter the result and hurt the other side, and data processing is more rushed and prone to errors.

REVIEW QUESTIONS

MULTIPLE-CHOICE QUESTIONS

1. In polling, a sample could **BEST** be described as

    (A) using complex computer programs to determine public opinion.

    (B) a representative group of the total population to be surveyed.

    (C) predetermined criteria for participation.

    (D) picking all of the potential political groups to possibly call.

    (E) using only computers to select who is called.

2. Last-minute polls often have results that are different from those of earlier polls. This is probably due to

    (A) the use of large numbers of questions.

    (B) the use of different questions.

    (C) an increase in sampling errors.

    (D) the lack of proper questions.

    (E) the lack of random controls.

3. The political opinions of the majority of the country have been stable over time about all of the following **EXCEPT**

    (A) support for the two major parties.

    (B) a generally low interest in politics.

    (C) a general emphasis on personal liberties.

    (D) a general level of concern about jobs.

    (E) a general mistrust of government.

4. National polling organizations tend to be

    (A) biased toward particular parties.

    (B) accurate.

    (C) inaccurate.

    (D) governmental agencies.

    (E) All of the above

5. Which issue is **LEAST** controversial among the various regions of the United States?

    (A) Abortion rights

    (B) Gay marriage

    (C) Defense spending levels

    (D) Social Security

    (E) Public school prayer

FREE-RESPONSE QUESTIONS

1. The U.S. public tends to view political polls in a positive light, while political leaders tend to have negative opinions of polls.

   (A) Explain two ways in which the public views the use and results of polls.

   (B) Explain two ways in which political leaders see the same polls in a negative light.

2. Political socialization is the way voters create their beliefs and attitudes toward government.

   (A) Identify three forms of political socialization.

   (B) Explain these three forms.

   (C) Identify the most important form of political socialization.

ANSWERS AND EXPLANATIONS

MULTIPLE-CHOICE ANSWERS

1. B

In polling, a sample is a small number of people drawn from and analyzed as representative of the entire population that will be surveyed.

2. C

Polls closer to an election tend to have problems such as skewed samples. Issues around questions or controls are usually not at stake, despite the last-minute factor.

3. A

Support for the majority parties has shifted considerably over time. The other issues have largely remained stable over time with regard to public opinion.

4. B

Major polls use very consistent methods that have yielded correct predictions far more often than not.

5. D

Because personal economic issues tend to be consistently supported by the public, Social Security would have the most support from citizens in all regions of the United States.

FREE-RESPONSE ANSWERS

1. 4-point Rubric

2 points in part (A): (two ways the public sees polls positively)

- The leaders are listening.
- The media is paying attention.
- The public has an influence.
- The agenda will be formed by the public.
- Parties will know who is supportive.

2 points in part (B): (two ways leaders see polls negatively)

- The public may not tell the truth.
- The public is fickle.
- The public intentionally misleads.
- The public has little knowledge or information.

2. 7-point Rubric

3 points in part (A): (identify three forms)

- Family
- Gender
- Media
- Education
- Age
- Wealth
- Race and ethnicity
- Religion

4 points in parts (B) and (C): (explain these three forms; identify the most important)

- Parents are the most important influence.
- More education leads to more liberal views.
- Wealthier residents vote more and are more conservative.
- Whether one is union or nonunion influences voting and liberalism.
- More religious citizens tend to be more involved and conservative.

CHAPTER 8: POLITICAL PARTIES

IF YOU LEARN ONLY SIX THINGS IN THIS CHAPTER . . .

1. The two-party system has dominated the American political system, with the major parties adopting new goals over the years.

2. The Democratic Party started as a party supporting states' rights for local control and is now a party supporting more federal power. The Republican Party started as a party supporting federal power and is now a party emphasizing states' rights.

3. The parties have also switched areas of dominance geographically. The Democrats used to control the South and rural areas; the Republicans used to control the Northeast and the West Coast. These areas of support have flipped.

4. Voting for only one party has diminished as a pattern.

5. Financial and grassroots support for parties has increased.

6. The two major parties are diverging more and becoming more polarized issues.

INTRODUCTION

Political scientists consider political parties as essential to a healthy republic. Even though the general public has historically been wary about political parties and holds negative views about how they work, elections without parties would be difficult.

FUNCTIONS OF POLITICAL PARTIES

The fundamental goals of political parties are to win elections, control the political system, and enact their agenda.

Recruit and Label Candidates	Parties search for candidates, nominate them, and help to define their viewpoints.
Influence Voters	Parties try to build coalitions of like-minded citizens.
Gather Funds	Parties raise hundreds of millions of dollars for their campaigns.
Get Information Out	Mailings, social media platforms, and other forms of communication can build support.
Oppose	No party is in control of all levels of government all of the time. Parties are the "loyal opposition," trying to force compromises.
Run the Government	Political parties play a major role in running the government. Both Congress and state legislatures are organized along party lines. Most political appointments to positions in the federal executive and judicial branches are made along party lines.

DOMINANCE OF TWO PARTIES

The Democratic and Republican parties have dominated the political landscape in the United States since the 1860s. Their core supporters focus on basic interpretations of the Constitution, goals of government, and issues of personal beliefs. Third parties have occasionally gained pockets of support but have not been able to replace either major party or create and sustain a large national following over time. In part, this is because Democrats and Republicans have been able to address the issues brought forth by political minorities.

The factor that most supports two-party dominance is the structure of national elections. Most states have rules allowing the two major parties an automatic place on the ballot. Third parties must raise a large number of petition signatures to gain access to the ballot, and even then, access is not maintained for future elections. The Electoral College system requires parties to win the plurality of a state vote to get any College votes, thus making that occurrence rare for third parties.

National elections now cost millions of dollars, thus limiting third-party chances. When third parties are able to win local and state elections, the structure of legislative committees often limits their access to positions of power. Out of frustration, no doubt, some third-party leaders have gone on to join the major parties in an attempt to make changes internally. In that position, they have had greater success in advancing their political agendas.

One of the strengths of the two major parties is their ability to adapt, absorb, and expand. When the Republican Party was created, for instance, it advocated federal power. But with industrialization and Republican control of politics for most of the late 19th century, the Republican Party began to advocate for less federal power and a laissez-faire approach to the economy.

CHANGES IN PARTY GOALS

After the presidential administration of Theodore Roosevelt, Republicans focused on supporting big business. Democrats began their support for the goals of organized labor and other working-class Americans, interests that came to the forefront as a result of the Great Depression and New Deal.

The goals of the Civil Rights Movement fit well with New Deal goals, making Democrats the modern liberals who tend to side with unions and racial and ethnic minorities.

The parties had, in fact, traded liberal and conservative positions from the prior century, something reflected by national election patterns. In the 1800s, Republicans could count on the Northeastern and West Coast states, while Democrats had the support of the South and rural areas. Today, this support is reversed. Moreover, within the philosophical framework of the Constitution, Republicans are now more focused on states' rights, and the Democrats more on the national level.

SIGNIFICANT CHANGES IN PARTY SUPPORT

The two major parties still dominate American electoral politics. However voter independence grew significantly in the late 20th century. Fewer ballots than ever before were cast for each major party. Republicans lost support in many urban areas and in the rapidly growing west. Democrats lost farmers and the South. Millions voted for protest candidates such as George Wallace, Ralph Nader, and Ross Perot. In each case, however, the major parties adjusted and regained voters. Democrats took control of urban votes and the West Coast, while Republicans found new strength in the South.

Future party alignments will probably hinge on immigration patterns. Hispanic American voters continue to grow in number, especially in the key electoral states of California, Texas, Florida, and New York. Will immigrants' traditional alignment with Democrat support for civil rights be broken up by concerns over abortion rights? Will the eventual rise of Hispanic workers into higher-wage jobs create a more conservative business orientation? Can Democrats become the majority party by forming stronger coalitions of minority groups and liberal European Americans? Will the Republican Party continue to benefit from strong support in the Sun Belt and the South?

BRIEF HISTORY OF THE DEMOCRATIC PARTY

Democrats trace their heritage to the Jeffersonian coalition of the early 1800s. This coalition overwhelmed Federalists and dominated the country for decades. When regional interests split the Democratic-Republican majority in the late 1820s, westerners emerged as Democrats under the dynamic leadership of Andrew Jackson. The donkey symbol, in use since the mid-1800s, was originally a cartoon insult for a set of leaders perceived to be stubborn, but it soon became a source of pride.

DEMOCRATIC PARTY

Era	Issues/Beliefs/Support Areas
Jacksonian Era 1830–1860	Individual freedoms, frontier independence/states' rights, and agricultural interests were the basis of early Democratic coalitions. Support was mostly in the South and West (frontier areas). This gave Democrats an advantage, because the population was growing rapidly in these regions. There was also mistrust of the wealthy elites who dominated politics in the cities of the Northeast, where class distinctions seemed counter to the new spirit of democracy.
Post–Civil War 1870–1900	When federal troops left the South in the late 1870s, Democratic policies returned to states' rights and rural issues. Segregation gave power to whites and their socially conservative views. Some "liberal" support in the Northeast (e.g., Grover Cleveland) did exist, especially in urban centers where political machines manipulated various voting blocks.
Progressive Era 1900–1920	States' rights remained powerful in the South, while support for worker interests was growing in the North. Democrats built on this progressive/Southern coalition to win the elections of 1912 and 1916.
Great Depression 1930–1945	New Deal coalitions and economic liberalism flourished. Growing support came from northern African Americans, northeastern liberals, and southern farmers. The public programs of World War II solidified economic changes, and Democrats flourished with large majorities.
Civil Rights Era 1945–1970	Civil rights liberalism, Great Society programs, antiwar sentiments, and the modern women's movement were dominant forces for the party. Southern conservatives became frustrated and protested by running separate candidates in several presidential elections (e.g., for Strom Thurmond in 1948 and George Wallace in 1968).
1970 to Present	Environmental issues, more civil liberty issues, more women's issues, and opposition to the rise of Reagan conservatism has defined recent Democratic support.

The following groups largely support the present-day Democratic Party:

- African Americans

- Pacifists

• Environmentalists

• Feminists

- Latinos

- Members of organized labor

The following news outlets are largely identified as Democratic leaning: *Washington Post*, *The Nation*, *New Republic*, MSNBC, and Air America Radio.

BRIEF HISTORY OF THE REPUBLICAN PARTY

In the 1850s, Republicans were centrist and liberal reformers who emerged from the collapse of the Whigs and moderate Democrats. Republican Party dominance of American government was in effect from 1860 to 1932. During this era, Republicans controlled the federal executive and legislative branches. This dominance ended with the rise of the Democrats' New Deal coalition.

The label *Grand Old Party* (*GOP*) was originally a reference to English political traidtions, but it was a label that stuck. And while the elephant symbol was originally a satirical reference to a large, uncontrollable, and rampaging beast, it too became a source of pride and has been a symbol of the party since the late 1800s.

REPUBLICAN PARTY

Era	Issues/Beliefs/Support Areas
Lincoln Era 1854–1876	National leadership, emancipation, unionism, and Reconstruction dominated the agenda. Support in the industrial North and the West Coast was sufficient for many election victories because the South was still in political chaos.
Gilded Age 1876–1900	Growing support for capitalism was dominant. Support in the North and West was massive, especially with rapid industrial expansion.
Theodore Roosevelt Era 1901–1912	Regulations of trusts and monopolies, along with the adoption of many progressive ideas, were goals of T. Roosevelt. Wide support outside the South was won due to T. Roosevelt's personal appeal, foreign policies, and historically high levels of patriotism.
Business Era 1912–1932	Pro-business forces ended T. Roosevelt's influence after 1912. Industrial development became the core issues in the face of isolationist reaction to World War I and growing concerns about communism. Strengths lay in the heavily populated Northeast. Leadership under Warren G. Harding and Calvin Coolidge flourished, with calls for less governmental interference in the economy.
New Deal 1932–1945	Opposition to Franklin Roosevelt and his programs was the beginning of a more libertarian approach toward federal authority. Republicans vehemently opposed increasing federal powers.

(continued on next page)

REPUBLICAN PARTY (con't)

Era	Issues/Beliefs/Support Areas
Cold War Era 1945–1980	Patriotism and intense anticommunism helped raise support. Issues about states' rights surfaced, as did opposition to civil rights. The Southern strategy was used to capture electoral votes in traditionally Democratic areas (for Barry Goldwater in 1964 and Richard Nixon in 1968 and 1972). The process came to fruition with the landslide elections of Ronald Reagan in 1980 and 1984.
Reagan Era 1980 to Present	Economic libertarians joined with social conservatives. Core support areas became the South, agricultural regions, and mountain states.

The following groups largely support the present-day Republican Party:

- Neo-conservatives
- Business interests
- Wall Street and financial interests
- Supply-side conservatives
- Religious conservatives
- Southern conservatives
- Mountain states conservatives (more libertarian)

The following news outlets and personalities are largely identified as Republican leaning: *Washington Times*, *National Review*, *The Wall Street Journal*, Fox News, and Rush Limbaugh.

PARTIES IN DECLINE?

Some of the original sources of power for political parties were cities. Political "machines" often took advantage of immigrants by doling out jobs in exchange for voter loyalty. These machines built large party coalitions that endured for decades.

Today, this type of corruption has been reduced, and party bosses have been eliminated. Some people believe that the major parties are now in decline. Party loyalty is no longer critical for economic advancement, and easy movement across the country has fragmented loyalties, families, and connections. An increasing number of voters are claiming independence from parties. Polls show at least one-third of all voters today claim no strong ties to either party. Other pieces of evidence include low levels of voter turnout and declarations by voters that they distrust parties and their leaders. The sudden popularity of candidates such as John Anderson, Ross Perot, and Ralph Nader is seen as evidence of weak major political parties.

There is, however, other evidence that parties are still strong and flourishing. The vast sums given to parties indicate continued party loyalty. Many readily give at every opportunity. Participation in meetings, demonstrations, message campaigns, and other party activities remains strong. Moreover, voter turnout among those who are registered is stable.

A possible myth may have been created about party decline during the dominance of relatively liberal policies between 1930 and 1980. When conservatives resurfaced in the 1980s and 1990s, more party involvement occurred. With the parties diverging more and more, party loyalty may be resurfacing.

RECENT VOTING PATTERNS (ELECTIONS OF 2000 AND 2004)

Northeast States	Democratic
Southern States	Republican
Midwest States	Split
Great Plains States	Republican
Mountain States	Republican
West Coast	Democratic
Men	Republican, especially "NASCAR dads" of the South, farmers, and business leaders (white-collar)
Women	Democratic, except "soccer moms" who are not employed outside of the home
European Ancestry	Republican
African Ancestry	Democratic
Hispanic Ancestry	Democratic. George W. Bush won substantial support from Hispanic voters in Texas while governor and won record numbers of such votes in the 2004 election.
Protestant	In the North: Democratic In the more "evangelical" South: Republican
Roman Catholic	In the North: Democratic In the more Hispanic churches of the South: growing Republican support
Jewish	Democratic
Nonreligious	Democratic
Wealthy	Republican
Middle Class	Split
Poor	Democratic
Urban Centers	Democratic
Suburbs	Republican
Rural	Republican

REVIEW QUESTIONS

MULTIPLE-CHOICE QUESTIONS

1. Which statement about political parties in the United States is **MOST** correct?

   (A) Parties have been stable since they were founded.

   (B) Broad changes in party power structures have often occurred.

   (C) Two major parties have dominated consistently.

   (D) Parties have grown in influence with the increasing power of presidents.

   (E) Parties have stable beliefs and goals.

2. How can two-party dominance during much of U.S. history **BEST** be explained?

   (A) Parties were able to absorb new political goals.

   (B) Parties have controlled the Electoral College.

   (C) Major parties have vast sums of campaign funds.

   (D) Urban party "machines" blocked the formation of other parties.

   (E) Citizens had general distrust of parties as a whole.

3. The future balance of Democratic and Republican support will probably hinge on

   (A) continued conservative dominance in the South.

   (B) continued loyalty of minority groups to liberal causes.

   (C) an increase in population in the urban centers of the North.

   (D) the ability of Democrats to access wealthy donors.

   (E) the possible switch in support of Hispanic voters due to social issues.

4. Progressives' demands for major changes in workers' rights affected

   (A) Republicans first.

   (B) Democrats first.

   (C) neither party.

   (D) voter loyalty to the major parties.

   (E) mostly the members of Congress.

5. Today, _____ would likely support most of the positions of Hamilton, and _____ would likely support most of the positions of Jefferson.

   (A) conservatives, liberals

   (B) Republicans, Democrats

   (C) Libertarians, Socialists

   (D) Socialists, Libertarians

   (E) Democrats, Republicans

Free-Response Questions

1. (A) Identify two key roles that political parties play in the politics of the United States.

   (B) Explain how the two roles you identified influence or control the agenda of the nation.

2. The Democratic and Republican parties are broad coalitions of major voting blocs.

   (A) Identify three of the major subgroups of each party's coalition.

   (B) Explain how each of these party coalitions has a form of unity in their beliefs.

   (C) Explain why each coalition has internal divisions.

ANSWERS AND EXPLANATIONS

MULTIPLE-CHOICE ANSWERS

1. C

While many aspects of the roles and power of the two major political parties have changed over time, the dominance of the Democrats and the Republicans has not.

2. A

The United States has experienced two-party dominance throughout its history because the parties adjusted to absorb new political goals. The other answer choices also contributed to some degree, but they are not as central in explaining why the two parties are so dominant.

3. E

Hispanics, the fastest-growing minority group, will likely prove to affect the future political balance. They helped elect Republican George W. Bush to office in 2004, but many Hispanics trended toward the Democrats in 2008 and 2012.

4. A

Through the leadership of Teddy Roosevelt and his administration, Republicans were the first to respond nationally to the progressives' calls for reforms.

5. E

Today, Democrats would likely support Hamilton's positions, while Republicans would support those of Jefferson. The first three answer choices are backward: Hamilton supported stronger national controls, especially over economic policies. Jefferson wanted more control at the state level, as do the modern Republicans.

FREE-RESPONSE ANSWERS

1. **4-point Rubric**

   2 points in part (A): (identify any two key roles)

   - Recruit and label candidates.
   - Influence the public.
   - Gather money.
   - Run the government.
   - Provide for opposition to the party in power.
   - Develop political agendas.

   2 points in Part (B): (explain how they, influence nation's agenda)

   - Parties look for qualified candidates who can get elected, and then they support these candidates.
   - Parties get the message of the party platform out to the public, provide information, run ads, etc.
   - Parties raise funds that can be used for ads, flyers, etc.
   - Parties control the operation of the legislative branch when they are the majority party.
   - Parties can band together as the "loyal" opposition to force compromises.
   - Parties canvas members for future issues and seek solutions to problems.

2. **10-point Rubric**

   6 points in part (A): (indentify any three groups in each party)

   - Democrats: African Americans, union members, liberal progressives, feminists, Hispanics
   - Republicans: Neo-conservatives, supply-side conservatives, religious conservatives, Southern conservatives, westerners

   2 points in part (B): (explain points of unity)

   - Democrats: Economic guidance by government, civil rights for minorities, pro-environmental programs, pro-worker rights
   - Republicans: Economic conservatism, states' rights, pro-business, less government

   2 points in part (C): (explain points of difference)

   - Democrats: Hispanics less loyal due to religious beliefs, splits over civil rights agendas, splits between unions and feminists
   - Republicans: Splits over religious beliefs, emphasis on business and taxes, North versus South

CHAPTER 9: CAMPAIGNS AND ELECTIONS

IF YOU LEARN ONLY SIX THINGS IN THIS CHAPTER . . .

1. Elections and campaigns in the United States are fairly frequent, time-consuming, and expensive.

2. From the Civil War until the New Deal, the Republican Party dominated American politics. From the New Deal to the 1960s, the second era of Democratic dominance occurred (the first happened from 1828 to 1860). The period from 1968 to the present day is often referred to as the era of "divided government" because neither party has dominated both the executive and legislative branches during this period.

3. The role of money in political campaigning has become a major point of controversy and has led to many attempts at reforms and restrictions; however, few restrictions have been enacted or have been effective.

4. Public awareness is heightened during presidential elections, and often it is the only time when divisions in political support expose themselves and shifts in party affiliation may be seen.

5. Because the number of electors each state has in the Electoral College is based on its population, larger states can heavily affect the outcome of presidential elections.

6. Campaign finance reform efforts have not had much success.

INTRODUCTION

Elections in the United States are noted for being numerous and open to universal participation. They are also expensive, especially at the statewide and national levels. They have become dominated by money, lobby groups, and the two major parties. Television and Internet media heavily influence reporting, campaigning, and debating. Campaigns aim at controlling media reporting, spinning information to benefit their cause, and avoiding any negative publicity. Recent elections have returned to 19th-century reliance on personal attacks, innuendo, and rumor. This appears to be increasing in frequency as there is more campaigning through independent groups that do not answer directly to the two major parties.

Individual voters, however, are still important to this process because they play critical roles in grassroots fundraising, lobbying leaders, and campaigning. Even with strict limits on personal donations, both parties have reaped huge amounts of money through other unlimited sources.

THE ROLE OF MONEY

The need for money gathering has also had an effect on the length of campaigns. So many funds are needed for a national campaign that candidates must start years in advance to gather the necessary amounts. This is a critical feature of presidential elections, where funding efforts start at least two years prior to the November vote. A tangential issue is the dominance of incumbents and early front-runners. With so much money at stake, key lobby and party groups will hesitate before venturing support for an outsider, especially if another candidate has a lot of support in early primaries.

THE ROLE OF THE ELECTORAL COLLEGE

The Electoral College also plays a role in the way campaigns are created and run. Because states with larger populations dominate the Electoral College system, campaign ads, funds, and speeches tend to be focused in these areas. Smaller states are often largely ignored. Another feature of the system comes into play when a state heavily favors one candidate. Why spend money and time there? Local leaders and their candidacies can suffer, and voter turnouts can drop.

THE ROLE OF MONEY AND REFORM ATTEMPTS

The influence of money in U.S. elections is controversial. In a nation of over 300 million people with voter turnouts of over 100 million, campaigning is expensive, and costs continue to rise dramatically. Television advertisements are a main component of these high costs, but radio, print media, and online media of a campaign add to these costs. With a significant percentage of voters claiming little loyalty to the two major parties, media images and favorable press are critical to attracting "swing" or independent votes each election.

The problem of money in politics is connected to a voter problem and a leadership problem. If voters weren't as easily influenced by superficial images and emotional pleas, then ads wouldn't be as effective. If voters were more critical in their analysis of the messages being presented, then attack ads and suggestive messages wouldn't as easily sway elections. There is also a legitimate concern that campaign contributions lead to policy changes that serve the interests of only large contributors, and that officials help only those individuals and groups who contribute. Even if it is not outright bribery, monetary assistance is still seen by many as an unfair, biased influence on the way the government operates. Efforts to control the flow of campaign contributions have been made for decades.

Efforts to make these contributions more public led to the creation of political action committees (PACs). This development, however, increased the money involved, however, because PACs can legally amass and donate vast sums in plain sight. Individual contributions are severely limited, but corporations and other powerful groups can "bundle" large numbers of such monies into one larger contribution. Internet communications have also allowed parties to reach millions of smaller contributors quickly and get money to many local races that never had such a level of national support. Most recently, the greatest end run around the rules is that of "independent" groups creating large ad campaigns that viciously attack "beyond" the control of a political party or its candidate.

When reforms and limits are argued, a counterattack is mounted: the issue of free speech. Does a restriction on being allowed to help a campaign restrict the right of political free speech? Recent Supreme Court rulings have sided with the idea that any giving of money is a form of speech. However, critics of the Supreme Court's ruling in the case of *Citizens United v. Federal Election Commission* (2008) maintain that this decision threatens to undermine the integrity of the American electoral system by effectively lifting limits on corporate contributions, which they say will favor pro-business interests at the expense of the average voter.

THE ROAD TO THE PRESIDENCY
(FOR THE MAJOR PARTY CANDIDATES)

At least 18 to 24 months before the election, possibly getting earlier now	Start fund-raising. Build a "war chest" of campaign funds. Contacts need to be made with support groups and party leadership.
Around 12 months before the election	Declare one's candidacy and form a national campaign committee. Build a campaign staff. Rules of campaign finance must be followed. Travel is extensive to cover various early primary and caucus states. Image and debate training is conducted with the staff.
February of the election year	Give speeches and "stump" in the early primaries and caucuses. Try to energize the party loyalists in states like Iowa and New Hampshire. A poor showing can doom access to funding support, as donors will put their support behind candidates who "have a chance."
March	Conduct a national campaign in the numerous "Super Tuesday" states. Capture needed delegate votes to obtain the nomination of the party. Attend intraparty debates as scheduled. Raise additional money.

(continued on next page)

THE ROAD TO THE PRESIDENCY
(FOR THE MAJOR PARTY CANDIDATES) (con't)

April–June	Complete the primary by campaigning in all corners of the country.
July–August	Settle on the VP nomination at the party convention. Work with party leaders to build a campaign platform.
Fall, especially after Labor Day	This is the traditional campaign season against the other major party's candidate. The candidate makes many scheduled speeches and appearances, then takes part in national debates with the opposing candidates.
First Tuesday after the first Monday in November of the election year (Election Day)	Receive the most electoral votes, based on individual state popular votes (currently 270 out of 538 are needed to win).
December	The Electoral College members cast their ballots.
January	With the start of the new session of Congress, the president of the Senate formally counts the electoral ballots.
January 20	The president is sworn into office.

PRESIDENTIAL ELECTIONS

SIGNIFICANT CHANGES IN PRESIDENTIAL ELECTIONS

Party meetings, caucuses, and conventions once dominated how candidates were selected. "Smoke-filled rooms," where insiders maneuvered to nominate candidates who were to their liking or under their influence, were the norm. The late 20th century saw drastic changes to this system. **Primaries** now select the presidential nominees for each party months before their conventions, committing party delegates to the public's choices.

This change has certainly opened the process to more candidates but has also created problems in terms of money and strategy. Many states hold primaries early in the election year, forcing candidates to try to gather vast campaign funds well before the elections. Lesser-known, though possibly well-qualified, candidates are often eliminated quickly because they do not have the funds to conduct these early campaigns in state primaries. National party summer conventions are now little more than pep rallies at which the candidates and party leaders make speeches and where little is decided. Another subtle, but important, feature of this primary system is that Southern states hold many of the early primaries. Therefore, this region of the country is very influential in determining who is nominated. Presidential aspirants must focus their campaign efforts on these and other early primaries to be serious contenders for their party's nomination. Recently, many states have been moving up the date of their presidential primaries in an effort to give them a greater impact on the nomination process. This development will certainly influence the future campaign strategies of presidential hopefuls.

KEY DIFFERENCES BETWEEN THE TWO MAJOR PARTS OF A PRESIDENTIAL CAMPAIGN

To win the *nomination* means to earn a place on the ballot for the general election and requires a nominee to capture the support of party regulars and loyalists. This often leads to a more conservative (Republican) or liberal (Democratic) stance on issues. Issues and party platforms are critical to gaining the support of the party's base of support during the primary campaign. Special attention must be given to party groups that can make or break a campaign. Republicans and Democrats must gain support from key support groups.

To win the *general election*, the candidate must appeal to the interests of the general public. This might require the candidate to adopt a more moderate stance without angering party loyalists. More emphasis is placed on personality and leadership during this phase. A compelling media image must be created. Quick quotes for the media ("sound bites") are highly valued. Polished answers to media questions and debate points are important in close races.

ELECTION PATTERNS

As mentioned in previous chapters, the two major parties have completely dominated national politics. They also tend to take turns dominating the political agenda for periods of time. Often, presidential elections are seen as points when parties establish or lose dominance. Chapter 6 summarized how liberalism and conservatism have seen periods of alternating control; the same has occurred for the Democrats and Republicans, as reflected by key elections. The modern starting point of this development is usually identified as the election of 1896. Traditions of traveling and campaigning, national media coverage, coordinated campaign staffs, and carefully managed candidates began with the contest between William McKinley and William Jennings Bryan.

MAJOR CRITICAL "REALIGNMENT" PRESIDENTIAL ELECTIONS SINCE 1896

Year	Candidates	Issues/Events
1896	McKinley—R Bryan—D	The first major national campaign trips by a candidate occur (Bryan). The first major use of campaign staff and managers occurs (McKinley). Both parties begin to emerge in their modern forms of pro-business Republican and pro-worker Democratic.
1912	Wilson—D T. Roosevelt—Progressive William H. Taft—R	Republicans split and ultimately reject T. Roosevelt's progressive programs.

(continued on next page)

MAJOR CRITICAL "REALIGNMENT" PRESIDENTIAL ELECTIONS SINCE 1896 (con't)

Year	Candidates	Issues/Events
1920	Harding—R James Cox—D	The emergence of the Republican Party as pro-business is firmly established.
1932	F. Roosevelt—D Herbert Hoover—R	The emergence of the Democrats' liberal New Deal agenda that will dominate politics for 50 years.
1948	Harry S. Truman—D Thomas Dewey—R Thurmond—(States' Rights; Democrat)	The first sign of a split within the Democratic Party marked by Strom Thurmond's protest candidacy that was precipitated by early civil rights issues.
1960	Kennedy—D Nixon—R	TV campaign coverage becomes influential, as debates take the center stage.
1964	Johnson—D Goldwater—R	Republicans select one of the most conservative candidates to date. The election is a landslide and ultimately the high watermark of civil rights liberalism. Goldwater becomes a hero to conservatives and influences later Republican candidates (such as Reagan).
1968	Nixon—R Humphrey—D Wallace—American Independent	Vietnam War protests disrupt the campaign. Wallace's candidacy further splits Southern Democrats from the party.
1980	Reagan—R Carter—D	The emergence of modern conservatism, which will dominate the political landscape and begin the massive shift of Southern whites to the Republican Party.
2000	Bush—R Gore—D	The Electoral College mess is resolved by a controversial ruling by the Supreme Court in the case of *Bush v. Gore* (2000).
2008	Obama—D McCain—R	After eight years of the Republican Bush administration, this election puts not only a Democrat in the White House, but also the first African American.

THE ELECTORAL COLLEGE

The **Electoral College** was created to balance the views of the electorate with the power of political leaders, because some argued that citizens are unable to make wise choices due to their limited grasp of the issues involved. However, if Congress selected the president, then too much power would be in the hands of the legislative branch. It was one of the final compromises made at the Constitutional Convention. The Electoral College, which was proposed by Alexander Hamilton, has the president selected by a special body of **electors**, who may not be members of Congress. Under Hamilton's proposal, electors would be chosen in each state as directed by the state legislature.

Each state receives the number of electoral votes equal in number to its senators and representatives, for a national total of 538. (There are 435 representatives and 100 senators; per the 23rd Amendment, there must be three for Washington D.C.—the same number as the least populated state.)

To win the general election, a candidate needs 270 electoral votes. The largest state, California, had 55 electoral votes in 2004 and 2008. The smallest states (like Wyoming, for example) have three electoral votes. California has more electoral votes than many of the lesser populated states combined. It is possible for a candidate to carry the electoral majority with the votes of only 10 states.

The votes are reapportioned after each census (this was done in 2010 for the 2012 election). States that grow faster than other states take electors from slower growing states. New York used to have the most electoral votes, but now stands third behind California and Texas.

The popular vote winner in each state gets all of the electoral votes from that state (except for possible vote splits in Maine and Nebraska). To win the popular vote, a candidate does not need to receive the majority of ballots cast; rather they only need to receive a plurality. Electors are expected to vote for the popular vote winner, are bound by tradition to do so, and in some cases are required to do so by state law. However, electors are not bound by the Constitution to follow the state popular vote results. Some electors have ignored their state mandates in the past, but none have ever caused a candidate to lose. Electors meet in December, usually at the state capitol, and cast their ballots. Each ballot is sealed and sent to Congress, where the president of the Senate (the vice president) will open and count the ballots in January. The media does ask electors how they voted in December, and they usually answer.

The House selects from the top three presidential candidates, and each state gets one vote. (Washington, D.C., does not get a vote.) The winner is the candidate who receives 26 state votes. If no candidate gets 26 votes, the House keeps revoting until someone wins. If the Electoral College does not have a majority winner, the vote reverts to Congress. The Senate selects from the top two vice presidential candidates, and each senator gets one vote. The majority vote winner (51) can then be sworn in as vice president. This way, a fallback leader is set if needed.

This event has almost occurred in close elections, such as in 2000. State congressional delegations may have a majority opposite of the public vote. Would the congressional party leaders vote for the opposition party candidate? This would have happened in George W. Bush's home state of Texas, where one of the more conservative electorates would have been represented by a slightly Democratic delegation in the House.

OBJECTIONS TO THE ELECTORAL COLLEGE SYSTEM

Many people object to the Electoral College system because it is not a system of direct, popular election, and many feel that this is needed for modern times. They reason that voters are now informed enough to make a direct election desirable.

Also, the popular vote winner can lose the electoral vote. (This occurred in the presidential elections of 1824, 1876, 1888, and 2000.) This is seen by many as limiting the public's control, which is a fundamental principle of our government. Moreover, highly populated states, as was mentioned earlier, totally dominate the system. Also, states with large differences in party loyalties cause votes for the less popular party to be meaningless, because the less popular party is unlikely to win that state's electoral votes.

REASONS THE ELECTORAL COLLEGE SYSTEM REMAINS

The costs of having to campaign equally across the country would raise national campaign costs beyond the already massive amounts that are now needed. Furthermore, any change would have to come through a Constitutional amendment, and large states will not easily give up their dominance.

CAMPAIGN FINANCE REFORM

National campaigns are very expensive. There have been numerous debates about the need for such amounts of money, the sources of such funds, and the propriety of such collections. How fair is the system? Who controls the elections? What promises are made for contracts, jobs, votes, or influence when so much money is involved? How can the poor or middle classes compete? How much free speech is involved in the giving of money? Many of these issues came to the surface during the elections of the 1960s and 1970s, when television advertising became the central cost and feature of modern electioneering.

MODERN CAMPAIGN FINANCE REFORM EFFORTS

Hatch Act, 1939	Federal employees and companies doing business under federal contracts were forbidden to contribute to elections.
Elections of 1968 and 1972, Watergate	Reactions to "slush funds," secret accounts, and money used for illegal activities gave rise to calls for federal reforms of money collections.
Federal Election Campaign Act, 1971, and amendments through 1979	Limits were placed on individual and PAC contributions, the Federal Election Commission (FEC) was created for oversight, and disclosure rules were established.
Buckley v. Valeo, 1976	In this Supreme Court ruling, the Court allowed Congress to limit some contributions to candidates but protected other forms of funding to parties as forms of free speech.
McCain-Feingold-Cochran Reform Bill (Bipartisan Campaign Act, 2002)	Efforts were made by Congress to limit "soft money" contributions and the influence of PACs.

KEY TERMS OF CAMPAIGN FINANCE

Term	Definition	Related Issues
Political Action Committees (PACs)	A group registered with the FEC and used to raise campaign funds is registered under this label.	This attempt at reform in the 1970s actually funneled more money into campaigns and raised more reform issues.
527s	IRS Section 527 allows nonprofit organizations to collect money and use it for political causes, such as TV ads.	Not regulated by the FEC, this loophole is not "connected" with campaigns; it therefore allows the creation of more vicious attack ads, such as those used in the election of 2004 (e.g., Swift Boat Veterans).
Hard Money	Money from individuals and PACS for specific candidates is regulated by the FEC.	The per-election limit is $1,000 per individual for a candidate and $5,000 for PACs.
Soft Money	Money used by parties for activities such as "party building" or voter registration efforts is not supposed to go directly to a candidate's campaign (but there is some debate about whether it does).	How can we differentiate between these activities?
Matching Funds	Federal money is given to candidates to help level the financial playing field, based on hard money collected.	Candidates receive a dollar-for-dollar match for donations of less than $250, if at least $5,000 is gathered from at least 20 states.
Independent Expenditures or Independent Advertising	Money is spent by individuals or groups for their own ads. They might only suggest support for a party or candidate (or criticize a candidate) without being "part" of the party.	What is the line between campaign, candidate, and private spending on ads? What are the controls on attack ads? Who is responsible if the ads are misleading?
Candidate Spending	Money from personal wealth is often used by candidates on their own campaigns.	If a candidate accepts matching funds, then the limit of candidate spending is $50,000 of the candidate's personal wealth.
Bundling	Putting together individual contributions (hard money) into group checks is often done by companies using multiple employee contributions.	Is this legal? Do the employees know this is happening?
Federal Election Commission (FEC)	This six-member agency was created in 1974 to monitor election funds.	Are the powers of the FEC sufficient?

SUMMARY OF CURRENT FINANCE ISSUES

The main questions revolve around the ability of large corporations and the super-rich to sway elections and the free speech rights of individuals, corporations, and interest groups.

The controversies surrounding campaign finance reform remain generally unresolved. Those who benefit the most from current advantages see little to gain by restricting the ways in which they can collect campaign funds.

BASIC RIGHTS AND LIMITS TO CONTRIBUTIONS

Individual contributors. Contributions to candidates for specific elections are limited in amount and must be reported. Contributions to party organizations are completely unlimited.

Political parties. There are restrictions on how monies can be spent for national campaigns, when ads can occur, and whether or not they can mention federal candidates. Parties can spend unlimited amounts on "party-building" activities.

Interest and lobby groups. There are now limits on spending on ads that mention candidates or parties but few limits on issues advocacy.

Political action committees. PACs have limits on how much can be collected for campaigns of specific candidates and when these monies can be spent.

527 groups. They have few limits on spending on ads that refer to the issues that candidates support or oppose or to the personal lives of candidates.

Candidates. There are limits on how much of a candidate's personal wealth can be used in campaigns, especially if the campaign collects federal matching funds.

COMMENTS ON LOCAL AND CONGRESSIONAL ELECTIONS

Local politicians and members of the House of Representatives come up for reelection frequently. Some local races may be annual events. House members stand for election every other year. This has created the "constant campaign." The positive side to this is that leaders must listen to their constituents, because corrections can be quickly made by the ballot. As a negative, the constant need for campaign fundraising takes a large portion of leaders' time and energy. Incumbents in the House usually have tremendous advantages by being able to keep in constant contact with important donors and constituents.

Donors are reluctant to support challengers because a loss will cost them influence. Challengers have less time to plan and campaign inside the two-year cycle. With these pressures, House incumbents spend much more time making sure their constituents are being helped and represented by their votes. They have fewer opportunities to be independent for any length of time. Senate races, especially in larger states, resemble presidential races in terms of need for money and organization. The Internet has also changed campaigns in both areas. The Internet enables candidates to disseminate more information to a national audience; this way, both parties can focus on key seats and key states. Also, the practice of funding campaigns from out of state has increased dramatically in recent years.

REVIEW QUESTIONS

MULTIPLE-CHOICE QUESTIONS

1. A major difference between elections of presidents and members of Congress is that

   (A) more voters cast ballots in presidential years.

   (B) congressional races are less competitive.

   (C) presidential races are easier to fund.

   (D) presidents must be more partisan.

   (E) congressional candidates must be more partisan.

2. A recent trend in presidential campaigns has been

   (A) an increase in personal attacks on candidates.

   (B) a push from party leaders to return to using state caucuses.

   (C) successful limits being imposed on the raising of funds.

   (D) the rise of successful third-party candidates.

   (E) the critical role of television debates.

3. Campaign finance reform efforts have been minimal because

   (A) political action committees have actually increased contributions.

   (B) the issue of free speech has limited restrictions.

   (C) lobbies and interest groups seem to find ways around spending limits.

   (D) those who win under the current system see little reason for change.

   (E) All of the above

4. National party conventions are now primarily used

   (A) as pep rallies.

   (B) to reward the party faithful with jobs.

   (C) to set the campaign agenda.

   (D) to support the nominee.

   (E) All of the above

5. A major issue in trying to get elected as president is

   (A) pleasing party loyalists enough without alienating the majority of the electorate.

   (B) trying to raise funds in all states.

   (C) having to raise funds after the nomination.

   (D) having to debate on television.

   (E) having the right campaign staff who know all the effective campaign strategies.

FREE-RESPONSE QUESTIONS

1. Most efforts at restricting campaign contributions have generally failed.

    (A) Identify the difference between "hard money" contributions and "soft money" contributions.

    (B) Identify two reasons efforts at restricting contributions have failed.

    (C) Explain at least one reason some insist that campaign-funding restrictions should fail.

2. The Electoral College is an anti-democratic anachronism.

    (A) Explain two reasons the Electoral College is opposed.

    (B) Explain two reasons the Electoral College is still in place.

ANSWERS AND EXPLANATIONS

MULTIPLE-CHOICE ANSWERS

1. E

A major difference between elections of presidents and members of Congress is that congressional candidates must be more partisan. Congressional candidates answer to smaller constituencies that are more likely to be partisan. Choice (A) is incorrect because, though true, it is not a difference between the two types of elections. Choice (B) is incorrect because congressional races are very competitive at times. Choice (C) is incorrect because national races are harder to fund. Choice (D) is incorrect because presidents must be less partisan in order to reach a broader electorate.

2. A

An increase in personal attacks on candidates has been a recent trend in presidential campaigns. This is a return to earlier patterns and seems to reflect the growing splits between liberals and conservatives. Choices (B), (C), and (D) are false statements. Choice (E) is incorrect because many contend that debates do not really affect voter behavior.

3. E

Campaign finance reform efforts have been minimal for all of the reasons listed: political action committees have increased contributions, the issue of free speech has limited restrictions, lobbies and interest groups seem to find ways around controls, and those who benefit from the current campaign contribution system have little incentive to change it.

4. A

National party conventions are now primarily used as pep rallies to give party speeches in front of television audiences. Though conventions have dwindling numbers of viewers, those with a strong interest in the party still watch them. Choice (B) is a false statement. The agenda is usually set by the candidates' campaign staff well before the convention. The nominee already has the support of delegates and the party.

5. A

Pleasing party loyalists enough without alienating the majority of the electorate is a major dilemma when trying to get elected as president. Choice (B) is incorrect because candidates don't need funds from all states to win; they only need key votes in electoral states. Choice (C) is incorrect because candidates must raise most funds early in the process (before they've received the nomination) to remain viable. Choice (D) and choice (E) are problems that candidates must face, but they are not serious issues.

FREE-RESPONSE ANSWERS

1. **4-point Rubric**

   1 point in part (A): (hard contributions versus soft contributions)

   - Hard money contributions are regulated contributions given directly to candidates for their campaigns; soft money contributions are less-regulated monies given to parties for activities such as "party building."

   2 points in part (B): (two reasons restrictions have failed)

   - Too many loopholes.
   - Party building is difficult to define.
   - Little incentive to change for those in office who benefit from current rules.

   1 point in part (C): (one reason restrictions should fail)

   - People should be able to spend their money to support candidates.
   - Restrictions penalize the wealthy.
   - Free speech would be limited.

2. **4-point Rubric**

   2 points in part (A): (two reasons to oppose)

   - Too biased toward large states.
   - Too biased toward states dominated by one party.
   - Biased against small parties.
   - Is anti-democratic.

   2 points in part (B): (two reasons the system remains)

   - Large, politically powerful states benefit.
   - Reduces costs of campaigning everywhere.
   - Difficult to replace.

CHAPTER 10: INTEREST GROUPS, LOBBIES, AND POLITICAL ACTION COMMITTEES

IF YOU LEARN ONLY FOUR THINGS IN THIS CHAPTER . . .

1. Lobbyists and special interest groups are often seen in a negative light because a favor-for-favor relationship is suspected. However, lobby forces have access to decision makers and serve an important function in the relationship between the public and government leaders.

2. Interest groups are concerned with a wide range of topics and show support for both Republican and Democratic issues, as well as independent issues.

3. Interest groups have the ability to access leaders, and they have many ways of exerting their influence.

4. Lobby leaders are key players in the development of policies and in the funding of campaigns.

INTRODUCTION

James Madison and other U.S. founders had negative views of groups trying to influence policy formation. Madison referred to "factions" in the *Federalist Papers* and hoped that the federal system would protect the government from excessive influence by such groups. He was particularly concerned that elites would gain control of the states, blocking access to government by deserving constituents. Under the new Constitution, protections from the federal government would guarantee that no faction could do so by creating layers of authority.

CURRENT VIEWS

Today, the public perception of interest groups continues to be relatively negative due to excessive sums spent by groups to influence elections. However, interest groups run the spectrum of political beliefs and are sometimes the most effective way for citizens to make their voices heard by the government. Interest groups often hire professional representatives to lobby for their interests in the national and state capitols.

The rapid creation of so many interest groups has become an issue for many. Conflicts revolve around the power of interest groups. Is their ability to donate vast sums of money the decisive factor between those who influence leaders and those who are ignored?

FUNCTIONS OF INTEREST GROUPS

Interest groups use four major strategies to do their work: lobbying, electioneering, litigating, and influencing public opinion.

The most powerful way interest groups try to affect government is through *lobbying*. Lobbyists prepare memos for Congress, meet and debate, give evidence at hearings, petition, raise campaign funds, and even draft potential legislation. Lobbies are notorious for hiring recently retired members of Congress and then using their inside experience to outmaneuver other groups. Suggestions of impropriety caused Congress to create rules requiring a waiting period before former members can begin such private consulting. Even stricter rules apply to former members of the executive branch who want to be hired for large salaries to lobby their former agencies. Because some major lobbies have vast resources, their influence over campaigns and parties remains controversial. Current examples include Republican connections to energy company lobbies and Democratic connections to union lobbies.

Interest groups also engage in **electioneering**, because they have a vested interest in getting the right people into office and making sure they remain there. Thus, interest groups are very active in political campaigns.

If an interest group is unable to get a desired result from Congress or a federal agency, it may resort to **litigating**, or turning to the judicial system to reach its goal. Perhaps the most famous example of this occurred when the NAACP was able to get the Supreme Court to rule that segregation of America's public schools was unconstitutional.

Lastly, interest groups attempt to shape public opinion through the use of media outlets, publishing the findings of research studies, and staging public events.

The proliferation of interest group activity reflects a positive aspect of the American system of government. With over 4,600 political action committees registered, all kinds of groups and opinions have open access to public officials. Any group, mainstream or radical, has an opportunity to register, gather supporters and funds, and contact leaders.

TYPES OF INTEREST GROUPS

Economic Interest Groups	These organizations form to serve the economic interests of their members, such as labor groups.
Social Action and Equality Groups	When a social change is desired, people may join together to help get this change made.
Public Interest Groups	Some organizations exist to work for their perception of the public's best interests.

MAJOR INTEREST GROUPS
(ALSO REGISTERED AS LOBBIES)

To increase their membership numbers and have more influence, almost all interest groups are registered as lobbies. Most have also created political action committees (PACs) to properly donate to campaigns.

LOBBY GROUPS

American Association of Retired Persons (AARP)	The very powerful lobbying force of citizens over age 55 has tremendous influence on issues such as Social Security and prescription drugs.
American Bar Association (ABA)	This large and well-funded group represents the legal community.
American Civil Liberties Union (ACLU)	This group of legal experts focuses on civil rights and civil liberties.
Chamber of Commerce	Chamber of Commerce represents the business community all across the nation.
Common Cause	This social action group lobbies for many liberal causes and "open, accountable" government.
American-Israel Public Affairs Committee	Support for Jewish communities and Israel are this group's focus.
American Federation of Labor–Congress of Industrial Organizations (AFL-CIO)	For decades, this group has headed the labor movement in the United States and has lobbied for worker rights.

(continued on next page)

LOBBY GROUPS (con't)

Eagle Forum	This conservative group advocates for family values issues and laissez-faire economic policies.
Earth First!	This radical environmental group has been the source of controversial, violent protests, especially from splinter groups.
Heritage Foundation	This very conservative group started as a research center for policy and now lobbies Congress in favor of reducing the federal bureaucracy and less government.
League of United Latin American Citizens (LULAC)	This group defends the civil rights of Hispanic citizens.
Mothers Against Drunk Driving (MADD)	This rapidly growing organization forced major changes in many state laws concerning the penalties for driving under the influence of alcohol.
The National Association for the Advancement of Colored People (NAACP)	For over 100 years, this organization has been an advocate for African Americans' civil rights.
National Rifle Association (NRA)	Focusing on 2nd Amendment rights, this well-funded and powerful lobby has conservative and anti–big government roots.
National Right to Life Committee	This issue-oriented group seeks to make abortion illegal.
National Organization for Women (NOW)	Central in the failed attempt to pass the Equal Rights Amendment in the 1970s, NOW continues to support women's rights and generally takes liberal positions, such as supporting abortion rights.
People for the Ethical Treatment of Animals (PETA)	Advocates for animal rights.
Promise Keepers	Formed in 1990, this group represents many evangelical Christians and their more conservative views.
Sierra Club	This environmental group focuses on conservation issues and maintaining clean air and water standards.

LOBBY GROUP BASICS

Almost all of the major interest groups, and thousands of others, have offices in Washington, D.C., and other governmental centers. They employ professional lobbyists who spend time working with members of Congress and their staffs. The lobbyists' goal is to create legislation that helps the interests of the members of the group in question.

LOBBYIST ACTIVITIES

Testify	Lobbyists attend committee hearings and bring their biases and points of expertise. They have important things to say about the possible impact of bills, especially for or against the goals of their group.
Meet	Personal contacts are critical ways to make political arguments. Controversial versions of such meetings are *paid junkets*, where lobby organizations pay for trips and vacations for members of government. Open bias and bribery are issues.
Research	Lobbyists and their staff have time and resources to gather data that can sway members of Congress when bills that the lobby supports or opposes come to a vote.
Lead	Lobbyists can sway the masses within the organization to call and write to the members of government.
Fund	Possibly the most powerful action is the raising and contributing of campaign funds.
Litigate	Lobby leaders can turn to the courts to attack acts, rules, and regulations that they feel are unfair to their group.

POLITICAL ACTION COMMITTEES (PACs)

When interest groups want to go the extra step and support specific candidates or parties, they may do so through PACs. The committees register with the Federal Election Commission and then may give financial support to candidates.

PACs may give money directly to candidates' campaigns. This is called *hard money* and is closely regulated by the Federal Election Commission. Even with these rules, millions of dollars are given in this manner.

PACs also give money to parties. This is called *soft money*. Limits to soft money donations and expenditures are a subject of constant debate.

Committees can use their money to create ads or messages for "issues," without specifically supporting a particular candidate. These kinds of expenditures are unregulated, even when it is clear that a particular candidate is being supported. (Additional details of spending rules are covered in Chapter 9.)

REVIEW QUESTIONS

MULTIPLE-CHOICE QUESTIONS

1. There are thousands of interest groups in the United States because

    (A) the political system is stable.

    (B) many desire to shape public policy.

    (C) the political system is open to all.

    (D) the political system is rapidly changed by public input.

    (E) the two major parties are unable to control the political agenda.

2. Most interest groups

    (A) help their members by supplying them with benefits.

    (B) support both major parties.

    (C) bring out large numbers of voters.

    (D) support only one party.

    (E) hire lobbyists to work for them.

3. The political power of interest groups lies in

    (A) bringing money to campaigns.

    (B) lobbying leaders and persuading them.

    (C) gathering many members to contact political leaders.

    (D) picking key issues.

    (E) All of the above

4. The **MOST** powerful interest groups tend to be

    (A) representatives of major industries.

    (B) representatives of citizens' groups.

    (C) representatives of minority groups.

    (D) only concerned with conservative issues.

    (E) the most professional.

5. Madison and other early leaders feared that "factions" would

    (A) split the country into party groups.

    (B) stop the ratification of the Constitution.

    (C) take control of regions and block minority groups.

    (D) have too much influence on national leaders.

    (E) All of the above

FREE-RESPONSE QUESTIONS

1. Interest and lobby groups have increased dramatically in number and influence.

    (A) Explain two reasons for the increase in interest groups and lobby organizations.

    (B) Explain two reasons why lobby groups are viewed negatively.

2. Lobbyists wield many forms of power in Washington, D.C.

    (A) Identify three ways in which lobbyists wield power in Congress.

    (B) Explain reasons why these forms of power are effective.

ANSWERS AND EXPLANATIONS

MULTIPLE-CHOICE ANSWERS

1. B

There are many interest groups in the United States because many want to shape public policy. Even though access may be limited and controlled by the richest lobby groups, many believe in trying to have an influence.

2. E

Most interest groups hire lobbyists to work for them. Some groups do some or all of the other items, but most groups do not.

3. E

The political power of interest groups lies in bringing money to campaigns, lobbying leaders and persuading them, gathering many members to contact these leaders, and picking key issues. All are major ways in which groups wield influence.

4. A

The most powerful interest groups tend to be those with the greatest financial resources. Economic interest groups that support big business have a decided advantage due to current campaign finance and lobbying regulations.

5. C

Madison and other early leaders feared that "factions" would take control of regions and block minority groups from having any political power. Madison correctly worried that the regions and states would need a central government that could protect minority groups of all kinds.

FREE-RESPONSE ANSWERS

1. **4-point Rubric**

   2 points in part (A): (two ways why an increase in lobby groups)

   - Is now legal to make campaign donations.

   - Is also legal to lobby.

   - More single-issue groups have been formed.

   - There is a more diverse population to represent.

   2 points in part (B): (two reasons why a negative image)

   - Too dominant

   - Suppress minorities

   - Too divisive

   - Too controlling

   - Too powerful if wealthy

2. **6-point Rubric**

   3 points in part (A): (three forms of influence)

   - Testifying before Congress.

   - Publishing research findings

   - Contributing funds to campaigns

   - The threat of litigation

   3 points in part (B): (explain why powerful)

   - Access to committees in Washington at critical debate times

   - Expertise and staff resources that even Congress might not have

   - Contributing lots of money to campaigns

   - Funds to go to court and sue

CHAPTER 11: MEDIA AND ITS FUNCTIONS

IF YOU LEARN ONLY FIVE THINGS IN THIS CHAPTER . . .

1. Media coverage has shown a tendency toward biased political coverage of different candidates and parties.

2. The media plays a major role in setting the public agenda.

3. The media has a significant influence on campaigns and elections.

4. Most media venues are owned by multimillion-dollar corporations that often are more concerned with their profit margins than with delivering quality news.

5. The growth of the Internet as a major news source is rapidly expanding media accessibility.

THE HISTORY OF MEDIA

The media's role in presenting political information is as old as U.S. politics. However, the idea that the media should be unbiased is as much a 20th-century concept as radio and television. Essays, leaflets, and books in colonial times were often printed to sway public opinion. The advent of daily papers aided in the distribution of political news, but early newspapers would be considered quite biased by today's standards. Later, the development of radio and television allowed a person to actually see or hear a political speech as it happened, thus enabling people to process political information that had not been filtered by the media. But the Internet has truly transformed the ways in which political news is gathered and disseminated. Instead of choosing from two different newspapers, or from among the major news networks, people can now select from a seemingly infinite pool of news websites, government reports, and individually produced political blogs.

Today, the media is as much a part of American politics as the three branches of government, earning it the nickname "the fourth branch." This is not to be confused with the federal bureaucracy, which is also called the "fourth branch" by some. Political parties, through the selective use of the media, attempt to advance their political agendas. Media outlets try to balance the need to make a profit, competition with other sources, and the difficult task of staying impartial. Added to this mix are governmental regulations requiring certain levels of "equal time" for party ads and statements.

During the first presidential campaigns, daily newspapers did not yet exist. Early political reporters worked for party leaders, and presented a biased agenda and attacked opponents, often viciously. What the supporters of John Adams and Thomas Jefferson said about each other in the media was certainly not balanced or neutral; in fact, it was often openly slanderous.

This type of reporting continued late into the 19th century, when the development of the telegraph and transcontinental transportation allowed early media companies to expand nationally. Essays and pamphlets were replaced by newspapers and magazines. Newspapers such as *The New York World* and *The New York Journal* used scandalous headlines and salacious stories to attract readers. With growing newspaper circulation came increasing influence. Newspaper publishers like William Randolph Hearst and Joseph Pulitzer used their newspapers as a platform to propagate their political biases and to prevent the spread of any opposing viewpoint. For example, when the illustrator Frederic Remington requested to return home from an apparently uneventful stay in Cuba during the Spanish-American War, Hearst famously responded, "You furnish the pictures, and I'll furnish the war."

Throughout the late 19th and early 20th centuries, newspapers and their editorial staffs were widely seen as overwhelmingly favoring Republican candidates. The invention of radio and television seemed to create a a more unbiased presentation of political news. Political journalists became national stars themselves. Men and women such as Walter Cronkite, Edward R. Murrow, and Barbara Walters became household names with significant influence.

By the 1960s, the media began to be seen as more liberal. Those who subscribe to this theory of the increasing liberal perspective of the media often point to television coverage of the Vietnam war to support their analysis. They claim that the media's coverage was biased and fostered opposition to the war from the American public. Regardless of whether this increasing liberal bias existed, Richard Nixon's presidency and the Watergate scandal helped cement the media's role as a watchdog of the government. Indeed, every president since Nixon has been the target of increased media scrutiny.

GOALS OF THE MODERN MEDIA/CONCERNS ABOUT THE MEDIA

For a representative democratic government to function properly, it needs to connect citizens to the policy-making process. Traditionally, political parties and interest groups have played that role. As various forms of mass media have developed, however, they have become more influential in two main areas: political campaigns for election and the public agenda.

The media responds to and participates in the political process. As observers, journalists report and reflect on the operation of government. By doing these things, the media helps to influence public opinion. When media outlets choose to focus on certain stories, they help to set the government's priorities. In this way, mass media not only reflects but also helps to create public opinion. Regardless of what political leaders want to do, they often have to spend time addressing issues raised by the media. For example, President Clinton spent much of his second term answering questions about alleged personal misconduct instead of advancing his legislative agenda.

Now, because most people turn to various media sources for information about candidates—rather than merely following the candidates themselves—each media outlet can affect how a candidate is perceived. This development is leading candidates to hire media professionals to help shape their media image and to gain favorable coverage. Although it appears that additional coverage of candidates' actions and beliefs would lead to a more-informed public, some argue that style is becoming more important than substance. One of the greatest concerns is over the increasing use of attack ads aimed at undermining support for political opponents.

Again, the primary medium through which news is disseminated has changed from the newspaper to the television. Newspaper articles, which can run several thousand words, rely on thorough reporting, descriptive language, and an abundance of quotes from primary sources to create an accurate and compelling story. Televised news does not need to delve as deeply into an issue, because as the old adage goes, "A picture is worth a thousand words." Famous images, such as a distraught young woman kneeling next to a fellow student who has been shot by a National Guardsman at Kent State University, don't need much of an explanation; the image provides its own.

The change in format, from news articles to news broadcasts, has also drastically shortened the amount of time necessary to present a news story. People no longer have to read about an event after it has happened. They can now see and hear an event live, often as it is happening. Unfortunately, many important stories concerning public policy are not covered by television news because they do not lend themselves to brief images and quick sound bites.

As people demand more content in less time, the popularity of Internet-based news organizations has grown. Finding news on the Internet can be summed up in the phrase "what you want, when you want it." Vast numbers of articles, public records, and even video segments are available for immediate consumption. Another benefit of the Internet is the global reach of its content. While a newspaper only can be printed a finite number of times and distributed to a limited number of locations, an online version of that same newspaper can be viewed by people anywhere there's an Internet connection. Unfortunately, the power to disseminate information can also be harnessed to disseminate disinformation. Rumors can be generated in seconds, and opinion is often confused with fact. The issue of accuracy among many of the more independent news sources is a growing concern. This is especially true of political blogs. Established news organizations have editors and large staffs that can verify reports and confirm accusations. What level of truthfulness is available on the thousands of individual Internet outlets?

THE MANIPULATED MEDIA

The media has also become a tool of the president and Congress. Playing to the camera has become almost as important as a candidate's platform. Speeches are carefully orchestrated to meet television coverage times. Press conferences are completely controlled by limiting the number of questions asked and by only allowing selected persons to ask questions. Both the House and Senate have media rooms where leaders enjoy access to television coverage.

STAGES OF THE DEVELOPMENT OF MEDIA IN THE UNITED STATES

Late 1700s to the mid-1800s	Almost no daily newspapers existed. Instead, news was distributed via pamphlets and essays (e.g., *Common Sense* by Thomas Paine). Organized reporting was done for political reasons and was directly controlled by supporters of different party groups. The media was intended to be partisan. The *Federalist Papers* were created with a partisan agenda. Political attacks were personal and often vicious.
Late 1800s	Newspapers became national businesses (e.g., the Hearst Syndicate) and profits were their goal. Selling stories was central. News organizations took pride in influencing public opinion (*yellow journalism*) or policy (*muckraking*). Newspapers were also central in helping to enact progressive reforms. Stories about the powers of trusts such as Standard Oil were good business and created pressure for political changes. This was an early form of the press setting the political agenda.
Early 1900s	Teddy Roosevelt established the "bully pulpit" through newspapers and the developing "press corps." His administration took the first steps in creating media events and press conferences. Getting inside information from the White House became a status symbol. The press came to rely on the president and was often openly supportive to continue getting information (the "lapdog" function). A reporter who was overly critical would be shut out from conferences and inside information.

Mid-1900s	The development of radio opened new forms of communication between leaders and the public. FDR used "fireside chats" as a form of agenda setting. The presidential staff knew they could reach millions with personal messages. News also became used for war propaganda. The first major use of news as war propaganda in the United States was in pro-British, anti-German coverage during the early years of WWI. Press conferences grew as media outlets, again controlled by the executive branch.
Late 1900s	The development of television and the Internet created instant information and polling of public support. The 1960s brought candidate image to the center of campaigning. Media events such as the Cuban Missile Crisis came to the forefront.
Vietnam and Watergate	The media took on the role of investigator (the "watchdog" function). Growing public mistrust of government led to media focus on government flaws and mistakes. The government's reaction was to try to carefully choreograph almost any contact between the press and political leaders. Presidents now only answer questions within strict guidelines. Teleprompters give the impression that presidents are speaking off-the-cuff, and radio transmitters allow for answers to questions to be sent to the president's ear.
Post-Vietnam	The creation of the Internet and explosion of talk radio has led to the prevalence of "attack journalism" (the "junkyard dog" function). Fame is gained by those with the most outrageous attacks and stories (Clinton scandals), and conservative and liberal groups try to outdo each other in media attacks.

MEDIA BIAS

Modern-day conservative groups maintain that the American media is very biased toward liberal issues and candidates. Polls taken by conservative groups claim that the vast majority of people working in media vote Democratic. Polls taken by moderate or nonpartisan groups, however, show that the media is relatively unbiased and that personal voting habits do not significantly influence media coverage of issues or candidates.

Clearly, some magazines tend toward different ends of the political spectrum, but the bulk of political reporting tends to be unbiased. Though the mainstream media generally tries to avoid biased coverage, there are distinct pockets of support for both conservatives and liberals, such as *The Nation*, *National Review*, *The Weekly Standard*, and *The New Republic*, each of which exists to support certain viewpoints. Nationally syndicated columnists such as George Will and Paul Krugman are famous for thoughtful commentary on political issues from particular perspectives.

EFFECTS OF MEDIA ON MODERN POLITICS

- White House staff members shield the president from many questions and control when questions are asked, how they are asked, and who asks them. Presidents universally use teleprompters, earphones, charts, and the like so they appear more prepared and in command.

- Campaigns and debates are now events that are completely crafted down to the finest detail. The public sees only what has been thoroughly planned by the campaign staff and nothing else.

- Staff groups who try to control every media image attempt to orchestrate election debates. Only certain debate questions are allowed, and each campaign team spends days in preparation.

- Special media rooms, created by congressional leaders, afford them instantaneous access to television coverage.

- Debates and speeches are timed to take advantage of news cycles or C-SPAN coverage times. C-SPAN has two channels that provide constant reporting of the activities of Congress.

- Press conferences are usually held only when issues can be effectively addressed.

- Presidential staffs have created a "constant campaign" that presents the president in a favorable light and at key events in order to keep popularity polls at their highest. It is as if the election campaign never stops.

- Candidates now use websites for national attention and fundraising. Elections that used to be relatively local in scope can now target a much wider audience and collect money from around the nation.

- Personal attacks on parties and candidates have escalated dramatically through the use of the Internet, particularly through blogs. Any and every group can disseminate propaganda to a vast audience, without much control of facts or biases.

THE MEDIA AND THE SHRINKING ATTENTION SPAN OF THE PUBLIC

The dominance of television and video images has dramatically reduced the amount of time spent presenting issues and candidates. Instead of presenting an entire speech, news organizations will use only the most relevant snippets of sentences, a technique known as *sound bite* news. Since the 1960s, the average time spent by the media reporting candidate's speeches has dropped from about a minute to sound bites under 10 seconds. As a result, campaign staffs focus their efforts on presenting easily digestible messages, memorable lines, or quotes. Much effort is also given to trying to find memorable mistakes by the other side, thus presenting a quick but lasting negative image of the other party. Being able to sum up an agenda in 10 words or less is key to advancing that agenda to the American people.

The Media and the Setting of the Political Agenda

Media outlets look for events and issues that sell well or offer controversy. These items often become the "crisis of the day" that politicians must address, or at least appear to address. The selection of such events can show a media bias toward parties and leaders, change the directions of policies, or enflame public anger. Recent examples include illegal immigration and coverage of the Tea Party movement.

REVIEW QUESTIONS

MULTIPLE-CHOICE QUESTIONS

1. Which goal of the U.S. media is **MOST** historically correct?

   (A) Promotion of free speech

   (B) Information access

   (C) Political fairness

   (D) Promotion of party bias

   (E) Dissemination of national information

2. Daily news reporting became a national phenomenon because of

   (A) the invention of radio.

   (B) the invention of television.

   (C) the invention of coast-to-coast telegraph systems.

   (D) the creation of national, for-profit news companies.

   (E) All of the above

3. Media agenda setting is criticized for all of the following reasons **EXCEPT**

   (A) it gives the power of setting the priorities of problems to media leaders.

   (B) it stops political leaders from setting the political agenda.

   (C) the media is biased.

   (D) the media spends too little time on key issues.

   (E) the media spends too much time on issues of little importance.

4. The **MOST** consistent trend in media coverage in the country has been

   (A) its generally neutral stand on most party issues.

   (B) its expansion of coverage of candidates' personal lives.

   (C) its reduction of story time and coverage.

   (D) its shift toward more constant coverage of politics.

   (E) its lack of coverage of the differences between party groups.

5. The **BEST** description of the general relationship between presidents and the media would be

   (A) mutual distrust.

   (B) mutual trust.

   (C) the media forces presidents to create political priorities.

   (D) presidents hate media scrutiny.

   (E) the two need each other and use each other for gain.

FREE-RESPONSE QUESTIONS

1. The media has been described as a powerful force in influencing the development of the government's political agenda.

    (A) Identify three ways in which the president or Congress attempts to control media access and influence.

    (B) Explain two ways in which the media secures its influence.

2. The impact of media coverage on American politics has changed over time.

    (A) Describe any two of the periods of media coverage.

    (B) Describe a goal of the media in trying to affect/bias the political agenda.

ANSWERS AND EXPLANATIONS

MULTIPLE-CHOICE ANSWERS

1. D

Throughout the history of media, party bias has been a media goal. Media in the United States has always been profit driven and was very biased in colonial times and in the first days of the republic. Free speech, access to all, fairness, and national dissemination of information are also goals of media, but these have not been consistently pursued over time.

2. E

The invention of radio, the invention of television, the invention of coast-to-coast telegraph systems, and the creation of national news companies have all helped make daily news reporting a national phenomenon.

3. B

It is not true that media agenda setting stops political leaders from setting the political agenda. Political leaders often use the media in many ways to set their agendas. Choices (A), (C), (D), and (E) are all true criticisms of media agenda setting.

4. C

The most consistent trend in media coverage in the United States has been the reduction of information into sound bites. Choice (A) is incorrect because media has often been very biased. Choice (B) is incorrect because media actually reduced personal coverage during the 20th century. Choices (D) and (E) are incorrect because media outlets have reduced coverage of politics and party differences.

5. E

The best description of the general relationship between presidents and the media would be that the two need each other and use each other. Choices (A) and (B) are incorrect because the level of trust between the two groups varies; some media and political leaders work closely together, while others do not. Choice (C) is incorrect because the media does not force the president to create political priorities. Choice (D) is incorrect because, in many instances, the president and his staff control media access to events and often get many benefits out of media-covered appearances.

FREE-RESPONSE ANSWERS

1. **5-point Rubric**

   3 points in part (A): (three ways leaders attempt to control the media)

   - Carefully managed press conferences
   - New leaks to select members of the media at key times
   - Timed interviews, reports, access via government-run studios
   - Crafted campaign strategies and sound bites
   - Carefully controlled legislative debates
   - Control of press conferences
   - Control of who gets to ask the questions
   - Party- and partisan-controlled Internet sites (blogs)

   2 points in part (B): (two examples of media's influence)

   - Selecting the stories to cover
   - Creating bias in coverage
   - Controlling time and space given to stories
   - Controlling reports on the public's reactions/support

2. **3-point Rubric**

   2 points in part (A): (two periods of media coverage)

   - Political pamphlets/essays that were for or against candidates during colonial times
   - Regional biases (slavery crisis)
   - National corporate news to sell issues during the early 20th century
   - Radio/television news in the mid-20th century
   - Internet reports from very biased and personal viewpoints in the present day

   1 point in part (B): (goal of media in bias)

   - Support specific candidates or parties because the media outlet agrees with them.
   - Make money by selling crisis stories.
   - Support political agendas, such as progressivism.
   - Make profit by exposing political scandals.

CHAPTER 12: THE LEGISLATIVE BRANCH

IF YOU LEARN ONLY SIX THINGS IN THIS CHAPTER . . .

1. The Constitution focuses on the powers and responsibilities of Congress.

2. Congress has created a complex process for creating laws, making it extremely difficult to pass new laws or amendments to current ones.

3. One of the biggest duties of Congress is the creation of the federal budget.

4. Party leaders control the legislative process.

5. Federal laws expanded the role of the national government during the 20th century.

6. Incumbent members of Congress are very difficult to remove from office.

THE HOUSE AND THE SENATE

Congress was originally designed to be the branch of government that is most responsible for the development of the republic, and it was the only federal branch where the people directly elected political leaders (the House). Presidents are chosen by electors, senators were originally chosen by state legislators, and federal justices are nominated by the president and confirmed by the Senate. Congress was also given the bulk of the duties listed in the Constitution (see Chapter 4; also refer to Article I of the Constitution). Even today, the House and Senate are the only parts of the federal government that are directly elected by citizens.

DUTIES AND THE COMMITTEES

Congress exists to create laws. This critical duty is designed to be complex and deliberate, with the vast majority of potential ideas being rejected. Large-scale compromise is often required and the overall legislative process is usually messy and lengthy. The job is also overwhelming. Congress attempts to deal with thousands of pieces of legislation each session, and no single member can master, or even be knowledgeable of, all of the details covered. Therefore, the committee system was devised to divide these duties into smaller units. This committee system requires that members of Congress handle areas of expertise and that all members support some of the decisions of other members. Leaders of the chambers of Congress and its committees must have strong powers to determine legislative priorities. The power to set the legislative agenda and prioritize problems is immense. Members of Congress are also expected to monitor other departments of government and to represent the views of constituents.

CONSTITUTIONAL POWER AND DUTIES

Article I, Section 8 of the Constitution lists the key powers of the federal legislature. Major powers include taxation, regulating interstate commerce, declaring war, and organizing the military. Interstate commerce powers have become a major area where Congress has expanded its powers, because many issues, such as civil rights, are connected to the business of interstate trade. As mentioned previously, the last paragraph of this section (Clause 18) includes the phrase "all Laws which shall be necessary and proper." The "Elastic Clause" has allowed Congress to add to its powers.

SPECIFIC CONGRESSIONAL POWERS AND DUTIES IN THE CONSTITUTION

A1S2C5	House: Choose a Speaker and other officers; have the power to impeach
A1S3C5	Senate: Choose officers; try all impeachments
A1S4C2	Congress: Meet once a year
A1S5	Congress: Judge elections of members; compel attendance; determine rules; punish members; possibly expel members; keep a journal of its proceedings
A1S6	Congress: Be privileged from arrest during sessions; can't hold other offices
A1S7	Congress: Start revenue bills in the House; present laws to the president
A1S8	Congress: Levy and collect taxes; pay debts; provide for the common defense and general welfare; borrow money; regulate interstate commerce; set rules for naturalization of citizens; make laws covering bankruptcy; coin money; fix the standards of weights and measures; set the punishment for counterfeiting; establish post roads and offices; promote the sciences and the arts; create copyright laws; create federal courts; define and set punishments for piracy; declare war; grant letters of marque and reprisal; raise and support armies, provide for a navy and call for the militia if needed; organize and discipline militias; govern the nation's capital district; regulate national forts and arsenals; make all laws that may be "necessary and proper"

A1S9	Congress: Do not suspend *writs of habeas corpus* unless emergencies require it; pass no bills of attainder or *ex post facto* laws; levy no taxes without a census; do not tax exports; do not make preferential laws for ports or coastal states; do not draw money from the Treasury without authorization; do not grant titles of nobility
A1S10	Congress: Monitor states' actions over imports and exports; monitor states' actions with other countries
A2	Congress: Set the times of the workings of the Electoral College
A3	Congress: Decide whether to create federal courts; set court salaries; direct where some federal trials are heard; declare the punishment for treason but do not include the families of those accused as possible recipients of punishment
A4	Congress: Admit new states; control federal territories; protect the states from invasion and domestic violence
A5	Congress: Help propose constitutional amendments
A6	Congress: Swear to uphold the Constitution

ASC = Article, Section, Clause

KEY DIFFERENCES BETWEEN HOUSE AND SENATE POWERS AND DUTIES

House of Representatives	Senate
Initiates revenue bills (both chambers must still vote on the final version)	
Initiates impeachment proceedings	Holds trial for those impeached by the House and votes on removal
Possibly requests discharge petitions for bills stuck in committee	Can filibuster bills being debated
House Rules Committee controls debate time limits	Allows for riders to unrelated bills
Must have a speaker as leader	Informal leaders are party heads, with president of the Senate (VP) in a mostly ceremonial role
Selects the president if the Electoral College can't	Selects the vice president if the Electoral College can't
	Approves the president's appointments to major federal posts and to the Supreme Court
	Approves treaties initiated by the executive branch
	Approves ambassadors as they are nominated by the executive branch

CREATED PROCEDURES

To streamline the tremendous task of reviewing bills, several traditions and procedures have been created. The most important are the traditions of seniority in deciding membership in committees and majority rule of committees. Members who have more years of service get more important positions. In addition, the majority party chooses all committee chairperson positions, therefore guaranteeing that one party can dominate the legislative process.

Within the Congress, differences between the House and Senate are noteworthy. Representatives must stand for re-election every other year, causing a focus on campaigning and fundraising. Because there are four times as many representatives as there are senators, the amount of individual power is reduced in the House. Senators also have much larger constituencies, and those from smaller states have greater influence than their counterparts in the House, because in the Senate, every state has only two votes. The tradition of open debates in the Senate gives every senator the potential to close down the legislative process with a filibuster. Filibusters can be ended with cloture votes, which were established in the early 1900s. The number of votes needed for cloture is currently set at 60, but the number of recent filibuster threats has caused congressional leaders to question these rules and numbers.

CONGRESSIONAL STAFFS, SPECIALIZATION, AND CONFLICTING ROLES

Because of their numerous and complex duties, members of Congress rely on dedicated staffs to share their workload.

This has often isolated members from contact with constiuents and limited their ability to become policy experts. Most members try to specialize in areas of law that affect their districts or states, or they focus where they have personal expertise. This has led to roles that are often openly in conflict with one another.

Members must advocate for their constituents, their party, their leaders, their committees, and their own sense of what is right. They don't have time to be experts on everything and are limited in the number of committees on which they can serve. Voting on one issue may bring them into conflict with some of the various interests they represent. They must maintain power, however, to maintain their influence.

THE FEDERAL BUDGET

No duty is arguably more important than the development of the annual federal budget. Determining funding for federal programs entails many debates and compromises with the president and other members of Congress. The federal budget takes effect on October 1 and expires at the end of the following September, a period known as the fiscal year.

The executive branch's Office of Management and Budget creates the budget outline, but Congress must prioritize the thousands of items and approve it. Congress is also in charge of creating the tax system that will fund the budget. If Congress does not levy taxes that cover the budget, it must take responsibility for allowing the nation to borrow the funds necessary to cover the shortfall.

ADDITIONAL DUTIES

Beyond the creation of legislation, members of Congress have other key duties. They are expected to help constituents navigate the federal bureaucracy. They are expected to help with responses to local disasters and conflicts. They also work with local and state leaders.

Furthermore, they are expected to meet with civic groups. They must also react to a president's agenda and compromise on their own. Senators have further duties in approving presidential appointments.

CURRENT STATUS

Even though it was originally designed to dominate the federal system, the Congress of modern times has been superseded in the mind of most citizens by the powers of the president. Congress's slow pace often frustrates the public. Congress must struggle with compromise, leaving many dissatisfied. The public has trouble maintaining interest in or being informed about 535 leaders. Congress relies on the president to create legislative priorities. Congress relies on the vast federal bureaucracy to implement many laws and policies. In recent times, Congress is often led by the opposite party of the president or has different parties in control of its two chambers. All of these developments have weakened the influence of Congress.

THE BASICS OF CONGRESS

Thousands of ideas for potential laws are generated annually. Citizens, lobby groups, state and federal agencies, executive leaders, members of Congress, and their staff members all contribute ideas for potential laws. This work is organized through the committee system.

BASIC COMMITTEES OF CONGRESS

Standing Committees	These are the permanent committees that work on annual items. In the 2008 session, the House had 20 standing committees responsible for issues ranging from agriculture and the armed services to energy, homeland security, sciences, and ways and means. The Senate had 16 such committees that year.
Joint Committees	Members of the House and the Senate gather basic information for Congress on many subjects, such as economics. In 2008, there were four such committees on printing, taxation, the "Economic Committee," and the committee that runs the Library of Congress.
Select/Special Committees	Select/special committees are temporary and set up to investigate or research issues. These committees are disbanded when the issue or conflict is resolved. There have been special committees on energy independence, Indian affairs, ethics, intelligence, and aging.
Conference Committees	When bills emerge from House and Senate debates, there may be significant differences between the House bill and the Senate bill. To rectify this, a conference committee is created that includes the major sponsors of the bill from both chambers. This committee has the duty of reconciling the differences and presenting the House and Senate with a united bill.

LEADERSHIP AND ORGANIZATION OF CONGRESS

House of Representatives: 435 members (this number was set in 1929), elected for two-year terms from state districts, with seats being distributed according to state populations

Leaders:

1. The **Speaker of the House** (required by the Constitution) is elected by majority vote of members and, in modern times, has always been a member of the majority party.

2. The **majority leader** is chosen by the majority party to develop its goals and policies.

3. The **majority whip** is the assistant to the majority leader and pressures members to support party goals.

4. **Committee chairpersons** are from the majority party. Chairpersons help establish the legislative calendar and schedule committee hearings. Rules Committee members are House leaders selected to make the rules for legislative debates and amendment options for bills. They control the final agenda on the House floor.

5. The **House Rules Committee** can make or break a piece of legislation when it either restricts or loosens the time limits for and scope of debates.

6. The **minority leader** is the leader of the opposition, minority party.

7. The **minority whip** is the assistant to the minority leader and liaison to the minority party members.

8. The **House Republican Conference** guides GOP bills and agendas.

9. The **House Democratic Caucus** guides Democratic bills and agendas.

Senate: 100 members elected for six-year terms from an entire state (rather than from a specific district, as in the House; there are two senators per state), 33 or 34 elected every two years (staggered-term system)

Leaders:

1. The **President of the Senate** (required by the Constitution) is the vice president and can monitor debates, count electoral votes, and vote to break a tie vote of the senators.

2. The President *Pro Tempore* (*pro tem*) (required by the Constitution) serves when the vice president is not available. Generally, it is a ceremonial role given to the majority party senator with the longest tenure (most seniority).

3. A **majority leader** is elected by the majority party to lead procedures, set the agenda, and so on.

4. A **majority assistant** (some texts list this as Senate whip) has the same duties as the House majority whip.

5. **Committee chairpersons** are from the majority party, usually assigned through seniority. As in House committees, the chairperson can wield power over when bills are debated, how they are debated, and sometimes even whether or not they are debated.

6. A **minority leader** leads the interests of the minority party.

7. A **minority assistant** (Senate whip) has duties that parallel those of the House whips.

8. Each party has a **"Conference Caucus"** that guides policies and agendas for the parties.

THE BASIC STEPS OF CREATING LAWS

The Constitution requires that revenue bills start in the House, but most other bills are given simultaneous treatment by the House and Senate.

Some bills are processed by the Senate and then the House, others by the House and then the Senate. All bills must be considered and approved by both chambers of Congress to become law.

Process:

1. Staff members of House and Senate leaders assign bills numbers for processing (e.g., HR 1..., S 1...).

2. Leaders get bills assigned to committees.

3. Committee chairpersons assign bills to subcommittees for study and debate.

4. Subcommittees hold public hearings, amend bills, and vote on bills. This is known as the "markup" procedure. If the bill is approved, it is then referred to the full committee.

5. The committee can hold further hearings and debates, but it often votes based on subcommittee recommendations.

6. The committee refers the bill to the full House or Senate floor.

7. Floor debates can occur, and, if passed, the bill is referred to the other chamber.

8. The powerful House Rules Committee frames House debates, times, and so on.

9. Once both chambers have passed the bill, a conference committee is formed to reconcile the two versions into a single bill.

(continued on next page)

THE BASIC STEPS OF CREATING LAWS (con't)

10. Both the House and the Senate vote on the conference committee version of the bill.

11. If the bill is approved it's then sent to the president.

12. If the president signs it, the bill becomes federal law.

13. If the president ignores the bill for 10 days (not counting Sundays), it automatically becomes law without the president's signature.

14. If the congressional session has fewer than 10 days remaining and the president ignores a new bill, then the bill dies at the end of the session. This is the "pocket veto."

15. If the president vetoes the bill, the House and Senate can vote to override with a two-thirds majority.

MODERN ADDITIONS AND REVISIONS TO PROCEDURES

Traditional committee procedures for debates, amendments, and votes have been modified by Congress to allow for more efficiency. Here are examples:

- **Fast tracking.** No amendments allowed; take the bill as is, or not. Because amendments are often lengthy and difficult to debate, fast tracking speeds the entire process.

- **Slow tracking.** Sequential committee hearings are required; this is usually a sign of a bill being delayed through lengthier processing.

- **Multiple referrals.** Many bills need to be seen by different committees that cover areas of government under their control. To speed this process, bills can be sent to these committees simultaneously.

- **Outside amendments.** Some revisions can be made by congressional leaders outside of committee meetings.

- **Unanimous consent rules.** As an efficiency measure, such rules allow for the usual voting procedures to be suspended, as long as no single member objects. Long vote counts can be avoided.

- **King of the Hill votes.** This newer procedure has several amendment versions voted on in order. As long as amendments pass, the voting continues. When an amendment fails, the last one to win becomes the version selected for the bill. Prior amendments are then ignored.

- **Queen of the Hill votes.** This system gives the amendment with the biggest margin of approval the victory over all other amendments.

A SAMPLE OF CONGRESSIONAL EFFICIENCY
(DATA FROM THE 102ND CONGRESS)

Total bills introduced in the two-year term:	10,238 (100%)
Bills sent to committees by leaders:	10,178 (99.4%)
Bills referred out of committees:	1,205 (11.7%)
Bills referred from floor debates:	1,201 (11.7%)
Passed by both the House and the Senate:	667 (6.5%)
Finally becoming federal law:	590 (5.7%) of all bills introduced

MAJOR PLACES WHERE LEGISLATION CAN BE BLOCKED

- Leaders can assign bills to openly hostile committees or committee chairpersons.
- Chairpersons can delay the bill's consideration ("pigeonhole").
- Subcommittee and committee members can vote no. (This is done often.)
- Subcommittee and committee amendments can change the bill so much that the original sponsors withdraw their support.
- Lobby groups can create opposition and pressure to kill the bill.
- Debate rules can cause changes in votes or amendments.
- Members of the Senate can filibuster or threaten to filibuster. Senators can hold the floor as long as they can stand, thus delaying any other business. This tactic can force compromises when the minority cannot stop a vote in any other manner.
- Individual senators can place a "hold" on any bill and keep it from being debated on the floor.
- Floor votes in either chamber can be against a bill.
- The conference committee can change the bill enough to change support in the two chambers.
- The president can pocket veto or veto, and Congress isn't able to override that veto.

KEY COMMITTEES OF CONGRESS

House Committees:	Duties:
Appropriations	Federal expenditures are controlled here.
Budget	Oversight of government spending.
Rules	Debate rules, bill sequence, and rules of amendments are set.
Ways and Means	Taxation legislation, Social Security.

Senate Committees:	Duties:
Appropriations	Federal discretionary spending programs are set.
Budget	Oversight of government agencies and spending is done.
Finance	Duties are similar to those of the HR Ways and Means committee.
Foreign Relations	Policy debates and treaty votes are main duties.
Judiciary	Judges and justices are questioned and possibly confirmed.

WHO CREATES, CONTROLS, OR INFLUENCES THE AGENDA OF CONGRESS?

Senate and House Leaders	Bills are directed to committees, legislative priorities set, and party agendas formulated.
Committee and Subcommittee Chairpersons	Bills are prioritized, scheduled for hearings and debates, and possibly delayed or killed through pigeonholing.
Party Leadership Committees	Overall priorities for legislation are created, and committee memberships are determined.
Lobbyists	Their access to information, staff members, and campaign contributions helps influence bills and their content.
PACs and Interest Groups	PACs and interest groups control votes through member pressure and campaign fund access.
Congressional Staff Members	The level of expertise of congressional staff members on issues can guide Congress's votes.
Party Members, Party Leaders, and National Party Committees	These can be critical sources of media or campaign support. Pressure is applied for loyal votes and the advancement of the overall party goals.
The President and Staff	Media access, public support, leadership, and the setting of national priorities affect Congress's work.
Independent Agencies and Executive Agencies	Vast bureaucracies control the way issues are addressed, the way rules are administered, and the way laws are enforced.

OPINIONS OF CONGRESS

In recent years, citizens have been divided in their opinion about the members of Congress. The vast majority of citizens hold negative opinions about these leaders as a group and about their effectiveness. People don't trust Congress; they see the members as listening only to wealthy insiders and caring only for personal power. They believe that members of Congress are disconnected from the needs of the average citizen.

Yet, when polled about the work of individual representatives, opinions turn positive. People react favorably to pork projects that create local jobs, they appreciate contact with representatives through various forms of communication, and they trust their leadership. As partisan splits widen in the early 21st century, people also see members of Congress as important representatives of the majority beliefs in their congressional district.

SAMPLES OF MAJOR LAWS CREATED BY CONGRESS
(COMMON NAMES)

Pendleton Civil Service Reform Act	1883	Federal jobs through merit, not patronage
Sherman Antitrust Act	1890	First attempt to limit monopolies and trusts
Pure Food and Drug Act	1906	Control over food manufacturing and processing
Clayton Antitrust Act	1914	Bolstered the Sherman Act
Glass-Steagall Act	1933	Major banking reforms and regulations
Social Security Act	1935	New Deal safety net effort
Wagner Act	1935	Union and collective bargaining rights
Hatch Act	1939	Civil servant restrictions in partisan politics
Smith Act	1940	Can't advocate for the overthrow of the government
Employment Act	1946	Government responsible for stabilizing the economy
Taft-Hartley Act	1947	Restrictions on union rules and powers
National Security Act	1947	Creation of Department of Defense, CIA, NSC
Civil Rights Act	1957	Effort to secure voting rights for African Americans
Clean Air Act	1963	Antismog efforts start
Civil Rights Act	1964	Racial discrimination outlawed
Voting Rights Act	1965	Voting discrimination outlawed
Freedom of Information Act	1966	Partial or full disclosure of previously unreleased government records
Fair Housing Act	1968	Housing discrimination outlawed
Organized Crime Control Act	1970	Aimed at eliminating organized crime
Occupational Safety and Health Act	1970	OSHA formed to ensure safe workplaces
Federal Election Campaign Act	1971	First limits on campaign contributors
Title IX, Educational Amendments	1972	Equal funding for women's athletics
Endangered Species Act	1973	Protects threatened species from extinction
Budget Reform Act	1974	Title X bars impoundment of funds by the president
Superfund Act	1980	Federal authority to clean up hazardous waste sites
Gramm-Rudman-Hollings Act	1985	Effort at balancing the budget, debt limits

(continued on next page)

SAMPLES OF MAJOR LAWS CREATED BY CONGRESS
(COMMON NAMES) (con't)

Simpson-Mazzoli Act	1986	Required employers to attest to their employees' immigration status
Americans with Disabilities Act	1990	Civil rights for those with disabilities
Family and Medical Leave Act	1993	Maternity and sick leave protection
Patriot Act	2001	Reduced restrictions on law enforcement agencies' ability to search peoples' personal records and eased restrictions on intelligence gathering
No Child Left Behind Act	2001	Federal education standards and rules
McCain-Feingold Act	2002	Effort at limiting "soft money" campaign contributions
Sarbanes-Oakley Act	2002	Required corporate financial records to be accurate
American Jobs Creation Act Energy Independence and Security Act	2004 2007	Repealed the exclusion of taxes on extraterritorial (from outside the U.S.) income; focus on developing renewable energy, improving energy efficiency, and lowering energy costs for consumers

CONFLICTING DUTIES OF MEMBERS OF CONGRESS

Representative Duties	Members should represent the wishes of their districts/states and not necessarily their own wishes; often, members of Congress have views that conflict with those of their constituents.
Trustee Duties	Members should take care of the republic and do what is best for the long-term health of the country, not just what is best for their own districts.
Partisan Duties	These duties include supporting party goals and being consistent with the ideas of liberalism or conservatism.

ADVANTAGES OF INCUMBENCY

House members are more difficult to defeat in reelection attempts than senators, but both groups are difficult to unseat for the following reasons:

Name Recognition	After years of media exposure, undecided voters often select a candidate whose name is familiar to them.
Campaign Costs	Members of Congress have access to many groups that fund races, and senators are often privately wealthy enough to finance their campaigns.
Franking	Free communication with the home constituents throughout a term helps with name recognition.
Pork Projects and Claims of Credit	Local jobs and contracts help build local support, and members of Congress are not shy about reminding their constituents about the source of benefits.
Seniority Powers	As leaders get more influential positions, voters feel that they gain power in Congress as well. They hesitate to start over with a junior member.
Party Support	Party organizations are reluctant to turn on loyal members, who are also proven winners.
Lobby Support	Groups that give money to exert influence are reluctant to gamble on lesser-known outsiders.

REVIEW QUESTIONS

MULTIPLE-CHOICE QUESTIONS

1. Each of the following was true of the founders' goals for the legislature **EXCEPT**

    (A) the public could not directly select members.

    (B) the legislature should have controls placed on its powers.

    (C) the legislature should defer to the executive in foreign policy matters.

    (D) the legislature could set its own salary level.

    (E) the legislature should be the leading branch of the national government.

2. The founders wanted to limit the legislative branch's powers by

    (A) not letting them ignore certain rights in normal times.

    (B) having only the House create tax legislation.

    (C) having the Supreme Court decide the constitutionality of laws.

    (D) giving the executive the power to increase or decrease taxes.

    (E) giving the executive the power to create independent agencies.

3. The Senate became a more democratic institution in the 20th century because

    (A) filibuster and cloture rules were clarified.

    (B) more nonwealthy citizens were elected to it.

    (C) more states were added to the union, thus decreasing the powers of individual senators.

    (D) the seniority system was weakened.

    (E) elections were taken from state legislatures and given to the public.

4. Every 10 years, the House must

    (A) select a new Speaker.

    (B) reorganize its committees.

    (C) set national budget priorities.

    (D) determine the number of representatives the states have.

    (E) redistribute the powers of subcommittee and committee chairpersons.

5. One of the biggest problems members of Congress face when making political decisions is

    (A) following their party's wishes.

    (B) following the goals of their party leaders.

    (C) following the wishes of constituents.

    (D) balancing conflicting duties.

    (E) keeping lobby groups happy to get more funds.

FREE-RESPONSE QUESTIONS

1. The idea of "necessary and proper" powers has been used to expand the scope of Congress's authority.

   (A) Identify the political name of the use of these powers.

   (B) Identify the power listed in Article I of the Constitution that Congress has most often expanded.

   (C) Identify and describe how one of the following cases was used for such expansion of powers:

   Gibbons v. Ogden, 1824

   Heart of Atlanta Motel v. United States, 1964

2. Congress has created a system of lawmaking that is slow, difficult, and usually kills bills.

   (A) List and explain two ways Congress stops legislation.

   (B) Explain two reasons why this might be intentional and positive.

ANSWERS AND EXPLANATIONS

MULTIPLE-CHOICE ANSWERS

1. C

It is not true that the legislature should defer to the executive in foreign policy matters. The fact that the legislature must approve treaties is an example of its involvement in foreign affairs. Choice (A) is incorrect because the public did not originally elect senators. We know that choice (B) is incorrect because the founders placed checks on the legislative branch, such as presidential veto power. Choice (D) is incorrect because Congress does set its own salaries. Choice (E) is incorrect because the founders clearly intended the legislature to be the primary branch.

2. A

The founders wanted to limit legislative powers by not letting them ignore certain rights in normal times. These limitations are contained in Article I, Section 9, which states that Congress must not suspend *writs of habeas corpus* unless emergencies require it. Choice (B) is incorrect because the Senate must concur on tax bills. Choice (C) is incorrect because the power of judicial review was established by the Supreme Court in the case of *Marbury v. Madison* in 1803; it was not listed in the Constitution. Choices (D) and (E) are false: The executive does not have the power to increase or decrease taxes or the power to create independent agencies.

3. E

The Senate became a more democratic institution in the 20th century because elections were taken from the state legislatures and given to the public; this was done through the 17th Amendment in 1913. Choices (A), (C), and (D) are incorrect because although they are all true statements, none of these events were as significant as the 17th Amendment. Choice (B) is not true.

4. D

Every 10 years, the House must determine the number of representatives that the states have due to the constitutionally mandated census and reapportionment of the House.

5. D

One of the biggest problems members of Congress face is the balancing of their conflicting duties.

Free-Response Answers

1. 4-point Rubric

1 point in part (A): (identify)

- Elastic Clause

1 point in part (B): (identify)

- Commerce Clause

- The power to regulate interstate commerce

2 points in part (C): (identify issue and describe)

- *Gibbons v. Ogden*, 1824—regulation of interstate trade is in the hands of Congress, not in the hands of the states.

- *Heart of Atlanta Motel v. United States*, 1964—prohibited discrimination in public accommodations by private businesses if they conduct interstate trade or benefit substantially from interstate trade.

2. 6-point Rubric

4 points in part (A): (two ways Congress stops legislation)

- Chairperson or subcommittee chairperson—pigeonhole or delay bill to death

- Subcommittee or committee—vote bill down

- Floor debate—vote bill down

- Other chamber—vote bill down at some step

- President—veto or pocket veto and bill dies

- Congress—no override vote

2 points in part (B): (two reasons this might be positive)

- Deliberation is good.

- Majority approval is needed.

- Emotional issues need time to be considered.

- Agreement among multiple branches shows need.

- Plenty of input by the public, lobby forces, or other leaders is good.

CHAPTER 13: THE EXECUTIVE BRANCH

IF YOU LEARN ONLY FIVE THINGS IN THIS CHAPTER . . .

1. Executive authority has expanded steadily throughout U.S. history.

2. Public opinion of the president shifts frequently depending on recent developments in domestic and international affairs or how the media represented his actions.

3. Despite the negative backlash the president often takes for promoting or executing an unpopular idea or action, history has shown that Americans are usually willing to live with whatever it is after the fact.

4. It is not uncommon for citizens to hold presidents to an unreasonably high standard of behavior.

5. The history of the U.S. government is full of power shifts between Congress and the president.

THE PRESIDENT

The role of the U.S. president has changed greatly over the years. The original plan for the executive officer was for him to react to congressional laws and execute their implementation, to represent the nation in matters of foreign affairs, and to suggest national legislative priorities. The founding fathers did not trust a single, powerful leader and made almost all executive powers contingent on congressional involvement. The president could command the military, but funding and rules would come from Congress. Treaties and appointments were to become official only with legislative approval. Veto actions could be overridden, and suggestions for legislative priorities could be ignored.

Congress held Article I powers to deal with emergencies and was listed first in the Article IV powers to protect the states. The Senate first demonstrated its expectations of supremacy by ignoring George Washington's request to address a committee and have his bills debated. He never set foot in the Capitol again, establishing an informal rule that is followed today: Presidents are invited into the halls of Congress.

In modern times, presidents have a significantly more powerful role than they did years ago. Circumstances have demanded it, the public has wanted it, and Congress was unable (or unwilling) to stop it. Here are some examples:

- President Polk sent the military into Mexico, leaving Congress with the dilemma of either declaring war or calling for an unpopular retreat.

- Lincoln suspended basic civil liberties during the chaos of 1861.

- Teddy Roosevelt sent the American naval fleet into conflicts in Asia and dared Congress to order it home.

- Franklin Roosevelt's staff instituted economic policies without congressional approval.

More recent presidents have sent troops into serious and violent conflicts without any declaration of war by Congress, arguing that the nation does not always have time to wait for a debate and majority vote.

Also at the president's disposal is the federal bureaucracy. Its employees and agencies must follow executive orders and directives. The president also has a large, talented, and extremely loyal staff that can conduct research, give advice, and shield their leader from criticism. Citizens can't easily identify with all 535 members of Congress, especially when that body's work is slow and deliberate.

THE PRESIDENT AND THE MEDIA

Not every political development goes the way the president would like. As the center of media attention, a president often takes the blame for outcomes beyond his or her control. Congress is happy to avoid that blame, even if items such as taxes and budgets are actually its responsibility.

Congress has tried to scale back executive powers by limiting the extent to which the chief executive can commit American armed forces, barring him or her from impounding funds that were authorized by Congress, and rejecting presidential appointees to various positions in the government. The intense scrutiny of presidential actions through investigative counsels is another form of congressional counterattack.

Conversely, Congress increased the powers of the executive branch after the events of September 11, 2001. For example, it gave the president the power to allow the military to imprison suspected terrorists without charges or trial in U.S. courts. Federal courts upheld these new executive powers in the summer of 2005 and again in 2009. However, congressional and public opposition to this specific expansion of presidential power remains strong.

In addition to the Constitution's vague description of executive authority, the constitutional qualifications for the office are minimal. The founders included no requirement of experience, education, or skills. The only requirements that were listed are as follows:

- Must be at least 35 years old

- Must be a citizen (native born)

- Residency (14 years in the United States)

CONSTITUTIONAL REQUIREMENTS FOR THE PRESIDENCY

Must be a "natural born Citizen" (native born). Until recently, there has never been a challenge or question about a possible candidate who was born *jus soli* (in a U.S. territory) or *jus sanguinus* (of a U.S. citizen whose parents live overseas). However, President Obama's native citizenship has been questioned by some political opponents despite concrete evidence of his being born in Hawaii.

Must have "attained to the Age of thirty five Years." The youngest presidents were Teddy Roosevelt and John Kennedy, who were 43 years old at the time they took office. The oldest were William H. Harrison and Ronald Reagan, who were in their 60s when first elected.

Must have "been fourteen Years a Resident within the United States." No rulings about the nature of these 14 years have occurred. Must they be consecutive years? *Jus sanguinus* citizens must reside a certain number of years after age 14, but not potential presidents.

COMMON CHARACTERISTICS OF PRESIDENTS

Historically, citizens have chosen certain kinds of political leaders for the presidency. Clearly, trends change, but to date, here are the common characteristics of our presidents:

Male	Minor parties, even as far back as the late 19th century, have nominated female candidates. The vice presidential candidacies of Geraldine Ferraro and Sarah Palin have been the highest major party female nominations.
European American	Almost all presidents have had British ancestry. Even as late as the 1980s, the nomination of a Greek American (Michael Dukakis) was considered unusual. In 2009, Barack Obama was the first African American to become president of the United States.
Middle-Aged	No one in his 30s has been nominated for his first run; 72-year-old John McCain was the oldest first-time nominee in 2008.

(continued on next page)

COMMON CHARACTERISTICS OF PRESIDENTS (con't)

Wealthy	Certainly in the 20th century, presidential candidates were expected to come from prosperous backgrounds.
Protestant Christian	Kennedy's candidacy as a Roman Catholic was questioned enough that he decided to give a special campaign speech explaining how he would not let the Pope dictate U.S. policy.
Graduated from College	Truman was the last president not to attend college, and many before him had graduated. Now, even the grades a candidate received in college classes have become the objects of scrutiny and debate.
Is in Good Health	Much scrutiny is given to possible health issues.
Is Relatively Attractive	Columnists, cartoonists, and television and stage comics can add a ruthless level of attacks that give a lasting impression of weakness. This may be very unfair, of course, but it is effective.
Is Married	All presidents (except Buchanan) have been married. In past times, being divorced was considered a major issue, but Reagan overcame that easily.
Has Leadership or Military Skills	Prior experience as a governor or member of Congress is critical. Experience as only a member of the House is probably not sufficient. Only one former Speaker of the House (Polk) has become president, but he had also served as governor of Tennessee. Being a general is considered a plus. If military service has not been completed, an explanation may be needed.
Is from an Important Electoral State	U.S. presidents have come mostly from important electoral states. Exceptions such as Bill Clinton (from Arkansas) might be overcome by being from a key region like the South, where Democrats need all the votes they can get.
Debates Well	Post-1960, a president's TV image has been emphasized. There is some disagreement over the importance of the debates, but both parties spend a lot of resources to make sure their candidate performs well.

DETERMINANTS OF PRESIDENTIAL POPULARITY

Several factors contribute to whether a president is popular. Polls show that *party identification* is the primary factor in attaining popularity and staying popular. How does the party in control appear to be handling the country? Do independent voters feel more positive about that party? A good example of this dynamic is the 1932 election: Even with all the problems of the Great Depression in play, 40 percent of voters still opted for Hoover.

The *economy* is important as well. "It's the economy, stupid," was the Clinton campaign's catch phrase for the election of 1992, reflecting the priorities of voters. A century's worth of data supports this. Also important is whether we are involved in a war or crisis. Voters frequently rally around the president in a show of patriotism and solidarity.

Personal behaviors matter as well. Since Watergate, political opponents—and the media—are quick to point out every potential flaw and mistake they can identify. The *activities of associates*, too, can affect a president's popularity. Scandals involving relatives or friends in positions such as in the Cabinet reflect back on the leader.

Finally, *timing* matters: The presidential "honeymoon" ensures that a leader will be popular at first. Second terms tend to witness lower popularity numbers.

PRESIDENTIAL SELECTION AND TERM LIMITS

Must be selected by the Electoral College. A presidential candidate needs to garner 270 electoral votes to secure the presidency.

Must have previously served no more than one full term and can serve for no more than two full terms or for a total of six years. These limits were put in place by the 22nd Amendment.

PRESIDENTIAL POWERS AND DUTIES

The president fulfills a critical advisory role. The president is the leader of his party, supporting candidates and the platform. The president is the national focal point during times of emergency and crisis. The president works face-to-face with international leaders, representing the goals of the nation.

CONSTITUTIONAL DUTIES AND POWERS OF THE PRESIDENT
(ARTICLE II AND ARTICLE IV, SECTION 4)

Duties and Powers	Constraints
Serves as commander-in-chief of the military (national security leader).	Congress funds and organizes the military and makes the rules for the military.
Negotiates treaties with foreign governments (foreign policy leader).	The Senate must approve treaties for them to take effect.
Nominates top federal officials, including federal judges and justices of the Supreme Court.	The Senate must approve these nominations; by tradition, "senatorial courtesy" is often expected for nominations.
Vetoes legislation passed by Congress.	Congress can override a veto with a two-thirds vote in both chambers.
Can use a pocket veto.	No constraints exist if the president does not sign legislation passed with fewer than 10 days left in the session.
Faithfully administers federal laws (national policy leader); uses executive orders, proclamations, and memoranda to do so.	Congress has set up its own agencies to counter executive power (Congressional Budget Office versus the White House's Office of Management and Budget) and has given many powers to independent agencies.
Can pardon people.	Public outrage may imperil popularity and reelection chances (e.g., Gerald Ford's pardon of Nixon).

(continued on next page)

CONSTITUTIONAL DUTIES AND POWERS OF THE PRESIDENT (ARTICLE II AND ARTICLE IV, SECTION 4) (con't)

Duties and Powers	Constraints
Addresses Congress and the nation and sets legislative priorities (State of the Union message; legislative leader).	Congress can ignore presidential priorities
Acts as chief of state (bully pulpit; crisis manager).	These powers are not defined in the Constitution, and low approval ratings damage the president's leadership powers. The public and the press hold very high expectations of a president's reactions in difficult times.
"…protect each of them (states) against Invasion… against domestic violence."	Presidents are to act "when the Legislature cannot be convened." This is a major way that executives can expand their powers during times of emergency.

THE POWER OF EXECUTIVE PRIVILEGE

Presidents have used the concept of separation of powers to claim a status above the scrutiny of Congress or the federal courts. As leader of the executive branch, a president can claim that certain decisions, information, documents, and secrets of executive agencies are the private business of the president, the president's staff, and the military.

The most famous dispute in this area was over the Watergate tapes of Richard Nixon. When Congress requested those tapes as part of an investigation, Nixon refused to turn them over. He claimed that they were personal documents for his own use in creating his presidential memoirs. The Supreme Court eventually resolved the dispute in favor of Congress. Presidents cannot hide behind executive privilege to put themselves beyond the reach of the law.

PRESIDENTIAL DIRECTIVES

There are different types of presidential directives to the executive branch. They are as follows:

- An *executive order* has the force of law. It can affect any federal agency. Such an order is a very powerful policy tool. Many environmental policies and civil rights policies, such as affirmative action, began as executive orders to the bureaucracy.

- A *proclamation* is a ceremonial action and is not law.

- Memoranda are issued to specific agencies, usually for single projects, but they can affect the way that agency conducts its business.

INFORMAL AND EVOLVED PRESIDENTIAL DUTIES AND POWER

Implied by the Constitution or Created over Time	Checked/Restricted?
Pocket veto	Congress can revive the legislation the next session.
Executive agreements with other countries	They are only "informal" agreements and not treaties.
Executive orders to the executive branch	They only apply to the federal agencies controlled by the executive branch.
Executive proclamations	They do not have the force of law and are usually only ceremonial.
Executive memoranda	They only apply to specific agencies or departments.
Crisis manager	This is informal only and restricted by the fact that Congress must declare war.
Foreign policy leader	Congress must approve treaties and can establish trade restrictions.
Party leader	This is informal only and restricted by the powers of many other party leaders.
"Creation" of the federal budget through the Office of Management and Budget (OMB)	Congress must approve the budget and can ignore OMB guidelines. The Congressional Budget Office (CBO) helps Congress.

EXPANSION OF PRESIDENTIAL POWERS

Presidential powers are not fixed. They frequently expand. The following are major examples:

1846	Polk	As commander-in-chief, Polk ordered the army into disputed territories claimed by Mexico, thus starting a military conflict without Congress's permission or a declaration of war.
1861	Lincoln	Lincoln declared a domestic emergency during a congressional recess, changing the way a president can act during a crisis. Lincoln suspended *habeas corpus* rights, even though those are listed in Article I (the powers of Congress).
Early 1900s	T. Roosevelt	Roosevelt pushed economic reforms, used the press to promote his agenda, and even sent the American naval fleet on a mission without congressional approval.

(continued on next page)

EXPANSION OF PRESIDENTIAL POWERS (con't)

1930s	F. D. Roosevelt	As head of the executive branch, FDR created federal economic programs and reorganized the executive branch—without congressional approval. When the Supreme Court started to halt New Deal programs, FDR hit it with a "court packing" plan that failed, but he eventually changed the court's reaction by way of public pressure.
Late 1960s	Nixon	Nixon blocked congressional programs by "impounding" funds for programs he didn't support. Congress was forced to legislate changes in the spending of program monies. The Supreme Court supported Congress.
Early 1980s	Reagan	Through the Office of Management and Budget, Reagan's budget director, David Stockman, attacked social programs by eliminating them from the federal budget. Congress had to go into a reaction mode again to attempt some restoration of these programs.
Modern Times	(Several)	The power of the executive order has increased over time. By ordering the huge bureaucracy to follow specific orders about certain programs or the spending of funds, the president can effect sweeping changes in the government and economy.

RECENT EVENTS AND LAWS AFFECTING PRESIDENTIAL POWER

Gulf of Tonkin Resolution. This congressional resolution, which was in effect from 1964 to 1970, gave President Johnson authorization, without a formal declaration of war by Congress, for the use of military force in Southeast Asia.

War Powers Resolution (1973). Time limits were placed on the use of troops in combat without congressional approval. The resolution is viewed by some as being unconstitutional.

Increased surveillance powers for the FBI and CIA. Initially, Congress limited the ability of the FBI and CIA to conduct certain kinds of surveillance, especially on U.S. citizens while in the country. Significant changes occurred recently, however, when the Patriot Act reduced restrictions on the FBI and CIA's ability to search peoples' personal records and eased restrictions on intelligence gathering.

Budget Reform Act (1974). In reaction to Nixon's impoundment of federal funds for programs he opposed, Congress now requires the spending of all funds authorized by Congress.

Gramm-Rudman-Hollings Act (1985). This act specified a schedule of gradually declining deficit targets leading to a balanced budget in 1991. This legislation also led to calls for a *balanced budget amendment.* However, political leaders soon realized that such a measure would leave the government without the ability to run up deficits during recessions to stimulate the economy, as is prescribed by the widely supported Keynesian economic theory, and the calls for this constitutional amendment ceased.

Iron Law of Emulation. The idea is that organizations in conflict tend to emulate each other. As the executive branch has increased power through a growing bureaucracy, the legislature has countered with larger staffs and agencies such as the Congressional Budget Office.

Rise of the House of 1994. In 1994, Newt Gingrich led a newly elected Republican majority in trying to shut down the federal government by not passing Clinton's budget. The president turned to the public and reminded them that Congress was in charge of services being cut and Social Security checks not arriving. Pressure from the public forced Congress to capitulate. A second try also failed, damaging the power of Speaker Gingrich.

Increased use of committee powers. Senate committees, such as the Foreign Relations Committee, have increased their opposition to presidential nominations. Famous examples include Senator Jesse Helms's blocks of Clinton nominees and threats of filibusters over conservative judges by Democratic senators in 2005.

Increasing use of "independent counsels." Investigative committees have led to growing congressional attacks on presidents. Examples include Watergate, Iran-Contra, Whitewater, the Clinton impeachment, Dick Cheney's oil policy committee, and so on.

Evidence of incumbent presidential success (or lack of success) as of the election of 2008. In 18 elections, the incumbent president was successful in getting reelected. In 19 elections, he was not. This does not include elections where former presidents were unable even to receive their party's nomination.

REVIEW QUESTIONS

MULTIPLE-CHOICE QUESTIONS

1. The issue of presidential power began as a very controversial matter. The powers initially granted to the president by the Constitution are evidence that the

   (A) founders didn't want a strong, single executive.

   (B) founders wanted a strong executive.

   (C) founders wanted states to control the national government.

   (D) founders didn't trust Congress too much.

   (E) national government was meant to be unified under one leader.

2. In being effective, a modern-day president's **GREATEST** challenge is

   (A) selecting judges and justices with similar political aims.

   (B) working with Congress.

   (C) keeping a favorable image through the media.

   (D) keeping fellow party members in line.

   (E) All of the above

3. One power that presidents hold without congressional checks is

   (A) appointments to the executive branch.

   (B) creating the federal budget.

   (C) establishing a legislative agenda through the State of the Union message.

   (D) the ability to request that congressional committees hear their concerns.

   (E) the ability to pardon citizens.

4. Executive orders are very powerful because

   (A) they have the same authority as congressional laws.

   (B) they can direct federal agencies to conduct business in a certain way.

   (C) they can change the scope and direction of federal policies on issues like civil rights.

   (D) they can apply to the entire federal bureaucracy.

   (E) All of the above

5. All of the following tend to be true about U.S. presidents **EXCEPT**

   (A) they are European American.

   (B) they have some sort of military service background.

   (C) they are from rural areas.

   (D) they have significant personal or family wealth.

   (E) they have no major health issues.

FREE-RESPONSE QUESTIONS

1. Though the founders intended Congress to be the leading federal branch, presidents now find themselves with more power.

    (A) Identify and describe two ways this trend toward increased presidential power has occurred (excluding presidential authority over the federal bureaucracy).

    (B) Explain how presidential authority over the federal bureaucracy has increased executive powers.

2. Recent Congresses have attempted to regain authority from presidents.

    (A) Identify and describe at least two such efforts by Congress.

    (B) Identify and describe one way in which Congress has failed in these efforts.

ANSWERS AND EXPLANATIONS

MULTIPLE-CHOICE ANSWERS

1. A

The powers delegated to the president by the Constituion reflect the founders' desire to have a weak executive. They didn't think states would dominate; they thought they would be separate in powers. They did trust Congress to be the leading body of the national system.

2. B

Many recent presidents have presided over a "divided government" in which the opposition party controlled Congress. This situation presents great challenges to a president's ability to enact his or her legislative agenda.

3. E

One power that presidents hold without congressional checks is the power to pardon. Choices (A) and (B) are directly checked. Congress can ignore choice (C); no president since Washington has dared to try choice (D), because the first effort was soundly ignored.

4. E

Executive orders command a lot of power for all of the reasons listed: because they have the same authority as congressional laws, because they can direct federal agencies to conduct business in a certain way, because they can change the scope and direction of federal policies on civil rights, and because they can apply to the entire federal bureaucracy.

5. C

It is not true that U.S. presidents tend to be from rural areas. Rather, presidents tend to be from important electoral states that are not rural. Although Barack Obama became the first African American president of the United States, all other presidents prior to him were white.

FREE-RESPONSE ANSWERS

1. **6-point Rubric**

   4 points in part (A): (identify and describe two ways trend toward more power has occurred)

   - Military initiative; Polk's placing of troops in conflict and forcing Congress to act

   - Emergency initiative; Lincoln's suspension of *writ of habeas corpus* rights during the emergency of 1861

   - Economic initiative; FDR's creation of offices and agencies to help during the Great Depression crisis

   - Deregulation initiative; Reagan's starting of this trend (other examples of this nature would work)

   2 points in part (B): (identify and explain how presidential authority has increased power)

   - Executive orders; have power of law to require actions of the agencies

   - Executive memoranda; power of actions over certain agencies

2. **6-point Rubric**

   4 points in part (A): (identify and describe two efforts by Congress)

   - Limit military powers; War Powers Act

   - Restrict budget powers; no presidential impoundment of funds

   - Appointments; oppose vigorously appointments more

   - Investigate; openly attack presidential personal behaviors

   - Budget fights; try to force change by not passing budgets

   2 points in part (B): (identify and describe at least one failure by Congress)

   - Gingrich budget fights; public ended up blaming Congress

   - Impeachment; Clinton scandals didn't lead to removal

   - Crisis; powers went back to president after 9/11

CHAPTER 14: THE FEDERAL BUREAUCRACY

IF YOU LEARN ONLY FOUR THINGS IN THIS CHAPTER . . .

1. One of the most dramatic changes in the structure of the U.S. government has been the growth of the federal bureaucracy.

2. Because they have such widely varying views about the proper role and scope of the federal government, Americans have a vast range of opinions about the federal bureaucracy.

3. Federal agencies have policy-making capacities.

4. Although the powers of federal agencies are controversial, the bureaucracy plays a key role in the attempt to meet the needs of the public.

THE FOURTH BRANCH

One of the biggest changes in government has been the creation of the agencies and departments that make up the "fourth branch." In early years of the republic, presidents had a few officials run the few executive departments that existed. The jobs these departments provided were often given as payoffs for party support. Response to widespread of corruption and incompetence in the late 1800s led to major civil service reforms.

Most of this system was dramatically changed by the Great Depression, the Cold War, and the civil rights era as agencies were created to implement public policy. These agencies now have an impact on businesses, school systems, air, general welfare, and the safety of citizens. The Cabinet has grown to include 15 departments, and Congress has created over 150 independent regulatory agencies.

SCOPE OF POWERS AND CRITICISMS OF THE FEDERAL BUREACRACY

Perhaps the biggest controversy concerning the federal bureaucracy is the scope of its powers. Critics of the federal bureaucracy often claim that its wide-ranging regulatory powers adversely affect American businesses and consumers. They also claim that because its officials are not democratically elected, they lack legitimate political authority. Moreover, opponents of the federal bureaucracy object to the vast sums of tax revenues it has at disposal, arguing that those monies could be more efficiently used by the private sector to achieve the same results. These critics are invariably biased in favor of a small federal government that provides limited social services.

The federal bureaucracy has two central powers: **rule making** and **rule adjudication**. When agencies create rules that will govern their actions, they are seen by critics as exercising a form of legislative power. Agencies announce the creation of rules and hold public hearings to allow for input, but once the rules are finalized, the public has to abide by them. If businesses or citizens are found to be in violation of bureaucratic rules, the final authority is the agency itself. This form of power allows the agencies to impose fines or revoke licenses. Agencies such as OSHA (Occupational Safety and Health Administration) have a great deal of authority over regulating business practices and can punish them severely for breaking codes.

CONTROLS OVER THE FEDERAL BUREAUCRACY

The bureaucracy is not without oversight and limits. The president and the Office of Management and Budget control agencies' budgets. If no budget resources are allocated, then the agency loses power. Also, courts can make rulings to limit the power of agencies. Congress can revise the statutes that created the mission of these agencies. The Senate can change the approach of agencies by approving leaders who either want to contract or expand their powers. Congress can also send in the General Accounting Office to hold lengthy audits, checking the propriety of an agency's spending. The Office of Personnel Management controls the merit level of administrators and monitors their level of training.

BASICS OF THE BUREAUCRACY

Bureaucracies grow the most during economic crises and in periods of war. Because of the regulations and the numerous jobs they create, bureaucracies are very difficult to dismantle or reduce once established.

About 3 million people work for the federal government. This is economically very significant to many communities and states. Although many argue against the size of the federal bureaucracy, a reduction in the federal workforce would have a significant impact on American employment and, therefore, the economy. Additionally, a reduction in federal services—from safe highways and mail delivery to Medicare and Social Security checks—would disrupt the daily lives of most

Americans. Despite the frustrations it may cause, a system of bureaucracy is ultimately the most efficient way to fulfill the promises of the Constitution to establish justice, provide defense, and ensure domestic tranquility. Moreover, because modern-day national problems are so massive and complex, often only federal agencies are able to address them effectively.

Bureaucratic leaders are often experts in various disciplines, and that gives them high levels of influence. Most bureaucracies are staffed by highly qualified and well-trained professionals. The Pendleton Act of 1883 ended political patronage, and now tests such as the Postal Service Exam and the Foreign Service Exam are used to find qualified candidates.

THE MAJOR UNITS OF THE BUREAUCRACY

THE EXECUTIVE BRANCH

Executive Office of the President (EOP)	Includes the agencies and individuals who directly help the president; it was created by Franklin Roosevelt to coordinate his New Deal programs
The Vice President's Office (VP)	Includes personnel who support/advise VP
The White House Office (WHO)	Includes the daily staff of the president ("West Wing"), including the chief of staff.
The National Economic Council (NEC)	Created in 1946 to aid the president in his new role of chief economic planner; the council consists of three of the nation's leading economists as well as other economists, lawyers, and political scientists
The National Security Council (NSC)	Is made up of the VP, secretary of defense, secretary of state, leaders of the Joint Chiefs, CIA director, and NSC advisor
The Office of Management and Budget (OMB)	Creates the federal budget
The Cabinet: 15 Departments (as created by Congress)	Includes State Department and Homeland Security

THE LEGISLATIVE BRANCH

Congressional Budget Office (CBO)	Congress's budget experts
General Accounting Office (GAO)	Congress's agency that monitors the spending of federal funds

OTHER AGENCIES

Congress has created hundreds of ***independent agencies*** outside of the Cabinet departments. Most of these independent agencies are not completely free from presidential control. Several, however, are completely independent of the executive branch. Many of these agencies have regulatory powers, such as the EPA, while others, such as the U.S. Postal Service, are government corporations that compete with private companies for business.

RESPONSIBILITIES OF INDEPENDENT AGENCIES

Major Independent Agencies	Duty Areas
Consumer Product Safety Commission (CPSC)	Regulate product safety, recalls
Environmental Protection Agency (EPA)	Air, land, and water quality
Equal Employment Opportunity Commission (EEOC)	Fairness in the workplace
The Federal Reserve (The Fed)	National banking and U.S. bond markets, interest rates
Federal Emergency Management Agency (FEMA)	Federal assistance to disaster areas
National Aeronautics and Space Administration (NASA)	Federal space research
National Endowment for the Arts (NEA)	Funds for the arts
National Science Foundation (NSF)	Grants for research, especially to universities and laboratories
Nuclear Regulatory Commission (NRC)	Nuclear industry regulation
Peace Corps	International development assistance; international relationship building
Securities and Exchange Commission (SEC)	Financial markets regulations
The Smithsonian Institution	National museums and their collections
Social Security Administration	Retirement, surviving spouse, and disability benefits

IRON TRIANGLES OF POLICY MAKING

Federal agencies are a key part of a political power structure known as "iron triangles of power." Iron triangles are used to describe the subgovernments that make public policy. For example, the interaction of congressional committees, veterans' groups, and the federal agencies that distribute those benefits determine veterans' benefits. The individuals at all three points of this triangle exchange political favors and information with one another. These interactions lead to the development of significant power over specific areas of public policy.

Why Iron Triangles Are So Prevalent and Powerful

- Government issues are now so vast and complex that smaller governmental units find themselves in charge of specific areas of policy making.

- All three of the main groups that comprise triangles benefit from keeping them in place.

- Lobby and interest groups keep their supporters in power and maintain their contracts, jobs, and benefits.

REVIEW QUESTIONS

MULTIPLE-CHOICE QUESTIONS

1. Some Americans have a negative opinion of government. The bureaucracy probably contributes to this opinion by

    (A) not tackling national problems.

    (B) not following congressional and presidential directives.

    (C) existing far from the controls of the public.

    (D) not providing jobs for the public.

    (E) being comprised of political appointees.

2. One of the more controversial aspects of the "fourth branch" is that agencies

    (A) have quasi-legislative and quasi-judicial powers.

    (B) can change the scope of their own powers.

    (C) are often eliminated, costing many their jobs.

    (D) do not help local economies.

    (E) are mostly staffed by political appointees.

3. The federal bureaucracy is critical to our government because

    (A) it is so difficult to reduce in size.

    (B) modern-day problems are too vast and complex for Congress to handle.

    (C) it has no effective controls on its powers.

    (D) the executive branch wants more power.

    (E) the Supreme Court has ruled that it must exist to help Congress.

4. Ineffective and unwanted agencies are often difficult to eliminate. This is **BEST** explained by the fact that

    (A) iron triangles of power benefit from their existence.

    (B) members of Congress benefit from their existence.

    (C) local communities want the jobs that go with the agencies.

    (D) powerful lobbying forces support these agencies.

    (E) leaders of agencies benefit from their continued existence.

5. Which federal agency is in charge of monitoring the proper spending of federal monies?

    (A) Office of Budget and Management

    (B) Congressional Budget Office

    (C) General Accounting Office

    (D) National Economic Council

    (E) All of the above

FREE-RESPONSE QUESTIONS

1. The federal bureaucracy has gained power within the federal system.

   (A) Identify and explain a "legislative" power that the bureaucracy has assumed.

   (B) Identify and explain an "executive" power assumed by the bureaucracy.

   (C) Identify and explain a "judicial" power assumed by the bureaucracy.

2. Some see the bureaucracy as growing too rapidly and gaining too much power.

   (A) Identify how each of the three branches of the federal government can attempt to control the bureaucracy.

   (B) Explain at least one option the general public has in controlling bureaucratic powers.

ANSWERS AND EXPLANATIONS

MULTIPLE-CHOICE ANSWERS

1. C

The bureaucracy probably contributes to government's low levels of public approval by existing far from the controls of the public. The bureaucracy does tackle issues, follow directives, and provide many jobs. Patronage appointments do not apply to the vast majority of government workers.

2. A

One of the more controversial aspects of the "fourth branch" is that agencies have quasi-legislative and quasi-judicial powers. Agencies must rely on Congress for power changes, they are seldom eliminated, and they help local economies.

3. B

The system of bureaucracy is now critical to our government because modern-day problems are too vast and complex for Congress to address. Choice (A) is incorrect because this issue is not a critical feature. Choice (C) is incorrect because the agencies are controlled by budgetary decisions, court rulings, and congressional actions. Choice (D) is incorrect because the executive has a lot of power, though many independent agencies exist with marginal executive controls. Choice (E) is incorrect because the Supreme Court has not ruled that the system must aid Congress.

4. A

Ineffective and unwanted agencies are often difficult to remove because iron triangles of power benefit from their existence.

5. C

The General Accounting Office is in charge of monitoring the proper spending of federal monies. The Office of Budget and Management (A) creates budget priorities, the Congressional Budget Office (B) helps guide Congress in keeping its priorities in the budget, and the Economic National Council (D) gives advice to the president.

FREE-RESPONSE ANSWERS

1. **6-point Rubric**

   2 points in each part (A), (B), and (C) (identify and explain the powers of bureaucracy)

   - Legislative: Agencies create the rules and regulations needed to perform their duties, because Congress doesn't have the time or expertise.

   - Executive: Agencies enforce their rules, often after they have created the very rules they execute.

   - Judicial: Agencies rule on regulatory issues and can impose penalties and fines.

   - Congress does not have time.

   - Congress does not have the expertise.

   - The president does not have time.

   - The court system can't handle all possible agency problems.

2. **4-point Rubric**

   3 points in part (A): (identify how each branch can control the bureaucracy)

   - Legislative: Controls the budgets, creates new rules/restrictions, and can eliminate an agency.

   - Executive: Orders and memoranda direct agencies to follow presidential directives.

   - Judicial: If challenges are brought, the agency's actions can be cut down, overturned, and eliminated.

   1 point in part (B): (explain one option for public controls)

   - Lobby Congress.

   - Lobby the agency directly.

   - Challenge the agency in court.

CHAPTER 15: THE JUDICIAL SYSTEM AND CIVIL LIBERTIES

IF YOU LEARN ONLY FIVE THINGS IN THIS CHAPTER . . .

1. The judicial system of the United States is clearly divided into state jurisdictions and federal jurisdiction, with state controls over most civil and criminal cases.

2. The "incorporation" of the 14th Amendment represents one of the greatest legal shifts in the history of the nation. All states must now provide every citizen due process and equal protection rights.

3. Federal court judges and justices have individual political leanings and views. These views are expressed as liberal and conservative biases, and are used by judges and justices to try to steer the courts in certain political directions.

4. The Supreme Court hears a small fraction of the cases sent to it on appeal. Supreme Court rulings tend to be made on cases of national significance with regard to the constitutionality of government actions.

5. Courts have very carefully structured methods of deciding cases, defining rights, and identifying the groups of citizens who might be affected by cases.

INTRODUCTION

Legal issues in the United States are classified in two ways. *Civil cases* cover issues of claims, suits, contracts, and licenses. *Criminal cases* cover illegal actions or wrongful acts and can result in fines and imprisonment. When courts rule, they use four kinds of law. The first is *common law*, which is derived from precedents set by courts of the past. Common law traditions extend back to rights established in English, colonial, and some French courts (Louisiana). When legislative bodies create laws, these codes become *statutory law*. Because the public elects the representatives who create statutory laws, the courts consider the news more compelling than common law. When agencies create rules and regulations that concern their areas of influence, these become *administrative law*. *Constitutional law* covers the broad area of interpretation established under judicial review.

TWO-COURT SYSTEMS

The court structure of the United States is one of the best examples of the federal system. States have unique legal traditions, handle most civil and criminal cases in the country, and have separate systems for appeals of lower court rulings.

Federal courts work within the boundaries of federal law—cases that are *exclusive jurisdiction* of the federal courts include cases arising from interstate issues, conflicts with federal authorities, issues specific to the Bill of Rights, and federal crimes. In some cases, federal and state jurisdictions overlap. This situation is referred to as *concurrent jurisdiction*. Disputes involving people from different states may be resolved by either state or federal courts. If a citizen commits a crime that violates both federal and state laws, the case might be heard by either level of the judicial system.

BASICS OF THE DUAL COURT SYSTEM

The following fall under **state jurisdiction**:

- Most civil disputes between citizens are settled in state civil courts.

- Most criminal disputes in the United States are settled in state criminal courts.

- Appeals from state courts are sent to state appeals court systems. Such appeals may end in state supreme courts. Many of these are known as "courts of last resort."

The following fall under the **exclusive jurisdiction** of federal law:

- Federal civil disputes are heard in specific federal courts or federal district courts.

- Federal criminal cases are usually heard in federal district courts.

- Examples of **exclusive jurisdiction**:

  - Citizens of one state versus citizens of another state

  - The counterfeiting of U.S. currency

  - Kidnapping

  - Mail fraud

  - Interstate trade conflicts

  - National banking conflicts

  - Conflicts with federal officials, agencies, and the federal government

- U.S. border issues
- Crossing state lines with the intent to commit crimes (i.e., RICO laws covering interstate crime syndicates)
- Abridging or denying the civil rights of citizens
- Conflicts over patents, copyrights, and customs rulings

LAYERS OF FEDERAL COURTS

Both the states and the federal court systems consist of layers of courts. At the federal level, most cases begin in *district courts,* which are found in most urban centers. If appeals are granted, cases move to regional *courts of appeals* or *circuit courts*. There are 12 such federal courts of appeals.

If further appeals are allowed, the Supreme Court of the United States finalizes the case. A few cases listed in Article III of the Constitution are given *original jurisdiction*, which means they are heard first and only by the Supreme Court. Such cases involve ambassadors, public ministers, or states suing other states. In modern times, such cases are usually limited to state disputes concerning boundaries, water, or mineral rights. All cases brought to the Supreme Court on appeal from lower courts (appellate jurisdiction) can be accepted or rejected by the Supreme Court, unless a lower state or federal court has declared a law unconstitutional.

ESTABLISHMENT OF "JUDICIAL REVIEW"

The single most significant change in judicial history was the establishment of the power of *judicial review*. The Supreme Court used its decision in the 1803 case of *Marbury v. Madison* to establish its authority over interpreting the constitutional status of the laws of Congress and other government actions.

William Marbury headed a list of Federalist appointees that claimed that Jefferson and his Secretary of State James Madison were hiding their appointment papers. Marbury demanded that the Court force the delivery of the papers by using a law that Congress had created, giving the Supreme Court the power to make the ruling. Chief Justice John Marshall ruled that the law that gave them such powers was itself unconstitutional and, therefore, they couldn't give the order to the president. Jefferson and the Congress had to accept the idea of judicial review or grant the Supreme Court power to exert control over the other branches. The Court established the power to interpret the words of the Constitution.

THE "SECOND" CONSTITUTION

Within the dual court system, the greatest change has been the use of the 14th Amendment to apply many sections of the Bill of Rights to state laws. As previously mentioned, states have separate sets of jurisdiction. This was originally interpreted to mean that the civil rights listed in the Bill of Rights applied only to federal cases and the actions under the federal government. But when the Civil War ended, the 13th, 14th, and 15th Amendments were ratified to ensure the rights of African Americans. The 14th Amendment requires all states to provide all citizens with *due process* and *equal protection*.

Supreme Court rulings in the 20th century resulted in many of these specific rights being applied to states. This development is now known as the process of *incorporation*. Now states must, in their own courts and laws, give citizens protections guaranteed by the Bill of Rights.

Prior to the 14th Amendment (1868), dual federalism dominated views of federal laws. The legal sections of the Constitution applied to federal courts and claims. State constitutions covered state laws. The Bill of Rights held for federal courts, not state courts.

RIGHTS IN THE BILL OF RIGHTS THAT HAVE BEEN "INCORPORATED" THROUGH THE 14TH AMENDMENT VIA SUPREME COURT RULINGS

Note that not *all* of the rights listed in the Bill of Rights have been "incorporated," because some of the rights have not been challenged in federal court cases or have not been accepted for such challenges by the Supreme Court.

- Privacy (not listed in the Bill of Rights but implied and interpreted from several amendment cases)
- Free speech (1st Amendment)
- Free press (1st Amendment)
- Freedom of religion (1st Amendment)
- Assembly and petition rights (1st Amendment)
- "Association" (1st Amendment)
- Search and seizure (4th Amendment)
- Exclusion of evidence (implied in cases dealing with the 4th Amendment, such as *Mapp v. Ohio*)
- Self-incrimination (6th Amendment)
- Confront witnesses (6th Amendment)
- Impartial jury (6th Amendment)
- Speedy trial (6th Amendment)
- Right to counsel (6th Amendment)
- Public trial (6th Amendment)
- Prohibition of cruel and unusual punishment (8th Amendment)

STRUCTURE OF THE FEDERAL COURT SYSTEM

Lower Federal Courts (trial courts where juries may be present; run by federal judges)

- U.S. District Courts (94 as of 2009)

- Various military courts and tribunals

- Courts, hearings, panels of various federal agencies, including independent agencies

- Bankruptcy Courts (officially they are units of the District Courts)

- U.S. Court of Federal Claims (claims against the United States, 16 judges run this court)

- U.S. Court of International Trade

- U.S. Tax Court

- Courts of the District of Columbia

- U.S. Territorial Courts (Guam, Northern Marianas Islands, U.S. Virgin Islands)

- Foreign Intelligence Surveillance Court

Appeals Courts (also run by federal judges)

- Legislative Appeals Courts

- U.S. Court of Appeals for the Armed Services

- U.S. Court of Appeals for the Federal Circuit (from Federal Claims Court)

- The U.S. Courts of Appeals (13 circuits, including DC, 6 to 28 judges in each; these 13 courts hear appeals from the Federal District Courts)

The Supreme Court

- Nine federal justices (The number is set by Congress.)

- Original jurisdiction cases cover foreign diplomats, United States versus a state, a state versus another state, a state versus citizens of another state, a state versus a foreign country.

- Appellate jurisdiction covers cases from U.S. courts of appeals, state supreme courts, the U.S. Court of Appeals for the Armed Services, and the Court of Appeals for the Federal Circuit.

- The vast majority of cases appealed to the Supreme Court are denied hearings by the Supreme Court justices. Thousands of requests are made annually, but the Supreme Court will hear only about 100 cases. Those cases not granted hearings are returned (*remanded*) to the last court, where that decision stands.

FEDERAL JUDICIAL TERMS

Federal judges and Supreme Court justices can serve for life terms. This makes their initial selection important and very political. Members of the judiciary are expected by liberals and conservatives to express specific political viewpoints in their interpretation of the Constitution. The spectrum of opinions forms around the issue of the proper role and powers of government, just like the sides taken by the two major parties. When presidents are trying to fill the many court vacancies, they rely on advisers and members of Congress to suggest names of judges and lawyers whose political viewpoints are parallel to their own.

Once a nomination is made by the president, the Senate Judiciary Committee confirms or rejects the nomination depending on the nominee's political slant. Those who favor a more open interpretation of the powers of the Constitution are labeled *judicial liberals*, and those who oppose that view are *judicial conservatives*.

THE SUPREME COURT'S WORK

Justices of the Supreme Court must be nominated by the president and approved by the Senate. The work and decisions of the Supreme Court are the focus of national scrutiny. The vast majority (99 percent) of cases appealed to the Court are *remanded*, making the lower court's decision final. Constitutional issues can stem from business contracts, interstate trade, criminal cases, and events as simple as police traffic stops. Appeals are submitted through *writs of certiorari*, and cases are usually supported by national organizations that want to help the Court's ruling. These *"friends of the Court"* submit *amicus curiae* briefs to help persuade the Court. Groups such as the American Civil Liberties Union (ACLU) are famous for their legal teams that work to secure the civil rights of American citizens.

FUNCTIONING OF THE SUPREME COURT

The Supreme Court functions in a very egalitarian manner. The chief justice is a guide and meeting chairperson but has no special voting powers. The chief justice does not have to be part of the majority. Conferences and debates in the Court have traditionally been relatively secret events, with only recently published books and memoirs revealing how decisions are finalized. In the few times that public hearings have been held, the procedures have been formal. Attorneys are very limited in their time allotted for presentations, yet any member of the court can ask any question he or she considers important.

Once the Court has made a decision, it makes its ruling known to the public. The *majority opinion* becomes the guide to interpreting the decision's effects. If one to four justices disagree with the majority opinion, they can issue a *minority opinion* explaining their dissent. Minority opinions are often used by the legal community as the basis of future challenges. Sometimes justices who sided with the majority may not agree with the legal principles given in the majority opinion. They might then publish *concurrent opinions* to make a point not made in the majority opinion or to emphasize a point it did make.

JURISDICTION OF THE U.S. SUPREME COURT

- The Supreme Court hears original jurisdiction cases as listed in Article III of the Constitution.

- It also hears cases that are granted an appeal hearing by the Supreme Court from lower federal courts (*writ of certiorari* grants).

- If any four of the justices want to hear a case, the entire court hears it.

- If state laws are declared unconstitutional by a lower federal court, then challenges to them move to the Supreme Court.

- If federal laws are ruled unconstitutional by a state court, then challenges to them move to the Supreme Court.

- Appeals granted from cases in state supreme courts can be heard by the U.S. Supreme Court.

THE IMPORTANCE OF SUPREME COURT RULINGS

When the Supreme Court interprets the meaning and constitutionality of laws, it is also playing a large role in policy making. The Court exerts this policy-making influence through judicial review, setting legal precedents, and overturning the decisions of lower courts. An informal rule of judicial policy making is ***stare decisis***, which is a Latin for "let the decision stand." *Stare decisis* is based on the custom of making judicial rulings based on decisions made in earlier, similar cases. However, the Supreme Court has overruled its own precedent on many occasions. The policy-making power of the Court is the subject of controversy as is evidenced by support for judicial activism or judicial restraint in many cases.

JUDICIAL ACTIVISM AND RESTRAINT

Two basic beliefs inform Supreme Court decisions. When judges or courts make rulings that support a particular political agenda or have a direct affect on policy, they are often accused of ***judicial activism***. Some see this as a judge allowing personal beliefs regarding public policy to color his or her decision on a case. Supporters of this belief claim that while the two other branches of government usually make decisions that are fair for most citizens, individual rights sometimes suffer at the hands of the majority. For example, many supporters of judicial activism point to the Court's ruling in *Brown v. Topeka Board of Education* (1954) as evidence of the need for such policy-making powers for the judicial branch. Judicial activism is opposed by the belief in ***judicial restraint***. This belief posits that policy decisions should be left to the legislative and executive branches because the judicial branch's role is to interpret and apply the law, not to create it. As judges are nominated and confirmed, not elected by a general public, policy created by a court is less democratic than policy created by elected officials.

It is important to note that judicial activism and restraint do not necessarily correspond to liberal or conservative views. Judicial activism can be used to promote or oppose any kind of policy regardless of its political leaning. Similarly, although conservatives often support a system of fewer laws and restrictions, judicial restraint does not necessarily coincide with a conservative political outlook.

IMPORTANT SUPREME COURT CASES

The following table presents those cases likely to be mentioned in AP exams.

Marbury v. Madison, 1803	Judicial review established.
McCulloch v. Maryland, 1819	Expanded federal "implied powers."
Gibbons v. Ogden, 1824	Established Congress's power to regulate interstate commerce.
Dred Scott v. Sanford, 1857	Slaves are not citizens.
Munn v. Illinois, 1876	Established that states can regulate privately owned business in the public's interest.
Plessy v. Ferguson, 1896	Separate but equal facilities for African Americans are constitutional.
Schenk v. U.S., 1919	"Clear and present danger" principle can be used to limit speech.
Gitlow v. New York, 1925	Free speech "incorporated."
Near v. Minnesota, 1931	No "prior restraint" of publication based on freedom of the press.
Korematsu v. U.S., 1944	Government can intern citizens in wartime emergencies.
Brown v. Board of Ed., 1954	Overturned *Plessy* ruling with regard to public schools.
Roth v. U.S., 1957	Obscenity is not protected by free speech rights.
Mapp v. Ohio, 1961	Defined "unreasonable search and seizure," regulated use of warrants to obtain evidence.
Baker v. Carr, 1962	Defined "unreasonable search and seizure," regulated use of warrants to obtain evidence.
Engel v. Vitale, 1962	No school-led prayer in public schools.
Gideon v. Wainright, 1963	States must provide defendants with attorneys in state courts.
Heart of Atlanta v. U.S., 1964	Commerce Clause applies to private business/interstate activities.
Griswold v. Connecticut, 1965	Court may intervene in apportionment cases; every citizen's vote carries equal weight.

Miranda v. Arizona, 1966	Police must explain rights of the accused at the time of arrest.
Terry v. Ohio, 1968	Police can search and seize with probable cause.
Lemon v. Kurtzman, 1971	Some government aid to parochial schools is allowed (Lemon Test).
N.Y. Times v. U.S., 1971	Limited prior restraint of the press.
Miller v. California, 1973	Community standards determine obscenity.
Roe v. Wade, 1973	Established a woman's right to an abortion under specific circumstances.
U.S. v. Nixon, 1974	Executive privilege does not extend to criminal cases.
Gregg v. Georgia, 1976	Death penalty does not violate the constitution.
Buckley v. Valeo, 1976	Campaign money limits, but contributions are a form of speech.
Regents v. Bakke, 1978	No racial quotas allowed in admissions quotas, but race can be considered.
New Jersey v. TLO, 1985	School searches without warrants possible.
Hazelwood v. Kuhlmeier, 1988	School newspapers can be censored by teachers, administrators.
Texas v. Johnson, 1989	Flag burning is a form of political free speech.
Planned Parenthood v. Casey, 1992	States can put some restrictions on *Roe* rights.
Santa Fe ISD v. Doe, 2000	No school-led prayers at extracurricular events.
Gratz v. Bollinger, 2003	Affirmative action in college admissions process okay but limited.

THE CHIEF'S ROLE

Courts are named after their chief justice, but the chief has no special powers over the other justices. The chief organizes hearings and guides discussions, but all other justices have equal power. Any five justices make the majority ruling in a case, whether or not the chief is one of the majority. If the chief is part of the majority, he or she assigns the writing of the majority opinion to one of the justices.

IMPORTANT CHIEF JUSTICES

There have been 17 chief justices under 44 U.S. presidents. The following four are possibly the most famous and represent significant court eras and changes:

John Marshall	1801–1835	34 years	Helped establish many court powers
Roger Taney	1836–1864	28 years	Favored state power
Earl Warren	1953–1969	16 years	Major civil rights changes and cases
William Rehnquist	1986–2005	19 years	Major conservative influence

THE JUDICIARY AND THE POLITICAL SPECTRUM

Justices and judges, like most Americans, have political interests and agendas. The selection of Supreme Court justices has always been informed by a nominee's liberal, conservative, or moderate political beliefs. Presidents have a long and consistent record of nominating judges and justices with political beliefs similar to their own. Members of the federal courts tend to reflect the biases of the two major parties.

JUDICIAL LIBERALS AND CONSERVATIVES

Judicial Liberals	They tend to support the following: • Broad interpretations of the Elastic Clause ("necessary and proper") • Broad interpretations of civil rights acts and laws • Pro-choice decisions • Strict limits on the separation of church and state (no school prayer) • Affirmative action programs to end discrimination
Judicial Conservatives	They tend to support the following: • Stricter limits on the use of the Commerce Clause (less power for feds) • Limited uses of "necessary and proper" in context of Article I, Section 8 • More local and state control of civil rights questions • Pro-life decisions • Community standards for free speech and obscenity • Affirmative action as a form of reverse discrimination • Community limits to lifestyle choices

RELATIONSHIP BETWEEN THE JUDICIARY AND THE PUBLIC

Ways the judiciary is insulated:

- Judges and justices may serve for life.

- Not elected.

Ways the judiciary answers to the public:

- Judges and justices may be impeached and removed by Congress.

- Past records of opinions and actions are used to evaluate judges for their appointments.

- Congress can react to unpopular decisions by leading the charge to amend the Constitution.

REVIEW QUESTIONS

MULTIPLE-CHOICE QUESTIONS

1. Which of the following Supreme Court decisions established the power of judicial review?

   (A) *Plessy v. Ferguson*
   (B) *McCulloch v. Maryland*
   (C) *Griswold v. Connecticut*
   (D) *Marbury v. Madison*
   (E) *Buckley v. Valeo*

2. The Supreme Court has original jurisdiction in all of the following instances **EXCEPT**

   (A) cases covering foreign diplomats.
   (B) cases that involve the United States versus a state.
   (C) cases dealing with the armed forces.
   (D) cases where one state is opposing another state.
   (E) cases where one state is opposing a foreign country.

3. Which statement concerning the judicial system is **NOT** correct?

   (A) Civil cases cover issues of claims, suits, contracts, and licenses.
   (B) Common law is derived from precedents set in previous courts of the past.
   (C) Statutory law is made by legislative bodies.
   (D) Constitutionality of a law is determined using judicial review.
   (E) Administrative law is derived from French and English legal traditions.

4. Which of the following statements is **NOT** consistent with the beliefs of judicial conservatives?

   (A) They are supporters of local and state control of civil rights questions.
   (B) They are supporters of pro-life decisions.
   (C) They are supporters of expanded interpretations of the "Elastic Clause."
   (D) They are supporters of applying community standards to free speech and obscenity questions.
   (E) They feel that affirmative action is a form of reverse discrimination.

5. Most cases reach the Supreme Court as a result of which of the following?

   (A) *Amicus curiae*
   (B) *Writ of mandamus*
   (C) *Ex post facto*
   (D) *Writ of certiorari*
   (E) Eminent domain

FREE-RESPONSE QUESTIONS

1. The judicial system of the United States is still the most "federal" part of the government.

    (A) Explain how the court system is "federal" in structure.

    (B) Describe three kinds of authority federal courts control and explain how this authority is evidence of federalism.

    (C) Describe two kinds of authority state courts control and explain how this authority is evidence of federalism.

2. Cases can reach the Supreme Court in two main ways.

    (A) Explain the two ways cases can reach the Supreme Court.

    (B) Identify two kinds of cases that go directly to the Supreme Court and explain why they do.

    (C) Explain at least two steps that occur when cases are appealed and accepted by the Supreme Court.

ANSWERS AND EXPLANATIONS

MULTIPLE-CHOICE ANSWERS

1. D

The court case of *Marbury v. Madison* established the power of judicial review—the power to interpret the meaning of laws and their constitutional status.

2. C

Cases dealing with the armed forces do not fall under the original jurisdiction of the Supreme Court. The Supreme Court has original jurisdiction in cases covering foreign diplomats, in cases that involve the United States versus a state, in cases where one state is opposing another state, and in cases where one state is opposing a foreign country.

3. E

Administrative law is not derived from French and English legal traditions. Administrative law is created by government agencies through their rules and rulings.

4. C

Judicial conservatives would not support the expansion of Elastic Clause powers but would rather see limited implementation of its use.

5. D

About 90 percent of the cases that reach the Supreme Court are brought by *writ of certiorari*.

FREE-RESPONSE QUESTIONS

1. **8-point Rubric**

   1 point in part (A): (define)

   - Dual court system: two distinct levels of jurisdiction

   4 points in part (B): (three kinds of federal, explain evidence of federalism)

   - Federal civil law

   - Federal criminal law

   - Federal appeals

   - Constitutional jurisdiction: counterfeiting, interstate conflicts, state versus state

   - Crimes made federal: kidnapping, civil rights abuses, attacking federal officials

   3 points in part (C): (two kinds of state authority, label)

   - "General law/general jurisdiction"

   - State civil laws

   - State criminal codes

   - State appeals

   - Common law of state courts

   - State statutory laws

2. **6-point Rubric**

   2 points in part (A): (two ways to the Supreme Court)

   - Appeals from lower federal courts and from state

   - Original jurisdiction

   2 points in part (B): (two cases that go directly to the Supreme Court)

   - State versus state because original jurisdiction

   - Ambassadors and public ministers because original jurisdiction

   2 points in part (C): (two steps to acceptance)

   - Cases are argued before the Court

   - Opinions are issued

CHAPTER 16: THE FEDERAL BUDGET AND ECONOMIC POLICIES

IF YOU LEARN ONLY FOUR THINGS IN THIS CHAPTER . . .

1. The creation of the federal budget is one of the central tasks of national government.
2. The Office of Management and Budget creates the basic budget and uses this duty as a way to advance its legislative priorities. Congress counters this power with its own budget agency, the Congressional Budget Office.
3. There are opposing theories of the proper role of government in the economy.
4. The 20th century saw increased expectation that the federal government will moderate business cycles and stabilize the economy.

THE BUDGET PROCESS

The budget process itself is a form of policy making. The federal budget process prioritizes where funds go and what can be done with them. Economic growth has become the measure of how effective the government is at creating a stable infrastructure and atmosphere for improvement.

The federal budget year, called the *fiscal year*, goes from October 1 through September 30. The Office of Management and Budget (OMB), under the executive branch, is responsible for drafting the budget. The Congressional Budget Office (CBO) is the group responsible for analyzing the budget and balancing the OMB's expenditure priorities with those of Congress.

The Senate and House Budget Committees are in charge of issuing the first concurrent budget resolution, which then must be approved by the full House and Senate. After this, congressional committees and subcommittees work on appropriations bills and make any changes to revenue bills needed to make them consistent with the first budget resolution. Next, Congress passes appropriation bills followed by a second, binding budget resolution, both of which are sent to the president for him or her to sign or veto. If both are signed, the budget goes into effect.

The main focus of the budget is on discretionary programs, which Congress can choose to fund. Mandatory programs are already set for funding. Congress sometimes has to authorize borrowing to cover all these. The greatest political controversy regarding economic policy is over what constitutes appropriate types and levels of federal spending. For example, some view **entitlement** programs such as Social Security and Medicare, which are major examples of **mandatory spending**, as being wasteful and unnecessary. Others argue that **discretionary spending**, such as expenditures for the armed forces, must be reduced.

REVENUES AND EXPENDITURES IN 2011 PROPOSED BUDGET

	Approximate %
Revenues and Sources = $2.567 Trillion	
Individual Income Tax Receipts	44
Social Security Taxes and Contributions	38
Corporate Income Tax Receipts	12
Federal Excise Taxes	3
Deposit on Federal Earnings	2
Estate, Gift Tax Receipts	1
Federal Customs, Duties, Tariff Receipts	1
Expenditures and Sources = $3.834 Trillion	
Social Security Payments	20
Security Agencies (Defense, Energy, Homeland Security, Veterans Affairs)	23
Non-Security Agencies	14
Net Interest Payments on the Public Debt	7
Medicare Payments	13
Medicaid Payments	7
All Other Spending on Programs (running the government agencies, transportation funds, energy funds, court funds, etc.)	16

GOVERNMENT DEBT

Massive government *debt* has accumulated in record amounts since the 1980s. About 16 percent of the budget is now devoted annually just to keeping up with the interest payments on the debt.

In recent years, the debate has become even more political as foreign governments, such as South Korea and the People's Republic of China, have purchased substantial sums of the bonds that finance the debt.

There are key disagreements about the government's role in the economy. Federal statutes require that the government must try to keep the economy stable and growing, but there is no consensus on how this is best done or even if the government should try.

ECONOMIC POLICY

MONETARY POLICY

Monetary policy, which controls the money supply mainly through the Federal Reserve System, largely determines the interest rates that banks charge for loans and has the power to speed up or slow down the economy as appropriate. The Federal Reserve Board is responsible for monetary policy, or control of the money supply. The Board's seven members are appointed by the president, and must be confirmed by the Senate, for 14-year terms that cannot be renewed.

Monetarism, which is widely associated with the work of Milton Friedman, is the belief that variations in the money supply have the greatest influence on the economy and that economic stability is best attained by keeping the growth rate of the money supply steady.

FISCAL POLICY

Fiscal policy refers to altering levels of taxation and spending to promote economic stability. Two opposing theories have greatly influenced U.S. fiscal policy in recent years.

According to **Keynesian economics**, the government must manage consumer demand for goods and services. In times of economic stagnation, it should increase its level of spending to stimulate consumer demand. Conversely, in inflationary times, it should raise taxes to lessen consumer demand. Franklin Roosevelt based his economic policies on Keynesian economics.

In opposition to Keynesian theory, **supply-side economics** maintains that the government should focus its economic policies on stimulating the supply, not the demand, of goods and services. This theory maintains that tax cuts, especially those for corporations and the wealthy, will provide more funds for investment in businesses, thus leading to increased levels of employment and economic prosperity for all. Advocates of this approach claim that initial tax cuts will eventually be offset with new tax revenues from the economic growth that will ensue. However, during the 1980s, President Reagan embraced this theory, cutting taxes and some government spending, but the federal debt soared during his administration.

PRESIDENTIAL ECONOMIC PROGRAMS

Program	President	Description
Trust Busting/Progressivism	T. Roosevelt	Early 1900s These efforts were results of the late 1800s Populist votes and growing demands for industrial reforms.
New Deal	F. Roosevelt	1930s Massive help from government programs was needed and became key social efforts.
Fair Deal	H. Truman	Late 1940s Early efforts at civil rights equality began in federal programs such as the military.
New Frontier	J. Kennedy	Early 1960s Civil rights laws were passed. Early forms of affirmative action and environmental programs began.
Great Society	L. Johnson	Mid-1960s Vast attempts were made to rebuild inner cities, give jobs, and provide assistance.
Price Controls New Federalism	R. Nixon	Early 1970s Rapid inflation was met with attempts to stop price increases through mandates.
Whip Inflation Now (WIN)	G. Ford	Mid-1970s More federal attempts at stopping rapid price increases were required, but efforts did not help.
Reaganomics/Trickle-Down Supply-Side/Devolution New Federalism	R. Reagan	Early 1980s The goals were to cut federal programs and business regulations. Tax cuts in the name of expansion were central.

FEDERAL MANDATES AND THE BUDGET

Many recent forms of federal assistance have come with "strings attached"—mandated rules that must be followed by states that use the money. Highway funds of the past were controlled by speed limit and driving age rules. Education funds have recently been connected to testing requirements.

When the federal government passes rules without supporting funds, known as *unfunded mandates*, states can balk at the regulations. Recent suits by local governments over unfunded gun control rules were won by states, and the rules did not have to be followed. When states need the money for important social programs, however, they must follow national guidelines.

REVIEW QUESTIONS

MULTIPLE-CHOICE QUESTIONS

1. The Congressional Budget Office performs which of the following responsibilities?

    (A) It is responsible for giving Congress budget projections based on the Office of Management and Budget priorities.

    (B) It monitors committee spending.

    (C) It determines congressional salaries.

    (D) It manages the spending of congressional aides.

    (E) It monitors executive branch spending.

2. The Fair Deal economic program was developed by which of the following presidents?

    (A) Lyndon Johnson

    (B) John Kennedy

    (C) Franklin Roosevelt

    (D) Ronald Reagan

    (E) Harry Truman

3. Which of the following statements concerning economic policies is **NOT** correct?

    (A) The term *inflation* refers to overall rising price levels in the economy due to excessive consumer demand or increases in the costs of producing goods.

    (B) Discretionary spending deals with programs that Congress can choose whether or not to fund.

    (C) A flat tax is a tax rate that escalates the more income one earns.

    (D) The term *fiscal year* for the federal government refers to the period from October 1 to September 30.

    (E) Mandatory spending refers to budget items Congress is required to fund.

4. The term *fiscal policy* refers to which of the following?

    (A) Efforts to control the money supply

    (B) Efforts to stimulate the supply of goods and services

    (C) Efforts to cut taxes for people of all income levels

    (D) Efforts to stabilize the economy by altering levels of taxation and spending

    (E) Efforts to achieve economic stability through deregulation

5. Legislation used by members of Congress to gain favors for home constituents and to pad a congressperson's voting support from his or her local constituents is called

    (A) *ex post facto* legislation.

    (B) discretionary legislation.

    (C) *de jure* legislation.

    (D) *de facto* legislation.

    (E) pork barrel legislation.

FREE-RESPONSE QUESTIONS

1. The executive branch has taken over the initiative in the overall process of federal spending.

   (A) Identify and explain a way the executive branch has done this.

   (B) Identify and explain a way Congress has attempted to block this power of the executive.

2. Discretionary spending programs are often controversial.

   (A) Describe three reasons why.

   (B) Explain how the identified reasons have contributed to these controversies.

ANSWERS AND EXPLANATIONS

MULTIPLE-CHOICE ANSWERS

1. A

The Congressional Budget Office is made up of professionals responsible for giving Congress budget projections, among other things.

2. E

President Harry Truman's economic program was called the "Fair Deal." Choice (A) is incorrect because President Lyndon Johnson called his economic program the "Great Society." Choice (B) is incorrect because John Kennedy's program was called the "New Frontier." Choice (C) is incorrect because Franklin Roosevelt's economic program was called the "New Deal," and choice (D) is incorrect because Ronald Reagan's program was called "Reaganomics."

3. C

With a flat tax, the tax rate does not escalate the more one earns. Rather, the flat tax applies the same tax rate, regardless of the amount of income earned. Under a progressive tax, the rate increases as income increases.

4. D

The term *fiscal policy* refers to altering levels of taxation and spending to promote economic stability.

5. E

Pork barrel legislation is used by Congress to gain favors for home constituents. It is one of many reasons that defeating an incumbent is so difficult.

FREE-RESPONSE ANSWERS

1. **4-point Rubric**

   2 points in part (A): (identify and explain executive)

   - State of the Union; setting the overall agenda and getting public support for priorities

   - OMB; creating the budget, raising or lowering amounts for programs supported or opposed by the executive

   - Veto; threats are often sufficient to guide Congress's votes

   2 points in part (B): (identify and explain one way to block)

   - CBO to counter the information and expertise of the OMB

   - Potential to override veto

   - National attention/leaders trying to mobilize the public to their goals

   - Laws stopping presidents from impounding funds

2. **6-point Rubric**

   3 points in part (A): (identify three reasons)

   - Competing notions of the proper role of government

   - Politics/pork

   - Competing economic demands

   3 points in part (B): (explain each reason)

   - Some desire more and some desire less discretionary spending based on their basic views.

   - Controversial programs benefit only local districts.

   - More jobs or more money for defense?

CHAPTER 17: DOMESTIC POLICY DEVELOPMENT

IF YOU LEARN ONLY FOUR THINGS IN THIS CHAPTER . . .

1. The public has come to demand domestic programs that address various problems.

2. Many domestic policy priorities are set through financial assistance to states and local governments in the form of grants.

3. The federal government often sets domestic policy priorities based on a comparison between the potential costs and the potential benefits of programs being considered.

4. Domestic policy changes were often brought about by economic developments and demands for civil rights.

INTRODUCTION

In addition to economic policy, there are two other major categories of public policy: domestic policy and foreign policy. **Domestic policy** focuses on issues within the United States, while **foreign policy** concerns U.S. relations with the other nations of the world. National priorities have become more elaborate, and the scope of federal involvement in public policy has grown in recent times. As mentioned in several other contexts, the Great Depression was a key event that changed the way people perceived the role of government. Recent conservative movements have advocated for a decrease in the powers granted to the government during the Depression, but overall public opinion is favorable toward government programs such as Social Security, affirmative action, urban renewal, and public transportation. Debates will certainly continue about the effectiveness of government in trying to solve social problems or economic ills, but some reforms, such as the Securities and Exchange Commission (SEC), which regulates the stock market, and the Food and Drug Administration (FDA), which ensures that harmful foods and medicines are not sold to consumers, are supported by most citizens.

KINDS OF POLICIES

Domestic policies fall into three basic categories. The first category encompasses *distributive policies*. Distributive policies are aimed at specific groups and are very selective in nature. Farm and industrial *subsidies* provide billions to those who grow critical food supplies or produce important products. Prescription drug companies, energy providers, and the airline industry all benefit from government subsidy programs. These programs are also popular with political leaders, as they tend to create voter support among the employees of such companies, while also garnering generous campaign contributions from the corporations themselves.

Regulatory policies are aimed at individuals, businesses, and governmental institutions. These policies cover a wide range of activities and services, from advertising to public utilities. The Environmental Protection Agency (EPA) regulates the amount of pollutants that can be released into the air and water. The SEC is a regulatory agency that oversees the stock market as well as other financial exchanges. The SEC was initially created to prevent another depression; however, its modern role also includes investigating corporate corruption, such as the Enron scandal, and fraud, such as Bernie Madoff's Ponzi scheme in 2008.

Redistributive policies are aimed at giving assistance to those who are seen as needing financial assistance. Many of these programs originated during the Great Depression and have become a source of controversy in recent years. Public opinion remains divided on whether or not these policies should continue in their present form or if they should be substantially reduced.

GRANT PROGRAMS

The system of federal grants continues to be a source of controversy among conservatives with regard to policy and funding. Congress grants states money for programs that the states control but requires certain federal rules be followed. States sometimes chafe under federal rules but most follow them or lose federal funding. One example of this dynamic is how the federal government regulated highway speed limits, although that power was officially left up to the states. A 1973 law prohibited federal highway grants for states with interstate speed limits set higher than 55 mph. The law was repealed in 1995, but for more than 20 years, the federal government was able to regulate the speed limit on a national level. A more recent example of the effect of federal grant regulation can be seen in our public education system. The **No Child Left Behind** federal education plan emphasizes the accountability of public schools. However, the program has been accused of being an *unfunded mandate*. This means that the government has created stricter federal requirements but has not allotted any federal funding to help schools adhere to these new requirements. The Americans with Disabilities Act, which requires nearly all private businesses to be accessible to disabled citizens but does not assist business owners with the cost of conforming to the act, is another example of an unfunded mandate.

THE BASICS OF POLICY DEVELOPMENT

- **Agenda setting.** Modern-day presidents have often taken the lead in setting the government's legislative agenda and Congress also plays a major role in this process. Congress often listens to public opinion as a cue to what issues should be addressed. Polls and media reports often influence perceptions of what issues appear to be most important.

- **Policy formulation.** Proposed actions require studies of potential costs, logistical concerns, long- and short-term effects on the affected parties, as well as other considerations. To create a clearer picture of the effects of a proposed policy, political leaders look at *cost-benefit analysis* data to compare the probable costs with the projected benefits. If a problem exists but the proposed policy is costly, then the issue might be dropped.

- **Policy adoption.** This is the part of the process that receives the most media attention. A proposed policy is submitted as a bill to Congress. It is debated and revised until it either dies or passes through Congress to the executive branch.

- **Policy implementation.** Someone must implement any new policy. Depending on the scope of the policy, an agency within the executive branch may be selected. In response to the terrorist attacks of September 11, 2001, a new cabinet department was created to oversee homeland security. Independent government agencies, such as the SEC and the EPA, are more specialized and don't generally implement policies outside of their specific area of focus.

- **Policy evaluation.** The public and the government react to the new policies and programs and then decide whether or not any changes are needed.

MAJOR DEVELOPMENTS IN DOMESTIC POLICY

Late 1800s: Gilded Age and Populism	The beginnings of policies for workers developed. Major battles occurred over the issue of union rights. European reforms on child labor influenced the United States. The People's (Populist) Party platform of 1892 brought radical calls for policy changes. Examples included legalizing unions, funding for public transportation, civil service reform, a national currency, graduated income taxes, and new banking regulations.
Early 1900s: Progressive Era	The breakup of Standard Oil signaled moves to control monopolistic business practices and trusts. The Panic of 1907 brought calls for banking reforms and led to the creation of the Federal Reserve System. The collapse of the stock market in 1929 led to calls for financial regulation policy.

(continued on next page)

MAJOR DEVELOPMENTS IN DOMESTIC POLICY (con't)

Mid-1930s: The Great Depression, New Deal	The executive branch moved to the forefront of economic policy development. Social Security was adopted as a major social safety net. WWII military spending created a long-term reliance on military jobs, contracts, bases, and industries.
Late 1900s: Cold War Era, Great Society	Government led attempts to reduce poverty, support agricultural production through subsidies, control inflation, and spur economic growth. Medicare and Medicaid programs were established, and discussions were held concerning changes in medical care. Environmental protection programs were created, rights were established for those with disabilities, and the government moved to increase financial support for public schools.
Early 2000s	The environment has remained a major issue with renewable energy and less reliance on foreign oil having come to the forefront. Healthcare reform reemerged as an issue, especially since President Obama took office in January 2009.

MAJOR FORMS OF FEDERAL ASSISTANCE TO STATES AND LOCAL GOVERNMENTS

Grants-in-Aid (Categorical Grants)	Grants are given for specific policy programs.
Block Grants	Community development, law enforcement, and education programs are examples of purposes for specific blocks of money.
Formula Grants	Federal rules indicate who gets the grants and how they apply. If states want to use these funds, they must abide by the rules.
Project Grants	Competitive bids are required, and often some matching funds are required from state and local governments.

REVIEW QUESTIONS

MULTIPLE-CHOICE QUESTIONS

1. Which type of grants require competitive bids and often also require some matching state and local funds?

   (A) Grants-in-aid

   (B) Project grants

   (C) Formula grants

   (D) Block grants

   (E) None of the above

2. During which domestic policy period was Social Security adopted as a major social safety net?

   (A) Gilded Age

   (B) Cold War

   (C) Great Society

   (D) Progressive Era

   (E) Great Depression/New Deal

3. When redistributed programs require recipients to show the government proof of need, usually based on income levels, they are using which of the following?

   (A) Block grants

   (B) Cost-benefits analysis

   (C) Means testing

   (D) Earned income tax credits

   (E) Workfare policies

4. Which of the following describes unfunded mandates?

   (A) The federal government creates policies without allocating specific funds to implement the changes.

   (B) The federal government passes a law that requires no spending on a state's part.

   (C) The federal government only suggests that states follow certain policies.

   (D) The state government passes laws that require certain actions on the federal government's part.

   (E) None of the above descriptions fit the process of unfunded mandates.

FREE-RESPONSE QUESTIONS

1. When large-scale problems challenge the nation, solutions are attempted. The government works methodically to put solutions in place.

   (A) Identify and explain any three steps the government might use to address problems.

   (B) Describe how cost-benefit analysis can affect this process.

2. The government enacts different kinds of domestic policies.

   (A) Identify three major types of domestic policies the government enacts.

   (B) Describe the political goals of these three types of policies.

ANSWERS AND EXPLANATIONS

MULTIPLE-CHOICE ANSWERS

1. B
Project grants require competitive bids, and they also often require some matching funds.

2. E
Social Security was adopted as a social safety net during the Great Depression/New Deal period. It began as a program to aid the elderly and to help spur economic activity during the Great Depression. It was a part of the New Deal under Franklin Roosevelt.

3. C
When redistributive programs require recipients to show proof of need (usually based on income level), they are using means testing.

4. A
Unfunded mandates occur when the federal government creates policies without allocating specific funds that local and state governments can use to implement these changes.

FREE-RESPONSE ANSWERS

1. **7-point Rubric**

   6 points in part (A): (identify and explain three steps)

   - Agenda setting; decide legislative priorities based on needs, public opinion, and national concerns

   - Policy formulation; Congress identifies possible solutions, analyzes approaches, and debates solutions, laws, rules, funding, possible benefits

   - Policy adoption; put legislation together, create rules, establish funding

   - Policy implementation; agencies begin to carry out programs and policies

   - Evaluation; feedback may lead to revisions or the end of policies and the elimination of programs

   1 point in part (B): (cost-benefit analysis)

   - The financial costs of programs are compared to the possible financial benefits.

2. **6-point Rubric**

   3 points in part (A): (identify three types)

   - Distributive

   - Regulatory

   - Redistributive

   3 points in part (B): (describe the goals of each)

   - Give financial assistance to individuals, groups, or companies

   - Promote or limit certain behaviors and practices

   - Help those who need financial assistance or have been denied access and assistance

CHAPTER 18: FOREIGN POLICY: MILITARY AND ECONOMIC

IF YOU LEARN ONLY FOUR THINGS IN THIS CHAPTER . . .

1. The vast majority of military conflicts involving the United States were conducted without congressional declarations of war. This shows the primacy of the executive in the development of foreign policy.

2. Treaties have often been replaced by executive agreements that do not require Senate approval.

3. The president is able to rely on a large staff and support network when considering foreign policy decisions. Congress does not have this network at its disposal.

4. Not without controversy, the United States remains a leader of key international organizations such as the United Nations and the World Trade Organization.

INTRODUCTION

Foreign policy decisions have always been a special power of the executive branch. The need for forceful leadership, speedy decisions, and direct negotiations gives the president control over most interactions with foreign powers. Congress has authority to ratify treaties, confirm ambassadors, and control the budget, but the president's roles as negotiator, receiver of diplomats, and commander-in-chief are paramount. Foreign policy agreements can be unilateral (made by the United States alone), bilateral (made between the United States and another nation), or multilateral (made among the United States and two or more other nations).

The history of power changes in the government often details the history of presidents pushing foreign policy and military initiatives. The vast majority of past military conflicts have occurred because the president ordered the deployment of troops. In only five instances in the past did Congress actually declare war.

WARS DECLARED BY CONGRESS

- 1812: Against the United Kingdom
- 1846: Against Mexico
- 1898: Against Spain
- 1917: Against Germany, Austro-Hungary, Turkey
- 1941: Against Japan (Germany and Italy declared war on the United States after December 8, 1941.)

MILITARY CONFLICTS WITHOUT FORMAL DECLARATIONS OF WAR

- 1801: Barbary Coast
- 1817: Florida, Spain
- 1845: Mexico: Border fight
- 1861: Civil War
- 1899: Philippines
- 1899: Cuban insurgents
- 1900: China (Boxer Rebellion)
- 1917: Mexico (Pancho Villa)
- 1918: Russian Revolution
- 1950: Korea (until 1953)
- 1954: Guatemala
- 1958: Lebanon
- 1961: Cuba (Bay of Pigs)
- 1962: Vietnam (until 1972)
- 1965: Dominican Republic
- 1970: Cambodia
- 1980: Iran (hostage crisis)
- 1983: Grenada
- 1983: Lebanon
- 1987: Persian Gulf
- 1989: Panama (Noriega)
- 1991: Iraq/Kuwait
- 1992: Somalia

- 1999: Bosnia/Kosovo
- 2001: Afghanistan
- 2003: Iraq

MAJOR FOREIGN POLICY MAKERS

The primary duty of the **State Department** is national security. It performs this duty by trying to avoid or resolve any situation that could result in the use of American military force. To decrease the need for military force, the State Department negotiates with other nations, provides financial aid, promotes American business interests, and protects American citizens abroad. The president's chief foreign policy adviser is usually the secretary of state. He or she runs the State Department and has undersecretaries to fulfill duties in specific foreign policy areas. The secretary of state spends a significant amount of time meeting and negotiating with foreign leaders.

The **Foreign Service** is a division of the State Department, but it's representatives, such as **ambassadors**, represent all government interests and usually coordinate their work with various federal agencies.

Congress created the **National Security Council** (NSC) in 1947 to serve the president in forming foreign and economic policies that promote national security. The national security advisor, who is appointed by the president, often rivals the influence of the secretary of state in the formation of foreign policy.

Congress also created the **Central Intelligence Agency** (CIA) in 1947 to gather and analyze information needed to make foreign policy decisions. The CIA director, who is appointed by the president and approved by the Senate, and his or her staff monitor and report on developments around the world.

The **Department of Defense** (DOD) specializes in defense policy. Headquartered in the **Pentagon**, the DOD is comprised of all three branches of the military (Army, Navy, and Air Force), the leaders of which all work under the supervision of the secretary of defense. The **Joint Chiefs of Staff** is a five-member group that advises the president, the national security advisor, and the secretary of defense on military issues. It is made up of the chiefs of staffs of all three branches of the military, the commandant of the Marines, and a chairperson, who is a top-ranking military officer appointed to the role by the president.

THE RISE OF "AGREEMENTS" OVER TREATIES

In addition to military powers, the executive branch has diplomatic powers that the legislature does not control. Presidents make executive agreements with foreign leaders that do not require senatorial approval. These agreements are so common in modern times that treaties are less frequently proposed. Recently, treaties aimed at the reduction of nuclear weapons have been met with considerable congressional opposition. Presidential administrations find it much simpler to cut deals at the agreement level and then wait to see if they work. If formal treaties are then needed, they can be negotiated. The collapse of the Soviet Union significantly reduced the need for military alliances coordinated through treaties.

THE IMPORTANCE OF POLICY DECISIONS

Foreign policy decisions are critical and sometimes long lasting. They usually do not involve military actions. Most policies concern programs of financial assistance through grants, loans, or building projects. The United States also works with the major international organizations, such as the United Nations (UN) and the World Trade Organization (WTO), which takes a leading role in promoting free trade. The United States also remains a leading member of the North Atlantic Treaty Organization (NATO), the North American Free Trade Agreement (NAFTA), and other international associations. In August 2005, President George W. Bush signed the legislation establishing the Central America-Dominican Republic-United States Free Trade Agreement (CAFTA-DR).

UNITED STATES AND INTERNATIONAL TRADE

The United States will probably be increasingly affected by a world of increasing international trade and interlocking political connections. There are serious domestic debates between the two major parties about America's involvement in the UN and the WTO.

Many conservatives dislike the idea that the United States must cooperate with foreign governments. Many liberals dislike the abuses that some international corporations heap on workers and the environment under free trade agreements. This conflict will be difficult to resolve, but the arguments will not stop the continued interconnectedness of world governments and the internationalization of markets.

INTERNATIONAL ORGANIZATIONS AFFECTING FOREIGN POLICY

- **CAFTA.** The Central American Free Trade Agreement, enacted in 2005, forms a free-trade zone for this region.
- **European Economic Union (EEU, EU).** Although not a member, the United States is greatly affected by the formation of this large free-trade zone. The creation of the EU

requires the United States to deal with a united Europe when making foreign policy decisions that affect trade and defense.

- **G-8 summits.** These are meetings that are held by leaders of the United States, Great Britain, Russia, China, Germany, France, Japan, and Canada. The meetings are held to further international cooperation and economic development.

- **International Monetary Fund (IMF).** The United States is a leading member of this organization, which attempts to promote stable currency exchange rates, favorable balances of payments, and economic development through the enforcement of economic policies.

- **Multinational Corporations.** Foreign policy is being shaped by increasingly multinational ownership of property, financial instruments, and companies.

- **NAFTA.** The North American Free Trade Agreement was approved during the Clinton administration and created a free-trade agreement that affects the United States, Canada, and Mexico.

- **North Atlantic Treaty Organization (NATO).** Originally organized to protect Western Europe from communist aggression, NATO has changed and expanded greatly since the fall of the Soviet Union. NATO now includes former communist countries of Central and Eastern Europe.

- **United Nations (UN).** The UN attempts to promote world peace and human rights. It has 192 member nations and is headquartered in New York City.

- **World Bank.** This international organization gives loans to developing nations.

- **World Trade Organization (WTO).** Created in the late 1990s, the WTO's main goal is to expand free trade.

REVIEW QUESTIONS

MULTIPLE-CHOICE QUESTIONS

1. Which of the following is the international organization that gives loans and subsidies to many countries, especially developing nations?

    (A) EEU

    (B) UNICEF

    (C) World Health Organization

    (D) World Bank

    (E) World Trade Organization

2. Which definition describes the concept of bilateral agreements?

    (A) This type of agreement deals only with the issue of military bases in the Pacific basin.

    (B) This type of agreement is between two nations with the purpose of creating joint policies.

    (C) This type of agreement deals with offensive-type military weapons only.

    (D) This type of agreement deals only with missile deployment.

    (E) None of the above definitions describe the concept of bilateral agreements.

3. Which of the following statements about the European Economic Union is **TRUE**?

    (A) The formation of the EU has had no affect on American foreign policy.

    (B) The EU was created to restrict free trade in Europe.

    (C) EU economic policies have a significant impact on developing nations.

    (D) All European nations are required to be members of the EU.

    (E) The formation of the EU has affected the way the United States makes foreign policy for Europe.

4. Which of the following statements is **NOT** true concerning foreign policy that deals with military and economic matters?

    (A) Most military conflicts in which the United States has been involved have not resulted in a declaration of war by Congress.

    (B) Presidents make "executive agreements" with foreign leaders that do not require senatorial approval.

    (C) Foreign policy decisions are usually critical and long lasting and usually do not involve military actions.

    (D) The Department of Defense runs hundreds of embassies with legions of highly trained foreign service workers.

    (E) There is a large bureaucracy backing the president's foreign policy agenda.

FREE-RESPONSE QUESTIONS

1. NAFTA is a significant and well-known example of American foreign policy.

   (A) Identify and describe the goals of NAFTA or any other important international organization of which the United States is a member.

   (B) Identify and explain one reason why different U.S. political groups might oppose U.S. membership in an organization such as NAFTA or the organization you identified.

2. Executive decisions concerning foreign policy are checked by the legislative branch.

   (A) Describe two ways such policies are checked.

   (B) Identify and describe the major way such checks are informally avoided by the executive branch.

   (C) Explain why the president has more power than Congress to make foreign policy decisions.

ANSWERS AND EXPLANATIONS

MULTIPLE-CHOICE ANSWERS

1. D
The World Bank specializes in giving loans and subsidies to many countries, especially developing nations.

2. B
Bilateral agreements are agreements between two nations for the purpose of determining joint policies. This is in contrast to unilateral policies, when a single country announces changes in policies or relations with other countries.

3. E
The creation of the EU has affected the creation of U.S. foreign policy by requiring the United States to deal with a united Europe when making decisions that affect trade and defense.

4. D
It is not the Department of Defense that runs the hundreds of United States embassies around the world. That responsibility resides with the State Department.

FREE-RESPONSE ANSWERS

1. 4-point Rubric

2 points in part (A): (identify and describe goals)

- North American Free Trade Agreement; promote free trade
- United Nations; create global cooperation and restrict the use of warfare
- World Trade Organization; promote free trade

2 points in part (B): (identify and explain opposition)

- No protections for U.S. workers/unions
- No protections for foreign workers
- No protections for the environment
- Fewer protections for children
- Too much power for international corporations
- Too little independence for the United States
- Too much interference from other countries
- Too much support for hostile nations
- Stifling bureaucracies/costly organizations

2. 5-point Rubric

2 points in part (A): (describe two ways policies checked)

- Confirmation hearings for ambassadors
- Budget and rules for the State Department
- Treaty confirmation votes
- Budget controls over financial assistance to other nations
- Formal declaration of war

2 points in part (B): (identify and describe way to avoid)

- Executive agreements/deals between leaders
- No congressional approval needed
- Deploy troops without war declaration/approval from Congress

1 point in part (C): (explain presidential power)

- One-on-one meetings with world leaders
- Information, contacts via State Department/embassies
- Information from agencies such as CIA
- Speed and decisive action needed
- Public turns to executive and demands action

Part Four

PRACTICE TESTS

HOW TO TAKE THE PRACTICE TESTS

This section of this book contains two full-length practice tests. Taking a practice test gives you an idea of what it's like to sit through a full AP U.S. Government & Politics exam. You'll find out in which areas you're strong and where additional review may be required. Any mistakes you make now are ones you won't make on the actual exam, as long as you take the time to learn where you went wrong.

The two tests here each include 60 multiple-choice questions and four free-response questions. You will have 45 minutes for the multiple-choice questions and 100 minutes to answer the free-response questions.

Before taking a test, find a quiet place where you can work uninterrupted for three hours. Time yourself according to the time limit stated at the beginning of each section. It's okay to take a short break between sections, but for the most accurate results, you should approximate real test conditions as much as possible.

Remember to pace yourself. Train yourself to be aware of the time you are spending on each problem. Take note of the general types of questions you encounter, as well as what strategies work best for them.

When you are done, read the detailed answer explanations that follow. These will help you identify areas that might require additional review. But don't focus only on the questions you got wrong. For those you got right, you also can benefit from reading the answer explanations. You might learn something you didn't already know.

For the *free-response questions*, consider the following points:

1. Use your time carefully. Read all of the questions and answer the one you know the most about first.

2. Answer the parts of the question in the order they are asked. Each part is worth points, and real people are scoring these. Give them the opportunity to see these points made clearly.

3. Provide examples to help support your points but don't get lost in examples.

4. Answer in complete sentences. Don't answer the questions with bullets. AP does not allow incomplete sentences to score points.

5. Finally, and most obviously, ANSWER ALL PARTS OF THE QUESTION!

6. The sample free-response answers that follow the exam are intended to help you understand how a reader will look for the correct information.

Good luck!

HOW TO COMPUTE YOUR SCORE

SCORING THE MULTIPLE-CHOICE QUESTIONS

To compute your score on the multiple-choice portion of each test, calculate the number of questions you got right. If you got six questions wrong, your score would be a 54 for the multiple-choice portion of the exam. Then divide that number by 60 to get your percentage correct.

SCORING THE FREE-RESPONSE QUESTIONS

The readers will have specific points that they will be looking for in each essay (called a rubric). Readers use the rubric as the guide for assigning points. Each free-response question is worth a certain number of points, and each point is awarded based on the answers that you provide. Each piece of information that readers are able to check off in your essay is a point toward a higher score.

To figure out your approximate score for the free-response questions, look at the key points found in the sample response for each question. For each key point you include, add a point. Figure out the number of key points there are in each question. Add up the total number of key points earned, and divide that by the total number of possible points.

CALCULATING YOUR COMPOSITE SCORE

Your score on the AP U.S. Government & Politics exam is a combination of your score on the multiple-choice portion of the exam and the free-response section. The free-response section and the multiple-choice section are each worth 50 percent of the exam score.

To determine your score, obtain the percentage of points you earned in your free-response and multiple-choice sections. Multiply each of these scores by 0.5 and then add those amounts together. Multiply this number by 100 to get your final score.

Many students and teachers ask what kind of raw score will lead to a desired final score. Each year's scores differ based on the relative difficulty of the questions. Usually, a raw score of over 70 percent will earn you a 5. A composite score above 60 percent is within the usual range of a 4. The test is challenging but manageable. If you can manage 45 correct answers on the 60 multiple-choice questions and achieve 45 points on the free-response questions, you can achieve a high final score.

Practice Test 1 Answer Grid

1. Ⓐ Ⓑ Ⓒ Ⓓ Ⓔ
2. Ⓐ Ⓑ Ⓒ Ⓓ Ⓔ
3. Ⓐ Ⓑ Ⓒ Ⓓ Ⓔ
4. Ⓐ Ⓑ Ⓒ Ⓓ Ⓔ
5. Ⓐ Ⓑ Ⓒ Ⓓ Ⓔ
6. Ⓐ Ⓑ Ⓒ Ⓓ Ⓔ
7. Ⓐ Ⓑ Ⓒ Ⓓ Ⓔ
8. Ⓐ Ⓑ Ⓒ Ⓓ Ⓔ
9. Ⓐ Ⓑ Ⓒ Ⓓ Ⓔ
10. Ⓐ Ⓑ Ⓒ Ⓓ Ⓔ

11. Ⓐ Ⓑ Ⓒ Ⓓ Ⓔ
12. Ⓐ Ⓑ Ⓒ Ⓓ Ⓔ
13. Ⓐ Ⓑ Ⓒ Ⓓ Ⓔ
14. Ⓐ Ⓑ Ⓒ Ⓓ Ⓔ
15. Ⓐ Ⓑ Ⓒ Ⓓ Ⓔ
16. Ⓐ Ⓑ Ⓒ Ⓓ Ⓔ
17. Ⓐ Ⓑ Ⓒ Ⓓ Ⓔ
18. Ⓐ Ⓑ Ⓒ Ⓓ Ⓔ
19. Ⓐ Ⓑ Ⓒ Ⓓ Ⓔ
20. Ⓐ Ⓑ Ⓒ Ⓓ Ⓔ

21. Ⓐ Ⓑ Ⓒ Ⓓ Ⓔ
22. Ⓐ Ⓑ Ⓒ Ⓓ Ⓔ
23. Ⓐ Ⓑ Ⓒ Ⓓ Ⓔ
24. Ⓐ Ⓑ Ⓒ Ⓓ Ⓔ
25. Ⓐ Ⓑ Ⓒ Ⓓ Ⓔ
26. Ⓐ Ⓑ Ⓒ Ⓓ Ⓔ
27. Ⓐ Ⓑ Ⓒ Ⓓ Ⓔ
28. Ⓐ Ⓑ Ⓒ Ⓓ Ⓔ
29. Ⓐ Ⓑ Ⓒ Ⓓ Ⓔ
30. Ⓐ Ⓑ Ⓒ Ⓓ Ⓔ

31. Ⓐ Ⓑ Ⓒ Ⓓ Ⓔ
32. Ⓐ Ⓑ Ⓒ Ⓓ Ⓔ
33. Ⓐ Ⓑ Ⓒ Ⓓ Ⓔ
34. Ⓐ Ⓑ Ⓒ Ⓓ Ⓔ
35. Ⓐ Ⓑ Ⓒ Ⓓ Ⓔ
36. Ⓐ Ⓑ Ⓒ Ⓓ Ⓔ
37. Ⓐ Ⓑ Ⓒ Ⓓ Ⓔ
38. Ⓐ Ⓑ Ⓒ Ⓓ Ⓔ
39. Ⓐ Ⓑ Ⓒ Ⓓ Ⓔ
40. Ⓐ Ⓑ Ⓒ Ⓓ Ⓔ

41. Ⓐ Ⓑ Ⓒ Ⓓ Ⓔ
42. Ⓐ Ⓑ Ⓒ Ⓓ Ⓔ
43. Ⓐ Ⓑ Ⓒ Ⓓ Ⓔ
44. Ⓐ Ⓑ Ⓒ Ⓓ Ⓔ
45. Ⓐ Ⓑ Ⓒ Ⓓ Ⓔ
46. Ⓐ Ⓑ Ⓒ Ⓓ Ⓔ
47. Ⓐ Ⓑ Ⓒ Ⓓ Ⓔ
48. Ⓐ Ⓑ Ⓒ Ⓓ Ⓔ
49. Ⓐ Ⓑ Ⓒ Ⓓ Ⓔ
50. Ⓐ Ⓑ Ⓒ Ⓓ Ⓔ

51. Ⓐ Ⓑ Ⓒ Ⓓ Ⓔ
52. Ⓐ Ⓑ Ⓒ Ⓓ Ⓔ
53. Ⓐ Ⓑ Ⓒ Ⓓ Ⓔ
54. Ⓐ Ⓑ Ⓒ Ⓓ Ⓔ
55. Ⓐ Ⓑ Ⓒ Ⓓ Ⓔ
56. Ⓐ Ⓑ Ⓒ Ⓓ Ⓔ
57. Ⓐ Ⓑ Ⓒ Ⓓ Ⓔ
58. Ⓐ Ⓑ Ⓒ Ⓓ Ⓔ
59. Ⓐ Ⓑ Ⓒ Ⓓ Ⓔ
60. Ⓐ Ⓑ Ⓒ Ⓓ Ⓔ

PRACTICE TEST 1

Section I: Multiple-Choice Questions

Time: 45 Minutes
60 Questions

Directions: Select the answer choice that best answers the question or completes the statement.

1. The most common form of political activity by citizens of the United States is

    (A) participating in campaigns.

    (B) donating money to candidates.

    (C) voting in presidential elections.

    (D) placing political yard signs during statewide elections.

    (E) voting in local and state elections.

2. Which of the following factors is the **MOST** important for predicting the outcome of congressional elections?

    (A) The amount of money spent by the candidates

    (B) Voter turnout

    (C) The success of the parties' presidential candidate within the particular congressional district

    (D) Whether or not the candidate is an incumbent

    (E) Whether or not hot-button issues are raised during the campaign

3. Which of the following statements is **TRUE** concerning committee chairs in the House of Representatives?

    (A) They are always members of the majority party of the House.

    (B) They are chosen by the party whip.

    (C) They are always endorsed by the president.

    (D) They are nominated by the Supreme Court and approved by the full House membership.

    (E) They are always the people with the most seniority in the House.

4. The **MOST** important determining factor when people select a presidential candidate is

    (A) a candidate's stance on specific issues.

    (B) a candidate's position on fiscal policies.

    (C) the effectiveness of a candidate's mass media campaign.

    (D) the amount of time a presidential candidate has spent in a voter's district.

    (E) the candidate's political party.

GO ON TO THE NEXT PAGE

5. Who authored the *Federalist Papers*?

   I. James Madison
   II. Benjamin Franklin
   III. Alexander Hamilton
   IV. John Jay

   (A) II only
   (B) III only
   (C) I, II, and III
   (D) II and III
   (E) I, III, and IV

6. A closed primary is a

   (A) primary election that allows eligible voters to vote only within their district.
   (B) primary open to all voters, who may vote for candidates from any party for each office.
   (C) primary that is for local offices only, not statewide offices.
   (D) primary in which a voter is required to identify a party preference before voting and cannot split the ticket.
   (E) primary in which only presidential preferences are determined and lower offices are not decided.

Use the following table to answer questions 7 and 8.

VIEWS ON GAY MARRIAGE

	Favor %	Oppose %	DK %
East	42	50	8
South	23	67	10
Midwest	33	56	11
West	36	58	6
Urban	36	52	12
Suburban	38	54	8
Rural	22	69	9
White	32	60	8
African American	28	60	12
Hispanic	36	51	13

Source: Pew Research; Center for People and the Press

7. Which of the following statements is **NOT** true about attitudes toward gay marriage?

   (A) Opposition to gay marriages is equal among African Americans and Whites.
   (B) Opposition to gay marriage is strongest in rural areas.
   (C) The highest percentage of respondents who replied "don't know" were Hispanics.
   (D) People in the South are the most accepting of gay marriages.
   (E) People in the East are the most accepting of gay marriage.

8. The widest gap between those favoring and those opposing gay marriage occurs in

   (A) respondents from the West.
   (B) respondents who are white.
   (C) respondents from rural areas.
   (D) respondents of Hispanic descent.
   (E) respondents from the East.

GO ON TO THE NEXT PAGE

9. The formal writ used to bring a case before the Supreme Court is called a

(A) *writ of mandamus.*

(B) *writ of certiorari.*

(C) *writ of habeas corpus.*

(D) *writ of theocracy.*

(E) *writ of court consent.*

10. Which of the following statements concerning the Virginia Plan at the Constitutional Convention is **NOT** correct?

(A) It favored the more populous states.

(B) It called for a national legislature that would have supreme power on all matters over the states.

(C) It called for the members of one legislative chamber to be elected by the people and the members of a second chamber to be chosen by individual legislatures.

(D) It called for a strong national government with three branches—legislative, executive, and judicial.

(E) It prohibited a state's population from being a factor in determining representation.

11. The government officials directly elected by voters are

(A) justices of the Supreme Court.

(B) the president and vice president.

(C) Cabinet secretaries.

(D) House and Senate members.

(E) members of the Electoral College.

12. Which of the following sources contributes most to the workload of the Supreme Court?

(A) Cases referred by Congress

(B) Cases from its appellate jurisdiction

(C) Cases referred by regulatory commissions

(D) Cases arising from original jurisdiction

(E) Cases referred from the executive branch

13. The ruling in the Supreme Court decision of *McCulloch v. Maryland*

(A) established the important constitutional concept of eminent domain.

(B) denied the federal government jurisdiction in disputes between states.

(C) expanded Congress's ability to exercise its implied powers.

(D) established that only the federal government controls international trade agreements.

(E) established the popular election of U.S. senators.

14. Which of the following statements **BEST** describes the importance of Shay's Rebellion?

(A) It reinforced the fact that the institution of slavery was too controversial to deal with at the time the Constitution was written.

(B) It proved that Native American uprisings were only temporary and would soon come to an end.

(C) It illustrated the need for a strong national government that could protect property rights and maintain order.

(D) It illustrated a need for a national currency.

(E) It proved that federalism was viable.

GO ON TO THE NEXT PAGE

15. The individual rights listed in the Bill of Rights were later extended to apply to the states, due mostly to the Supreme Court interpretation of which Constitutional Amendment?

(A) 12th

(B) 14th

(C) 16th

(D) 10th

(E) 18th

16. Which of the following powers is **NOT** given to the president by the Constitution?

(A) The president has the power to grant pardons for federal crimes.

(B) The president can create new Cabinet-level departments as he or she feels necessary.

(C) The president has the power to veto bills sent to him or her by Congress.

(D) The president commissions officers in the various branches of the military.

(E) The president has the power to appoint ambassadors with the advice and consent of the U.S. Senate.

17. Due process rights protect a U.S. citizen from

(A) having his or her private property seized without just reimbursement.

(B) having untrue things written about him or her.

(C) being imprisoned without a public trial.

(D) being forced to house soldiers in his or her home.

(E) being required to register for military service.

18. When the House of Representatives debates a bill under a "closed rule," which of the following conditions exists?

(A) No amendments to the bill can be offered.

(B) The debate will not be a matter of public record.

(C) The vote on the particular bill will be kept confidential.

(D) The amount of debate time on the particular bill is set at 10 minutes for each representative.

(E) The debate will be limited to only the bill's sponsor and one opponent to the bill.

19. Which of the following best describes the view expressed in the *Federalist Papers* concerning the potential development of political parties and interest groups?

(A) They were viewed as necessary and beneficial to the expression of citizens' views and healthy for the country.

(B) They were viewed as an integral part of the constitutional process.

(C) They were endorsed numerous times as beneficial.

(D) The writers of the *Federalist Papers* considered them divisive and dangerous.

(E) They were discussed as being favorable, but they were proposed to be carefully monitored.

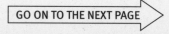
GO ON TO THE NEXT PAGE

20. The **BEST** definition for the term *interest group* is

(A) a formal organization of people with common political interests who support candidates.

(B) an organization of people with shared policy goals who enter the policy process at numerous places in an attempt to advance those goals.

(C) a group of individuals who are hoping to accomplish nonspecific goals for the general improvement of society.

(D) a formal organization that sponsors activities that are narrow in scope and focus; these groups pursue single issues.

(E) a group of people who share common ideas but have no formal organization and exert very little political influence.

21. Which of the following Supreme Court decisions dealt with the exclusionary rule and evidence being obtained by illegal means?

(A) *Mapp v. Ohio*

(B) *Korematsu v. United States*

(C) *Bakke v. Board of Regents*

(D) *Plessy v. Ferguson*

(E) *Munn v. Illinois*

22. Which of the following statements is **TRUE** of most bills introduced in the House of Representatives and Senate?

(A) Most bills are passed by committees but die from a lack of support in the respective chamber.

(B) Almost every bill in Congress dies from a lack of support in the House Rules Committee.

(C) Most bills are passed by one chamber of Congress but die from a lack of support in the other chamber.

(D) Most bills are withdrawn by the bill's sponsor before even being considered.

(E) Most bills are referred to the appropriate committees but are never sent to the full Congress; they simply die in committee.

23. Which of the following definitions **BEST** describes the term *iron triangle*?

(A) The close working relationship among the three levels of the judicial branch

(B) The cooperation among federal, state, and local governments

(C) The relationship among diplomats, the president, and the Senate in treaty negotiations

(D) The close relationship between a federal agency, a congressional committee, and an interest group that often becomes a mutually advantageous alliance

(E) Cooperation among the military, executive branch, and the legislative branch when planning and financing a military action

GO ON TO THE NEXT PAGE

24. Important industries experiencing extreme problems might expect government help in all of the following ways **EXCEPT**

    (A) intervening with subsidies.

    (B) passing tax break legislation.

    (C) funding product research and development.

    (D) setting prices.

    (E) guaranteeing loans to assist the industry through the difficult period.

25. According to the framers of the Constitution, one of the primary functions of government is to

    (A) expand the number of democracies in the world.

    (B) increase the population of the United States by establishing liberal immigration policies.

    (C) protect individual property rights in the United States.

    (D) develop an equitable system of taxation in the United States.

    (E) develop an educational system that serves all U.S. citizens.

26. Based on numerous studies, which of the following statements concerning the news media is **TRUE**?

    (A) A slight Democratic bias was discovered.

    (B) A strong liberal bias was discovered.

    (C) No bias was detected, and the news was generally determined to be neutral.

    (D) A slight conservative bias was discovered.

    (E) A strong Republican bias was discovered.

Use the following table to answer questions 27 and 28.

OVERALL PRESIDENTIAL APPROVAL RATINGS 1953–2001

	Average %	High %	Low %
Kennedy	70	83	56
Eisenhower	65	79	48
G. H. W. Bush	61	89	29
Clinton	55	73	37
Johnson	55	79	35
Reagan	53	65	35
Nixon	49	67	24
Ford	47	71	37
Carter	45	74	28

Source: Gallup Organization.

27. Which of the following presidents had the biggest difference between their highest and lowest approval ratings?

    (A) G. H. W. Bush

    (B) Clinton

    (C) Kennedy

    (D) Ford

    (E) Johnson

28. Which of the following presidents had the most consistent approval ratings?

    (A) Eisenhower

    (B) Reagan

    (C) Clinton

    (D) Nixon

    (E) Kennedy

GO ON TO THE NEXT PAGE

29. The overwhelming majority of criminal cases in the United States are tried in

   (A) federal district courts.
   (B) federal appellate courts.
   (C) state and local courts.
   (D) state appellate courts.
   (E) federal military courts.

30. Which of the following concepts are mentioned in the Preamble to the Constitution?

   I. Establish justice
   II. Provide for the common defense
   III. Secure the blessings of education
   IV. Promote the general welfare

   (A) III and IV only
   (B) I, III, and IV
   (C) I, II, and IV
   (D) I and IV only
   (E) All of the above are mentioned in the Preamble.

31. Which of the following was the **MOST** immediate effect of the Supreme Court decision in *Brown v. Board of Education* (1954)?

   (A) Surprisingly, an almost immediate end to segregated education took place.
   (B) A constitutional amendment was passed to strengthen the ruling.
   (C) Bussing of inner-city students to suburban schools was established voluntarily.
   (D) There was a rapid growth in private schools in the South.
   (E) There was a national show of support for this long-overdue Supreme Court decision.

32. Most of the delegates to the Republican and Democratic national conventions at the present time are chosen during

   (A) precinct caucuses.
   (B) regional caucuses.
   (C) state party conventions.
   (D) local party caucuses.
   (E) presidential primaries.

33. Which of the following conditions would **MOST** benefit retired persons on fixed incomes?

   (A) A period of low inflation
   (B) A period of high unemployment
   (C) A period of high inflation
   (D) A period of low unemployment
   (E) A period of stagnant employment

34. The largest single purchaser of health care in the United States is

   (A) charities.
   (B) private insurance companies.
   (C) doctor-owned HMOs.
   (D) private citizens.
   (E) the federal government.

35. Which of the following statements is **MOST** true concerning political parties over the past 40 years?

   (A) Party loyalty has remained relatively the same.
   (B) Party loyalty has decreased.
   (C) Party loyalty has increased significantly.
   (D) Party loyalty has grown only in urban areas.
   (E) Party loyalty has grown significantly in suburban areas.

GO ON TO THE NEXT PAGE

36. Which of the following is an action Congress can take if the Supreme Court declares a federal law unconstitutional?

(A) Congress can override Supreme Court decisions with a two-thirds vote.

(B) Congress can request that the executive branch veto the court decision with a simple majority vote.

(C) Congress can attempt to amend the Constitution.

(D) Congress can vote to have the federal appeals court start the case back through the judicial system for reconsideration.

(E) Congress can vote to have the Supreme Court issue a *writ of certiorari*.

37. Which of the following definitions **BEST** describes *inalienable rights*?

(A) Rights based upon the common consensus

(B) Rights established through the political process

(C) Rights based upon a military code of fairness

(D) Rights based on mutual rights

(E) Rights established by voting

Use the following table to answer questions 38 and 39.

Public Opposed to Overturning
Completely overturn Roe v. Wade?

	Yes %	No %	Don't know %
Total	30	63	7
Men	31	62	7
Women	29	64	7
White	31	63	6
Black	28	60	12
Hispanic	31	62	7
Ages 18–29	29	66	5
Ages 30–49	28	65	7
Ages 50–64	32	62	6
Ages 65+	34	57	9
College graduate	20	75	5
Some college	32	63	5
High school or less	35	57	8
Republican	48	47	5
Democrat	19	75	6
Independent	25	69	6
Conservative Republican	62	33	5
Moderate/Liberal Republican	25	71	4
Conservative/ Moderate Democrat	23	72	5
Liberal Democrat	13	82	5
White Protestant	37	56	7
Evangelical	52	41	7
Mainline	21	71	8
White Catholic	31	65	4
Secular	12	82	6

Attend Church

	Yes %	No %	Don't know %
Weekly or more	46	48	6
Sometimes	22	70	8
Seldom or never	17	77	6

Source: Pew Research; Center for Religion and Public Life, 2005.

GO ON TO THE NEXT PAGE

38. According to the table, which age group shows the **MOST** support for the *Roe v. Wade* decision?

(A) 18–29

(B) 30–49

(C) 50–64

(D) 65+

(E) None of the above

39. According to the chart, which of the following statements is **NOT** correct?

(A) The strongest support for overturning *Roe v. Wade* comes from conservative Republicans.

(B) Older people are more likely to want to overturn *Roe v. Wade* than younger people.

(C) The most evenly divided group is the group labeled Republican.

(D) The percentage of Hispanics not wanting to overturn *Roe v. Wade* is double that of the Hispanics wanting to overturn it.

(E) Women support overturning *Roe v. Wade* more than men.

40. Which of the following statements concerning the Speaker of the House of Representatives is **TRUE**?

(A) The Speaker is nominated by the president and confirmed by the Senate.

(B) The Speaker only votes when a House vote has ended in a tie.

(C) The Speaker is elected by members of the majority party in the House of Representatives.

(D) The Speaker must be at least 35 years of age.

(E) The Speaker must be endorsed by the Supreme Court because of the importance of the position.

41. Historically, bureaucracies in the United States have grown significantly during which of the following times?

(A) Periods of economic stability

(B) Periods of prosperity

(C) Periods of depression

(D) Periods of war

(E) Periods of recession

42. Which of the following determines the number of delegates to a national party convention and the rules under which they are chosen?

(A) State party conventions

(B) The national committee of the particular party

(C) State legislatures

(D) The state party leadership

(E) Local party caucuses

43. Which of the following Supreme Court decisions reversed the earlier decision in *Plessy v. Ferguson*?

(A) *Korematsu v. United States*

(B) *Mapp v. Ohio*

(C) *Marbury v. Madison*

(D) *Brown v. Board of Education*

(E) *Gideon v. Wainwright*

44. The person who serves as the president's chief civilian adviser on military matters is the

(A) chairperson of the Joint Chiefs of Staff.

(B) secretary of state.

(C) director of the Federal Bureau of Investigation.

(D) secretary of defense.

(E) national security adviser.

GO ON TO THE NEXT PAGE

45. Which of the following theories encourages the government to increase spending during a recession to stimulate consumer demand?

   (A) Supply-side economics

   (B) Marxist economics

   (C) Keynesian economics

   (D) Reaganomics

   (E) Monetarism

46. Which of the following **BEST** describes the impact of presidential coattails in recent elections?

   (A) This effect is stronger for Republicans than for Democrats.

   (B) This effect has been increasing over the last half of the 20th century.

   (C) This has rarely affected recent elections due to more ticket splitting.

   (D) This effect is seen more in House rather than Senate races.

   (E) This effect is stronger for Democrats than for Republicans.

47. *Franking privilege* is the

   (A) right of members of Congress to be exempt from income taxes.

   (B) power of the government to subpoena individuals and compel them to testify before Congress.

   (C) right of people to not testify against themselves.

   (D) right of members of the Supreme Court to be exempt from testifying in legal proceedings.

   (E) power of members of Congress to send mail to their constituents free of charge.

48. Which of the following statements is **NOT** true of the Electoral College?

   (A) Each state has as many electoral votes as it has U.S. senators and representatives.

   (B) Except for Maine and Nebraska, every state has a winner-take-all system.

   (C) If no candidate receives an Electoral College majority, then the election goes to the House of Representatives.

   (D) The state parties select slates of electors; these are often assigned as a reward for faithful service to the party.

   (E) Electors are bound by the Constitution to vote the way their state voted, and they cannot vote their conscience.

49. Which of the following powers is designated only to the national government?

   (A) The power to levy taxes

   (B) The power to take private land for public use

   (C) The power to make and enforce laws

   (D) The power to regulate trade with foreign nations

   (E) The power to create and maintain a judicial system

50. The 22nd Amendment to the U.S. Constitution did which of the following?

   (A) It repealed prohibition.

   (B) It limited U.S. presidents to two terms.

   (C) It established a system for presidential succession and presidential disability.

   (D) It lowered the voting age in the United States to 18 years of age.

   (E) It changed the method by which Congress can raise its salaries.

GO ON TO THE NEXT PAGE

51. Which of the following is the Latin term for "let the decision stand," the principle of using precedents in the judicial system?

(A) *Stare decisis*

(B) *En loco parentis*

(C) *Habeas corpus*

(D) *Writ of certiorari*

(E) *Pluribus principalus*

52. Which of the following statements is **NOT** true about the U.S. Senate?

(A) There is no rules committee to limit debate in the Senate.

(B) The vice president presides over the Senate and only votes in the event of a tie.

(C) Until the 17th Amendment, senators were elected by state legislatures.

(D) The membership of the Senate has always been made up of average citizens.

(E) It shares the power to declare war with the House of Representatives.

Use the following graph to answer question 53.

Children in poverty by race/ethnicity and residence, 2000

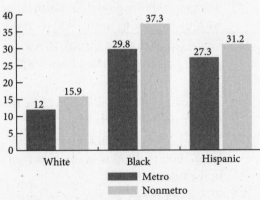

Source: Calculated by ERS from March 2001 Current Population Survey.

53. Which of the following statements concerning children in poverty is correct according to the graph?

(A) Poverty for metro White children and metro Hispanic children is essentially equal.

(B) Poverty for nonmetro Black children is lower than poverty for nonmetro Hispanic children.

(C) Poverty for metro White children is about equal to poverty for metro Black children.

(D) Poverty for metro Hispanic children is higher than poverty for metro Black children.

(E) Poverty for metro Black children is lower than poverty for nonmetro Hispanic children.

"A well regulated Militia, being necessary to the security of a free State, the right of the people to keep and bear Arms, shall not be infringed."

54. The above text is from which amendment to the U.S. Constitution?

(A) 5th Amendment

(B) 4th Amendment

(C) 10th Amendment

(D) 2nd Amendment

(E) 6th Amendment

55. A progressive income tax can **BEST** be described as a(n)

(A) innovative form of taxation that incorporates sales taxes and tariffs.

(B) system of taxation that is considered more fair because it taxes all citizens at the same rate.

(C) equitable tax, because only those who are wealthy are taxed.

(D) tax where those with more income pay a higher rate of tax on their income.

(E) regressive tax, because as a person's salary increases annually, his or her tax rate decreases, encouraging investment.

GO ON TO THE NEXT PAGE

56. News coverage by print and broadcast media is **BEST** described by which of the following?

(A) It is extensive and in depth.

(B) It is usually biased in its presentation.

(C) It is presented at a relatively high educational level.

(D) It is mostly superficial.

(E) It is mostly sensationalized.

57. The term *critical election* can be **BEST** described as a

(A) term used for elections where serious economic differences exist between the candidates.

(B) term used to describe elections when the nation is in a state of war.

(C) term used for elections where party realignment takes place.

(D) term for an election where Supreme Court vacancies are anticipated.

(E) term for any election where one party has won the previous three elections and this election is critical to the minority party.

58. Which of the following terms describes a president's ability to hold on to a bill if Congress is in the last 10 days of a session and let it die by not signing it?

(A) *En loco parentis*

(B) Hidden veto

(C) *Writ of certiorari*

(D) *Writ of mandamus*

(E) Pocket veto

Use the following graph to answer questions 59 and 60.

Distribution of Households by Size:
1900 and 1940 to 2000

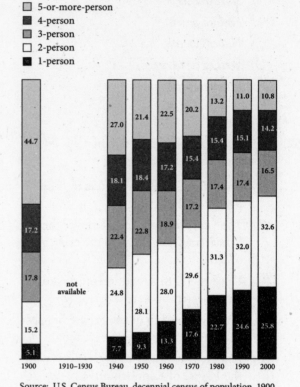

Source: U.S. Census Bureau, decennial census of population, 1900, and decennial census of housing, 1940 to 2000.

59. According to the graph, which of the following statements is correct?

(A) The graph shows growth in households with three persons from 1900 to 2000.

(B) The graph shows that growth in two-person households tripled from 1900 to 2000.

(C) The smallest decline is shown to be that of four-person households.

(D) The largest increase in household type from 1900 to 2000 is in single-person households.

(E) The graph shows an increase in four-person households from 1980 to 2000.

GO ON TO THE NEXT PAGE

60. Beginning in 1950, which decade shows the largest decline in five-or-more-person households?

(A) 1950 to 1960
(B) 1960 to 1970
(C) 1970 to 1980
(D) 1980 to 1990
(E) 1990 to 2000

STOP

Section II: Free-Response Questions

Time: 100 Minutes
4 Questions

Directions: You have 100 minutes to answer all four of the following questions. Unless the directions indicate otherwise, respond to all parts of all four questions. It is suggested that you take a few minutes to plan and outline each answer.

Spend 25 minutes to complete each question. In your response, use substantive examples where appropriate. Make certain to number/letter each of your answers as the question is numbered/lettered below.

1. A recent problem in American government has been the issue of legislative gridlock. This can occur within Congress or between Congress and the president.

    (A) Describe the condition of legislative gridlock.
    (B) Give an example of how gridlock might exist between the House and Senate.
    (C) Give an example of how gridlock might exist between Congress and the president.
    (D) Explain why gridlock has been more of a problem in recent years.

2. One of the politically divisive issues in recent times has been the selection process for Supreme Court justices.

    (A) Describe the process for the selection and appointment of Supreme Court justices.
    (B) Explain why this process has been more difficult recently by citing two reasons for this increased difficulty.
    (C) Explain one reason why Supreme Court appointments are very important.

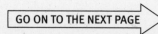 GO ON TO THE NEXT PAGE

Source: Cox and Forkum.

3. Using the cartoon provided and your knowledge of American government and politics,
    answer the following questions:

    (A) Explain what point the cartoonist is making about the 2004 election.

    (B) Define the term *independent expenditure* as it relates to political campaigns.

    (C) Explain one positive and two negative effects of independent expenditures
         by political groups.

4. The Electoral College is one of the most misunderstood aspects of the U.S. political system.
    Discuss the following concerning the Electoral College:

    (A) Explain one rationale for establishing the Electoral College.

    (B) Describe two major flaws that have been exposed in the Electoral College process over
         the years.

    (C) Explain two proposals for amending or replacing the Electoral College.

GO ON TO THE NEXT PAGE

GO ON TO THE NEXT PAGE

GO ON TO THE NEXT PAGE

STOP

ANSWER KEY

1.	C	22.	E	43.	D
2.	D	23.	D	44.	D
3.	A	24.	D	45.	C
4.	E	25.	C	46.	C
5.	E	26.	C	47.	E
6.	D	27.	A	48.	E
7.	D	28.	E	49.	D
8.	C	29.	C	50.	B
9.	B	30.	C	51.	A
10.	E	31.	D	52.	D
11.	D	32.	E	53.	E
12.	B	33.	A	54.	D
13.	C	34.	E	55.	D
14.	C	35.	B	56.	D
15.	B	36.	C	57.	C
16.	B	37.	D	58.	E
17.	C	38.	A	59.	D
18.	A	39.	E	60.	C
19.	D	40.	C		
20.	B	41.	D		
21.	A	42.	B		

PRACTICE TEST 1: ASSESS YOUR STRENGTHS

The following tables show how Practice Test 1 is broken down by topic, the same as it would be on the official AP U.S. Government and Politics exam. If you need help with the free-response section, refer back to Chapter 2: Strategies for Success.

Topics	Question	If You Missed These Questions, Study:*
Constitutional Underpinnings of U.S. Government	5, 6, 10, 25, 30	Ch 3, 4, 5
Political Beliefs and Behaviors	1, 4, 38, 39, 45, 46	Ch 6, 7
Political Parties, Interest Groups, and Mass Media	19, 20, 26, 32, 35, 36, 42, 56	Ch 8, 9, 10, 11
Institutions of National Government: The Congress, the Presidency, the Bureaucracy, and the Federal Courts	2, 3, 9, 11, 12, 13, 16, 18, 22, 27, 28, 29, 31, 40, 41, 43, 44, 47, 48, 49, 50, 51, 52, 57, 58	Ch 12, 13, 14, 15
Public Policy	14, 23, 24, 33, 34, 53, 55, 59, 60	Ch 16, 17
Civil Rights and Civil Liberties	7, 8, 15, 17, 21, 37, 54	Ch 15

* Although topics do not exactly coincide with the chapters in this book, they should be used as a general guideline of where you need to focus your studies.

Topics	Number of Questions	Answered Correctly
Constitutional Underpinnings of U.S. Government	5	
Political Beliefs and Behaviors	6	
Political Parties, Interest Groups, and Mass Media	8	
Institutions of National Government: The Congress, the Presidency, the Bureaucracy, and the Federal Courts	25	
Public Policy	9	
Civil Rights and Civil Liberties	7	

ANSWERS AND EXPLANATIONS

SECTION I: MULTIPLE-CHOICE QUESTIONS

1.   C

Statistics show that the most common form of political participation by U.S. citizens is voting during presidential elections.

2.   D

Incumbency has proven to be an extreme advantage in congressional elections. Connections to the funds of political action committees and other built-in advantages are hard for challengers to overcome.

3.   A

Committee chairs are always members of the majority party. This proves to be a very important advantage for majority parties.

4.   E

A candidate's political party identification is the most important factor in voter choice. This is a bit surprising as, in many ways, it goes against the trend toward independence; however, party identification still carries a great deal of influence.

5.   E

Benjamin Franklin had no role in the writing of the *Federalist Papers*. Alexander Hamilton wrote the bulk of the *Federalist Papers,* with James Madison and John Jay participating to a lesser degree.

6.   D

A closed primary requires voters to proclaim a party preference; they cannot vote for opposing parties.

7.   D

It is not true that the people of the South are most accepting of gay marriage. Only 23 percent of people from the South responded that they favor gay marriage. This figure is substantially below the 42 percent favorable rating among people from the East.

8.   C

The widest gap between those favoring and those opposing gay marriage occurs in respondents from rural areas. There is a 47 percent spread between those favoring and those opposing gay marriages in rural areas. This gap is by far the widest indicated by the chart.

9.   B

A *writ of certiorari* is the formal proclamation that forwards a case to the Supreme Court. This Latin term means "made more certain." It requires a lower court to send up its records of a case for review. This is how most cases reach the Supreme Court. It requires that at least four justices feel the need for a case to be reviewed.

10.   E

The Virginia Plan strongly favored the inclusion of a state's population in determining congressional representation. This would have been a big advantage for populous states such as Virginia.

11.   D

The government officials directly elected by the people are House and Senate members. House members were always chosen by the people; the 17th Amendment changed the election of U.S. senators from state legislatures to the people of the various states. These are the only federal officials directly elected by voters.

12.   B

Cases from the Court's appellate jurisdiction contribute to most of the workload of the Supreme Court.

13.   C

The landmark decision *McCulloch v. Maryland* expanded Congress's ability to exercise its implied powers by interpreting the scope of the Elastic Clause.

14.   C
Shay's Rebellion vividly illustrated the need for a strong national government because it showed how weak the government was under the Articles of Confederation. After this uprising, a consensus formed that something had to be done to strengthen the national government.

15.   B
The 14th Amendment, ratified shortly after the Civil War, had numerous aspects. One of those was that the rights listed in the Bill of Rights were extended to apply to the states. This process is referred to as incorporation.

16.   B
The president does not have the power to create Cabinet-level departments as he or she feels necessary. Only Congress can create new Cabinet-level positions. The president may request them, but it is Congress that creates them.

17.   C
Due process rights protect a U.S. citizen from being imprisoned without a public trial. Due process rights deal with the judicial system's treatment of accused criminals. The rights of the accused have been clarified and expanded by several landmark Supreme Court rulings.

18.   A
When the House of Representatives debates a bill under a closed rule, no amendments to the bill can be offered.

19.   D
The writers of the *Federalist Papers* saw political parties and interest groups as problematic. There is little argument that they had a very dim view of political parties and interest groups.

20.   B
Interest groups are based on common policy goals. Interest groups try to accomplish their goals through various means.

21.   A
Mapp v. Ohio dealt with the exclusionary rule and illegally obtained evidence.

22.   E
Statistically speaking, an overwhelming majority of bills introduced in the House of Representatives die in committee.

23.   D
Iron triangle is the term for the relationship among federal agencies, congressional committees, and interest groups. This working arrangement has proven to be advantageous to all three parties.

24.   D
Important industries experiencing extreme problems might expect the government to intervene with subsidies, tax breaks, funding for product research, or guaranteed loans. However, one thing the federal government has refused to do to help struggling industries has been to set prices.

25.   C
One of the most basic principles protected throughout U.S. history has been individual property rights.

26.   C
Despite a common belief that the media has a built-in liberal bias, a number of studies done by independent groups show no factual data to support this claim. The media has almost always been determined to be neutral in its coverage of politics.

27.   A
George Herbert Walker Bush had a 60 percent difference between his highest and lowest approval ratings. This is the biggest difference evident on the chart.

28.   E
President Kennedy had a high of 83 percent and a low of 56 percent in his approval ratings. According to the chart, this is the most consistent approval rating of these presidents.

29.   C

The vast majority of criminal cases are tried in state and local courts. Crimes must fit particular parameters to be considered federal crimes and, therefore, handled in federal courts.

30.   C

The Preamble to the Constitution mentions the establishment of justice, providing for the common defense, and the promotion of the general welfare. Education, while very important to the nation, is not mentioned in the Preamble to the Constitution.

31.   D

Immediately following the decision in *Brown v. Board of Education* in 1954, there was a rapid growth of private schools in the South. This put public education in the South in peril.

32.   E

Presidential primaries have grown in importance during the past 40 years. Today, the majority of delegates to both major political party conventions are chosen during presidential primaries.

33.   A

A period of low inflation would most benefit those on fixed incomes. Low inflation means that prices are not rising. When prices rise, those on fixed incomes are hurt the most.

34.   E

The government is the largest purchaser of health care services in the United States. Programs such as Medicare and Medicaid make these purchases.

35.   B

Party loyalty has decreased over the past 40 years. There is more ticket splitting than ever before. While individuals identify with parties during presidential elections, they are very willing to step outside the party fold in elections below that level.

36.   C

If Congress disagrees with a Supreme Court ruling it may attempt to amend the Constitution.

37.   D

Inalienable rights are considered to be basic rights based on natural rights. This implies that they are rights that government has no right to interfere with.

38.   A

18- to 29-year-olds show the most support for *Roe v. Wade*. According to the chart, 66 percent of this group opposes the overturning of *Roe v. Wade*.

39.   E

It is not true that women support overturning *Roe v. Wade* more than men do. In fact, the opposite is true. The chart shows that 31 percent of men support overturning *Roe v. Wade* in comparison to 29 percent of women. Men favor overturning this decision more than women do.

40.   C

The Speaker of the House is chosen by the members of the majority party. This position is important and powerful.

41.   D

Historically, wartime has proven to be a period of bureaucratic growth.

42.   B

The size or number of delegates to a national party convention is determined by a party's national committee.

43.   D

Brown v. Board of Education of Topeka reversed the Supreme Court's earlier ruling stating that separate but equal was constitutional. This ruling was reversed because separate was, in fact, very rarely even close to equal.

44.   D

The secretary of defense serves as the president's chief civilian military adviser. With an office in the Pentagon, the secretary works very closely with the military and keeps the president apprised of military affairs.

45.   C

The theory of Keynesian economics encourages the government to create jobs for people during periods of high unemployment. John Maynard Keynes, an English economist, believed it was beneficial for the government to create jobs during periods of high unemployment, thereby stimulating economic growth.

46.   C

As explained earlier, with increased ticket splitting, the effect of presidential coattails has decreased.

47.   E

Franking privilege is the power of members of Congress to send mail to their constituents free of charge. Members seem to use their franking privilege more during election years. This is only one of many reasons why it is difficult to defeat an incumbent.

48.   E

Electors are not bound by the Constitution to vote the way the state they represent voted. There are numerous examples of an elector voting his or her conscience or otherwise deviating from the way the state he or she represented voted.

49.   D

Only the national government can regulate trade with foreign countries. Sometimes, if a foreign government is at odds with the U.S. government, the national government will forbid trade with the offending country.

50.   B

The 22nd Amendment limited the president to two terms. This was passed following Franklin Roosevelt's having been elected to four terms as president. Before FDR, presidential candidates had limited themselves to two terms by tradition. Many were afraid that having presidents remain in office for longer than two terms could lead to innumerable problems.

51.   A

Stare decisis is a Latin term meaning "let the decision stand." The practice of basing judicial decisions on previously decided cases (precedent) comes from this term.

52.   D

The membership of the Senate has always been made up of the rich elite. The Senate has at times in our history been called the "Millionaires Club." Members of the Senate have tended to be wealthier than members of the House.

53.   E

According to the graph, poverty for metro Black children is higher than poverty for nonmetro Hispanic children.

54.   D

This is the text of the 2nd Amendment. Its interpretation in recent years has been politically divisive. Many people today support some form of gun control, while others refer to this amendment as supporting their unequivocal right to bear arms.

55.   D

The concept of a progressive income tax (also called a graduated income tax) is that the more an individual makes, the higher that person's tax rate should be. The income tax system of the United States is a progressive income tax system; it has proven to be a very complex system for many individuals to understand.

56.   D

It is the consensus that print and broadcast media coverage of the news tends to be mostly superficial. Many believe this is because news coverage has become more and more ratings driven.

57.   C

Critical elections are those elections where party realignment of some type takes place. This term refers to the fact that a certain segment of voters will change their loyalty from one party to the other. One example would be the Democrats losing the South to the Republicans.

58.   E

A pocket veto occurs when the president simply holds on to a bill and takes no action during the last 10 days of a congressional session, effectively killing that particular bill.

59.   D

The graph shows that the number of single-person households increased over five times during the period from 1900 to 2000.

60.   C

According to the graph, the sharpest drop in households with five or more persons after 1950 took place between 1970 and 1980.

SECTION II: FREE-RESPONSE QUESTIONS

RUBRIC FOR QUESTION 1: 5 POINTS TOTAL

Part (A): 2 points for defining legislative gridlock.

- Gridlock occurs when there is a lack of progress in the passage of legislation. Typically, this is the result of either conflicts between the political parties inside of Congress or in partisan arguments between Congress and the president.

Part (B): 1 point for explaining that gridlock might exist between the House and the Senate when one chamber is controlled by one party and the other chamber is controlled by the opposite party.

Part (C): 1 point for explaining that gridlock exists between Congress and the president when one party has a majority in Congress and the opposite party controls the presidency. It may be noted that the opposing party may only need to control one chamber of Congress.

Part (D): 1 point for explaining that legislative gridlock has happened more often due to the rise in split-ticket voting, which has resulted in increasing instances of divided government. Also, there has been more partisanship and less of a spirit of political compromise in recent years.

RUBRIC FOR QUESTION 2: 5 POINTS TOTAL

Part (A): 2 points for describing the process for selection of Supreme Court justices.

- The president nominates a person to the Supreme Court, and the U.S. Senate approves that nominee.

Part (B): 2 points for explaining the reason why the process has been more difficult recently.

- The recent problems can be traced to the fact that the Senate has often been controlled by the opposite party to that of the president.
- There has been an increase in partisanship within the Senate itself.

Part (C): 1 point for explaining that a president's Supreme Court appointments can advance his or her political goals long after he or she has left office.

RUBRIC FOR QUESTION 3: 7 POINTS TOTAL

Part (A): 2 points for explaining that the Swift Boat Veterans group had an important negative effect on Senator John Kerry's 2004 presidential campaign.

Part (B): 2 points for defining the term *independent expenditure*.

- An independent expenditure is money spent for a communication that expressly advocates the election of one candidate or the defeat of the other candidate. This money is not considered to be a campaign contribution, so independent expenditures are not limited. The individual or group making the expenditure cannot consult or coordinate with the campaign they are supporting.

Part (C): 1 point each (3 points total) for one positive and two negative effects.

Possible positives:

- Individuals can spend their money to support candidates of their choice in any amount that they wish because, technically, independent expenditures are not considered part of a candidate's campaign.

- This lack of limits can be viewed as securing political free speech as guaranteed by the 1st Amendment.

Possible negatives:

- It is difficult for voters to determine the difference between the candidate's campaign, the candidate, and the groups that support his or her candidacy.

- A candidate may not approve of or endorse the message of the ads produced.

- It is difficult to establish accountability if the ads are untrue or misleading.

RUBRIC FOR QUESTION 4: 5 POINTS TOTAL

Part (A): 1 point for explaining either

- that the framers did not want Congress to choose the president because it would have caused the presidency to be too much under congressional influence; or

- that the framers did not want to leave the election of the presidency in the hands of the popular vote because they did not think that most of the electorate were educated and informed enough about politics to make wise decisions regarding the selection of the president.

Part (B): 1 point each (2 points total) for describing two of the following:

- Electors are not bound by the Constitution to vote for the candidate that was the winner of the popular vote in the area they represent.

- As parties grew in strength, this process led to a president from one party and a vice president from the opposite party. (This was later corrected by the 12th Amendment.)

- The winner of the popular vote may not win the vote in the Electoral College.

Part (C): 1 point each (2 points total) for explaining two of the following:

- A district plan that would allocate electoral votes based upon popular vote results from each congressional district by congressional district

- A proportional plan under which a presidential candidate would receive the same percentage of a state's electoral votes as he or she received of the state's popular vote

- Direct election of a president based entirely on the popular vote

- A national bonus plan where a presidential candidate would receive a number of bonus electoral votes for winning the national popular vote, helping to ensure that the winner of the popular vote would almost certainly win the Electoral College vote

Practice Test 2 Answer Grid

1. Ⓐ Ⓑ Ⓒ Ⓓ Ⓔ
2. Ⓐ Ⓑ Ⓒ Ⓓ Ⓔ
3. Ⓐ Ⓑ Ⓒ Ⓓ Ⓔ
4. Ⓐ Ⓑ Ⓒ Ⓓ Ⓔ
5. Ⓐ Ⓑ Ⓒ Ⓓ Ⓔ
6. Ⓐ Ⓑ Ⓒ Ⓓ Ⓔ
7. Ⓐ Ⓑ Ⓒ Ⓓ Ⓔ
8. Ⓐ Ⓑ Ⓒ Ⓓ Ⓔ
9. Ⓐ Ⓑ Ⓒ Ⓓ Ⓔ
10. Ⓐ Ⓑ Ⓒ Ⓓ Ⓔ

11. Ⓐ Ⓑ Ⓒ Ⓓ Ⓔ
12. Ⓐ Ⓑ Ⓒ Ⓓ Ⓔ
13. Ⓐ Ⓑ Ⓒ Ⓓ Ⓔ
14. Ⓐ Ⓑ Ⓒ Ⓓ Ⓔ
15. Ⓐ Ⓑ Ⓒ Ⓓ Ⓔ
16. Ⓐ Ⓑ Ⓒ Ⓓ Ⓔ
17. Ⓐ Ⓑ Ⓒ Ⓓ Ⓔ
18. Ⓐ Ⓑ Ⓒ Ⓓ Ⓔ
19. Ⓐ Ⓑ Ⓒ Ⓓ Ⓔ
20. Ⓐ Ⓑ Ⓒ Ⓓ Ⓔ

21. Ⓐ Ⓑ Ⓒ Ⓓ Ⓔ
22. Ⓐ Ⓑ Ⓒ Ⓓ Ⓔ
23. Ⓐ Ⓑ Ⓒ Ⓓ Ⓔ
24. Ⓐ Ⓑ Ⓒ Ⓓ Ⓔ
25. Ⓐ Ⓑ Ⓒ Ⓓ Ⓔ
26. Ⓐ Ⓑ Ⓒ Ⓓ Ⓔ
27. Ⓐ Ⓑ Ⓒ Ⓓ Ⓔ
28. Ⓐ Ⓑ Ⓒ Ⓓ Ⓔ
29. Ⓐ Ⓑ Ⓒ Ⓓ Ⓔ
30. Ⓐ Ⓑ Ⓒ Ⓓ Ⓔ

31. Ⓐ Ⓑ Ⓒ Ⓓ Ⓔ
32. Ⓐ Ⓑ Ⓒ Ⓓ Ⓔ
33. Ⓐ Ⓑ Ⓒ Ⓓ Ⓔ
34. Ⓐ Ⓑ Ⓒ Ⓓ Ⓔ
35. Ⓐ Ⓑ Ⓒ Ⓓ Ⓔ
36. Ⓐ Ⓑ Ⓒ Ⓓ Ⓔ
37. Ⓐ Ⓑ Ⓒ Ⓓ Ⓔ
38. Ⓐ Ⓑ Ⓒ Ⓓ Ⓔ
39. Ⓐ Ⓑ Ⓒ Ⓓ Ⓔ
40. Ⓐ Ⓑ Ⓒ Ⓓ Ⓔ

41. Ⓐ Ⓑ Ⓒ Ⓓ Ⓔ
42. Ⓐ Ⓑ Ⓒ Ⓓ Ⓔ
43. Ⓐ Ⓑ Ⓒ Ⓓ Ⓔ
44. Ⓐ Ⓑ Ⓒ Ⓓ Ⓔ
45. Ⓐ Ⓑ Ⓒ Ⓓ Ⓔ
46. Ⓐ Ⓑ Ⓒ Ⓓ Ⓔ
47. Ⓐ Ⓑ Ⓒ Ⓓ Ⓔ
48. Ⓐ Ⓑ Ⓒ Ⓓ Ⓔ
49. Ⓐ Ⓑ Ⓒ Ⓓ Ⓔ
50. Ⓐ Ⓑ Ⓒ Ⓓ Ⓔ

51. Ⓐ Ⓑ Ⓒ Ⓓ Ⓔ
52. Ⓐ Ⓑ Ⓒ Ⓓ Ⓔ
53. Ⓐ Ⓑ Ⓒ Ⓓ Ⓔ
54. Ⓐ Ⓑ Ⓒ Ⓓ Ⓔ
55. Ⓐ Ⓑ Ⓒ Ⓓ Ⓔ
56. Ⓐ Ⓑ Ⓒ Ⓓ Ⓔ
57. Ⓐ Ⓑ Ⓒ Ⓓ Ⓔ
58. Ⓐ Ⓑ Ⓒ Ⓓ Ⓔ
59. Ⓐ Ⓑ Ⓒ Ⓓ Ⓔ
60. Ⓐ Ⓑ Ⓒ Ⓓ Ⓔ

PRACTICE TEST 2

Section I: Multiple-Choice Questions

Time: 45 Minutes
60 Questions

Directions: Select the answer choice that best answers the question or completes the statement.

1. Which of the following **BEST** describes the definition of "reserved powers" of the states?

    (A) Powers given to the states through the concept of implied powers

    (B) Powers not specifically granted to the national government or denied to states

    (C) Powers given only to Congress and are not available to the executive branch

    (D) Powers given only to the Supreme Court

    (E) Powers, such as regulating foreign trade, over which states maintain only a small amount of control

2. Candidates for president have been **LEAST** likely to come from which of the following sources?

    (A) The vice presidency

    (B) State governorships

    (C) The Cabinet

    (D) The House of Representatives

    (E) The Senate

3. Which of the following has the responsibility for creating additional federal courts and assigning the number of judges who will preside in them?

    (A) The secretary of the treasury

    (B) The attorney general

    (C) The secretary of the Department of Justice

    (D) The president

    (E) The Congress

4. Which of the following **BEST** describes the president's responsibilities under the War Powers Resolution?

    (A) The president must have the approval of Congress and the United Nations before committing troops for more than 10 days.

    (B) The president must propose a plan for financing a conflict within 30 days of committing troops.

    (C) The president must deploy National Guard units prior to asking Congress to reinstate a selective service system.

    (D) The president must bring troops home from hostilities within 60 days unless Congress votes approval.

    (E) The president must have approval of the Joint Chiefs of Staff before committing troops for more than 30 days.

GO ON TO THE NEXT PAGE

5. Which of the following labels describes the belief that government should not meddle with the economy?

(A) Keynesian economics

(B) Voodoo economics

(C) *Laissez-faire* economics

(D) Supply-side economics

(E) Monetarism

6. To create a balance of power without jeopardizing the independence of the presidency, which of the following measures did the framers of the Constitution take?

(A) They limited the president 's role in the area of national security.

(B) They created a weak president as a head of the executive branch.

(C) They checked or balanced presidential powers.

(D) They required the vice president to be from the opposite party.

(E) They created a presidency that had no powers over the military.

7. The Supreme Court decision in *Bakke v. California Board of Regents* dealt with which of the following issues?

(A) Segregation in student housing

(B) Censorship of a student newspaper

(C) Freedom of speech for college professors

(D) Affirmative action and reverse discrimination

(E) Fair salary schedules for female faculty members

8. Until the latter part of the 1800s, the primary mechanism for government employees to secure their job was which of the following?

(A) Nepotism

(B) Military accomplishments

(C) Patronage system

(D) Merit system

(E) None of the above

9. Which of the following is a power that state legislatures have in relation to the federal government?

(A) State legislatures recommend potential Supreme Court justices to the president.

(B) State legislatures determine who will represent each state in the Electoral College.

(C) State legislatures redraw the boundaries of congressional districts following a national census.

(D) State legislatures determine how often a national census should be conducted.

(E) State legislatures must independently vote on declarations of war following the vote of Congress.

10. Which of the following **BEST** describes the term *de facto segregation*?

(A) This is segregation based on social custom or economic factors, not by law or government action.

(B) This is the type of segregation that took place in the South prior to the Civil War.

(C) This is the type of segregation created by laws such as Jim Crow laws.

(D) This is a type of segregation affecting only economic opportunities, not social equality.

(E) This is segregation based on gender.

GO ON TO THE NEXT PAGE

Use the table provided to answer questions 11 and 12.

News Media Viewed More Favorably Than Political Institutions

Favorable opinion of...	2001%	2005%	Change
Daily newspaper	82	80	−2
Local TV news	83	79	−4
Cable TV news*	88	79	−9
Network TV news	76	75	−1
Major national papers	74	61	−13
Supreme Court	78	66	−12
Democratic Party	63	57	−6
Congress	65	54	−11
George W. Bush**	64	55	−9
Republican Party	54	52	−2

* In 2001, the cable news question listed only CNN and MSNBC as examples. In 2005, Fox News Channel was added to the question.

** Bush 2005 figure from March. Percentages based on those who could rate each.

Source: Pew Research, Center for People and Press.

11. According to the table, which type of media was viewed **MOST** favorably in 2001?

(A) Major national newspapers
(B) Daily newspapers
(C) Cable TV news
(D) Local TV news
(E) Network TV news

12. According to the table, which of the following political institutions or people experienced the largest decline in the public's favorable opinion rating from 2001 to 2005?

(A) Congress
(B) Republican Party
(C) Democratic Party
(D) George W. Bush
(E) Supreme Court

13. Which of the following was viewed by the framers of the Constitution as the primary policy maker?

(A) President's Cabinet
(B) Secretary of state
(C) President
(D) Congress
(E) Supreme Court

14. Presidents often have names for their legislative programs. Which president called his plan the "Great Society"?

(A) John Kennedy
(B) Ronald Reagan
(C) Lyndon Johnson
(D) Jimmy Carter
(E) George H. W. Bush

15. Which of the following Cabinet departments has the largest annual budget?

(A) Treasury
(B) Education
(C) Health and Human Services
(D) Commerce
(E) State

16. Which of the following is the party that initiates a lawsuit?

(A) Prosecutor
(B) Plaintiff
(C) Defendant
(D) Advocate
(E) Jurist

GO ON TO THE NEXT PAGE

17. Which of the following was **MOST** responsible for expanding the rights of accused criminals during the 1960s?

    (A) The president
    (B) Congress
    (C) The attorney general
    (D) The Department of Justice
    (E) The Supreme Court

18. Which committee in the House of Representatives is responsible for placing a bill on the legislative calendar and for establishing the time limits for debate and the types of amendments that will be allowed?

    (A) Ways and Means
    (B) Judiciary
    (C) Rules
    (D) Joint
    (E) None of the above

19. Which of the following amendments to the U.S. Constitution was intended to overturn the Dred Scott decision by the Supreme Court?

    (A) 18th
    (B) 20th
    (C) 19th
    (D) 16th
    (E) None of the above

20. Which of the following are Cabinet departments of the president?

    I. Veterans Affairs
    II. Agriculture
    III. White House Counsel
    IV. Transportation

    (A) I and IV only
    (B) I, II, and III
    (C) I, II, and IV
    (D) II, III, and IV
    (E) III and IV only

21. Which of the following statements concerning the federal income tax system is **NOT** correct?

    (A) When originally instituted, the federal income tax was declared unconstitutional by the Supreme Court.
    (B) The federal income tax provides only a small portion of the national government's revenues.
    (C) The federal income tax was created by the 16th Amendment.
    (D) The federal income tax is a progressive tax; the higher a person's income, the higher his or her tax rate.
    (E) Corporations as well as individuals pay income taxes.

22. Which of the following **BEST** defines the concept of "full faith and credit"?

    (A) It deals with economic policy, stating that the Federal Reserve will protect deposits.
    (B) It concerns Congress respecting the autonomy of the Supreme Court.
    (C) It deals with the federal government's maintaining a strong military.
    (D) It deals with cooperation between the executive and legislative branches on budget issues.
    (E) It concerns states being required to recognize the documents and acts of other states.

GO ON TO THE NEXT PAGE ⟹

23. Which of the following is **MOST** accurate in describing the U.S. House of Representatives?

   I. Members are elected every two years.

   II. It is a continuous body.

   III. Members must be at least 21 years old.

   IV. Members can only serve six terms.

   (A) I, II, and III

   (B) I and IV only

   (C) II, III, and IV

   (D) I, III, and IV

   (E) I and III only

24. Which of the following definitions **BEST** describes the concept of eminent domain?

   (A) It is the guarantee that citizens will not have to keep soldiers in their houses.

   (B) It is the idea that economic policy is best set by economists.

   (C) It is the belief that the United States is destined to expand its borders.

   (D) It is the right of the government to take private property for public use as long as the owner is fairly compensated.

   (E) It is the belief that no person may be held in jail unless the government shows just cause.

25. The president of the United States possesses the constitutional power to negotiate treaties with other nations, but the treaty is not considered final until which additional step is taken?

   (A) Congress votes to accept it by simple majority of both houses.

   (B) Congress votes to accept it by a two-thirds majority of both houses.

   (C) The House of Representatives votes to accept it by a two-thirds majority.

   (D) The Senate votes to accept it by a two-thirds majority.

   (E) The Senate votes to accept it by a simple majority, and the Supreme Court declares it constitutional.

Use the following graph to answer question 26.

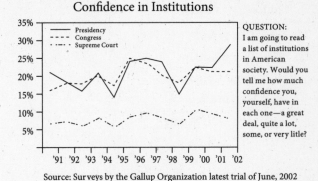

Confidence in Institutions

Source: Surveys by the Gallup Organization latest trial of June, 2002

26. According to the chart provided, which of the following statements is **NOT** true?

   (A) The confidence in the presidency sharply increased from 2001 to 2002.

   (B) The level of presidential confidence was declining between 1991 and 1993.

   (C) Confidence in the Supreme Court was higher than that in the presidency in 1995.

   (D) Confidence in the presidency rose from 1998 to 1999.

   (E) Confidence in the Supreme Court declined from 1994 to 1996.

27. At today's national party conventions, the majority of the delegates are chosen by which of the following methods?

   (A) They were delegates to previous conventions.

   (B) They are chosen by state party leaders.

   (C) They are chosen during state presidential primaries.

   (D) They are chosen through the caucus process.

   (E) They are state and national office holders from that party.

GO ON TO THE NEXT PAGE

28. Under the Articles of Confederation, the bulk of political power rested in which of the following entities?

    (A) Congress
    (B) The president
    (C) State legislatures
    (D) The military
    (E) The U.S. Senate

29. Bureaucratic agencies are originally created by which of the following?

    (A) Congress
    (B) The president
    (C) The federal courts
    (D) The Supreme Court
    (E) The president's Cabinet

30. Which of the following Supreme Court decisions established that an accused person has the right to be represented by a lawyer in state courts and that if a person cannot afford an attorney, the state must provide one?

    (A) *Miranda v. Arizona*
    (B) *Bakke v. California*
    (C) *Munn v. Illinois*
    (D) *Buckley v. Valeo*
    (E) *Gideon v. Wainwright*

31. Which of the following statements is **NOT** true concerning the White House staff?

    (A) The press secretary is a member of the White House staff.
    (B) The president relies on the White House staff for information, policy options, and analysis.
    (C) The national security advisor is a member of the White House staff.
    (D) The White House staff size and responsibilities grew enormously in the latter half of the 1900s.
    (E) Appointments to the White House staff are confirmed by the Senate.

32. Which of the following committees in Congress is responsible for reconciling differences in bills passed by the House and Senate?

    (A) Ways and Means
    (B) Rules
    (C) Domestic Affairs
    (D) Conference
    (E) Appropriations

33. Which of the following elections can legally use federal money during campaigns?

    (A) Gubernatorial elections
    (B) Local elections
    (C) Presidential elections
    (D) Congressional elections
    (E) None of the above

GO ON TO THE NEXT PAGE

34. Which historical events are generally seen as ending the friendly relationship between the press and politicians?

(A) World War I and World War II

(B) The Great Depression and Prohibition

(C) The Civil Rights Movement and the assassination of Martin Luther King Jr.

(D) The presidential debates and television

(E) The Vietnam War and Watergate

35. The term *establishment clause* refers to the part of the U.S. Constitution dealing with which of the following?

(A) It is the part of the Second Amendment that establishes the right to bear arms.

(B) It is the part of the Seventh Amendment that prohibits excessive bail and cruel and unusual punishment.

(C) It is the part of the First Amendment that states that Congress shall make no law respecting the establishment of religion.

(D) It is the part of the Fifth Amendment that guarantees that no person shall be forced to testify against himself or herself.

(E) It is the part of the 19th Amendment that establishes women's right to vote.

36. The process of initiative is **BEST** described by which of the following?

(A) It is the formal expression of congressional opinion that must be approved by both houses of Congress.

(B) It is a procedure allowing voters to submit a proposed law to a popular vote.

(C) It is a congressional process by which the Speaker may send a bill to a second committee after the first committee is finished acting on the bill.

(D) It is a brief, unsigned opinion issued by the Supreme Court to explain a ruling.

(E) It is an action taken by Congress following a presidential veto.

Use the following graph to answer questions 37 and 38.

Percent Distribution of the Total Population by Age: 1900 to 2000

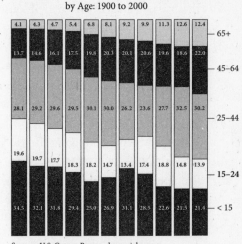

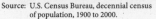

Source: U.S. Census Bureau, decennial census of population, 1900 to 2000.

37. According to the graph, which of the following groups decreased the most as a percentage of the population between 1900 and 2000?

(A) 65+

(B) 45–64

(C) 25–44

(D) 15–24

(E) < 15

38. According to the graph, which of the following statements is true?

(A) The 45–64 and 65+ age groups both grew by the same percentage between 1900 and 2000.

(B) The percentage of the population of the 25–44 age group declined from 1980 to 2000.

(C) The 65+ age group increased its percentage of the population in every decade from 1900 to 2000.

(D) The 15–24 age group increased in every decade from 1900 to 1950.

(E) The 25–44 age group increased in every decade from 1900 to 1960.

GO ON TO THE NEXT PAGE

39. Which of the following statements concerning the Speaker of the House is **NOT** correct?

    (A) The Speaker presides over the House when it is in session.

    (B) The Speaker exercises considerable control over how bills get assigned to committees.

    (C) The Speaker plays a major role in making committee assignments in the House.

    (D) The Speaker is third in line for succession to the presidency following the vice president and the secretary of state.

    (E) The Speaker appoints or plays a key role in appointing his or her party's legislative leaders and the party leadership staff.

40. The War Powers Resolution, which requires the president to get approval from Congress in order to deploy military forces, was passed in reaction to which historical event?

    (A) The sinking of the *Lusitania*

    (B) The bombing of Pearl Harbor

    (C) The Vietnam War

    (D) The Korean War

    (E) Operation Desert Storm

41. Bureaucratic agencies are initially created by which of the following governmental institutions?

    (A) The presidency

    (B) Federal courts

    (C) The Presidential Cabinet

    (D) Congress

    (E) None of the above

42. According to the Constitution, Congress is prohibited from passing a bill of attainder. Which of the following describes a bill of attainder?

    (A) It is a bill forcing citizens to pay for their own legal representation in criminal trials.

    (B) It is a law making something illegal after the fact.

    (C) It is a law that declares a person, without a trial, to be guilty of a crime.

    (D) It is a law placing a tax on items that are manufactured in the United States.

    (E) It is a bill that forces citizens to pay for the quartering of soldiers in their homes.

43. Which of the following statements concerning the U.S. Senate is **NOT** correct?

    (A) The U.S. Senate is a continuous body.

    (B) U.S. senators were elected by state legislatures until ratification of the 17th Amendment.

    (C) U.S. senators must be at least 30 years of age.

    (D) The U.S. Senate confirms presidential nominees to the Supreme Court.

    (E) The U.S. Senate, because of its size, has very strict rules and limitations concerning the debate of proposed bills.

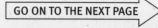
GO ON TO THE NEXT PAGE

Use the graph to answer questions 44 and 45.

	Poverty Rate
ALL PERSONS	13.3
RACE AND HISPANIC ORIGIN	
White	11.0
Asian or Pacific Islander	14.0
African American	26.5
Hispanic (persons of Hispanic origin may be of any race)	30.3
AGE	
65 years and over	10.5
18 to 64 years	10.9
Under 18 years	19.9
RESIDENCE IN	
Suburban areas	9.0
Midwest	10.4
Northeast	12.6
South	14.6
West	14.6
Nonmetropolitan areas	15.9
Central cities	18.8
MARITAL STATUS	
Married couples	5.2
Unmarried males	17.4
Unmarried females	24.4

Source: U.S. Census Bureau (Poverty Rates for Persons with Selected Characteristics, 1997).

44. According to the graph, which of the following groups had the highest poverty rate in 1997?

(A) People 65 years and over

(B) People from the Midwest

(C) Married couples

(D) People from the South

(E) People from suburban areas

45. According to the graph, which category is **NOT** identified for its poverty rate?

(A) Race and Hispanic origin

(B) Age

(C) Education level

(D) Marital status

(E) Residence

GO ON TO THE NEXT PAGE

46. Which of the following groups seeks to reduce the influence of the federal government and other governments in general?

(A) Socialists

(B) Liberals

(C) Conservatives

(D) Independents

(E) PACs

47. Which of the following Supreme Court decisions established the power of judicial review?

(A) *Miller v. California*

(B) *Mapp v. Ohio*

(C) *McCulloch v. Maryland*

(D) *Korematsu v. United States*

(E) *Marbury v. Madison*

48. Primaries where voters are presented with a list of candidates from all parties and voters may switch back and forth between parties are called

(A) closed primaries.

(B) caucus primaries.

(C) blanket primaries.

(D) candidate primaries.

(E) run-off primaries.

49. Which of the following definitions describes standing committees?

(A) They exist in a few policy areas, and their membership is drawn from both the Senate and the House.

(B) They are committees appointed for a specific purpose and a specific length of time.

(C) They are the committees formed only when the Senate and the House pass a particular bill in different forms.

(D) They are committees found only in the Senate that deal with continuous issues.

(E) They are permanently established committees formed to handle bills in specific policy areas.

50. Which of the following **BEST** describes the strict constructionist approach to judicial decisions?

(A) It is the view that judges should consistently be harsh in the sentences they hand down.

(B) It is the view that judges should decide cases on the basis of the exact language of the Constitution.

(C) It is the view that judges should apply local standards when deciding a case.

(D) It is the view that judges should apply a broad interpretation of constitutional authority.

(E) It is the view that judges should follow only judicial precedents and previous court decisions when deciding a case.

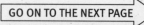 GO ON TO THE NEXT PAGE

51. According to the Constitution, which of the following has the power to pardon federal criminals?

    (A) Congress
    (B) The Senate
    (C) The Supreme Court
    (D) The president
    (E) None of the above

52. The Great Compromise, which blended the Virginia and New Jersey Plans, is sometimes called by which other name?

    (A) The Three-Fifths Compromise
    (B) The Albany Plan of Union
    (C) The Rhode Island Compromise
    (D) The Connecticut Compromise
    (E) The Pennsylvania Compromise

53. James Madison described political factions as undesirable but inevitable in which of the following?

    (A) The Declaration of Independence
    (B) The Preamble to the Constitution
    (C) The *Federalist Papers*
    (D) The body of the Constitution
    (E) None of the above

54. Which of these U.S. minority groups has consistently experienced the greatest level of poverty?

    (A) African Americans
    (B) Hispanic Americans
    (C) Eastern-European Americans
    (D) Asian Americans
    (E) Native Americans

55. Which of the following groups make up iron triangles?

    I.   Congressional subcommittees
    II. Interest groups
    III. Presidential Cabinet
    IV. Federal agencies
    V.   Joint Chiefs of Staff

    (A) II, III, and V
    (B) I, II, and IV
    (C) II, III, and IV
    (D) I, II, and III
    (E) III, IV, and V

56. Which of the following statements concerning the role of the vice president is **NOT** true?

    (A) In case of presidential disability, the vice president assumes the position of president.
    (B) The vice president presides over the U.S. Senate.
    (C) Since 1980, the role and activities of the vice president have been increased informally by presidents.
    (D) The vice president's constitutional duties include serving as chairperson of the Joint Chiefs of Staff.
    (E) The vice president only votes in the Senate if a legislative vote is tied.

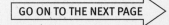 GO ON TO THE NEXT PAGE

57. Should the Supreme Court decide a case by a split decision, the justices on the losing side write their reasons for disagreeing with the majority decision. This is called which of the following?

   (A) *Writ of certiorari*
   (B) *Per curiam opinion*
   (C) *Writ of mandamus*
   (D) *Writ of habeas corpus*
   (E) Dissenting opinion

58. The party position in Congress responsible for making certain that party members are present for a vote and that they vote the way the party wishes is

   (A) the president *pro tempore.*
   (B) the chairperson of the caucus.
   (C) the minority leader.
   (D) the party whip.
   (E) none of the above

59. Which of the following types of federal grants do states prefer because they are for general purposes and relatively restriction-free?

   (A) Categorical grants
   (B) Grants-in-aid
   (C) Block grants
   (D) Mandates
   (E) Class-action grants

60. Whenever the Supreme Court announces a decision *per curium*, it means which of the following?

   (A) It signifies the decision was made by a unanimous vote of the Supreme Court.
   (B) It signifies the decision was made by a split vote of the Supreme Court.
   (C) It signifies the Supreme Court cannot decide the case and the lower court's decision stands.
   (D) It signifies the Supreme Court decision is being announced without legal explanation or without a majority opinion.
   (E) It signifies that the Supreme Court decision goes into effect immediately.

STOP

Section II: Free-Response Questions

Time: 100 Minutes

4 Questions

Directions: You have 100 minutes to answer all four of the following questions. Unless the directions indicate otherwise, respond to all parts of all four questions. It is suggested that you take a few minutes to plan and outline each answer.

Spend 25 minutes to complete each question. In your response, use substantive examples where appropriate. Make certain to number/letter each of your answers as the question is numbered/lettered below.

1. Ever since the Constitution was written in 1787, the federal government has attempted to balance the desires for liberty and order.

   (A) Describe one of the following provisions of the Constitution and, using a specific historical example, explain how this provision has been used to enhance or diminish the balance between liberty and order.

   • The due process clause as described in the 5th and 14th Amendments

   • Freedom of expression clause of the First Amendment

   (B) Explain a key provision of each of the following laws and related court decisions and explain how each of these laws and decisions has promoted order at the expense of liberty.

   • Executive Order 9066 (1942)—*Korematsu v. United States* (1944)

   • Espionage Act of 1917—*Schenck v. United States* (1919)

2. The two bodies of Congress, the House of Representatives and the Senate, operate in two very different manners.

   (A) Describe the role of each of the two listed institutional structures of the House of Representatives in terms of passing legislation. Explain how these structures make it difficult for the minority in the House of Representatives to have their ideas put into action.

   • Committee structure

   • Speaker of the House

   (B) Describe one institutional process unique to the Senate in terms of passing legislation. Explain how this process enhances the power of the minority party to influence the legislative process.

GO ON TO THE NEXT PAGE

3. During the 1960s, the Supreme Court experienced a very activist period under the leadership of Chief Justice Earl Warren.

   (A) Discuss the terms *judicial activism* and *judicial restraint.*

   (B) Explain the specific rights gained by accused persons in the following three Supreme Court decisions:

   - *Miranda v. Arizona*

   - *Gideon v. Wainwright*

   - *Mapp v. Ohio*

   (C) Explain the reaction the public had to Earl Warren because of these and other decisions.

4. Iron triangles have a significant impact on the legislative process.

   - Identify the components of an iron triangle.

   - Explain how iron triangles function.

   - Explain how iron triangles may be seen as an example of client politics.

GO ON TO THE NEXT PAGE

GO ON TO THE NEXT PAGE

_____

_____

_____

_____

_____

_____

_____

_____

_____

_____

_____

_____

_____

_____

_____

_____

_____

_____

_____

GO ON TO THE NEXT PAGE

STOP

ANSWER KEY

1.	B	21.	B	41.	D
2.	C	22.	E	42.	C
3.	E	23.	E	43.	E
4.	D	24.	D	44.	D
5.	C	25.	D	45.	C
6.	C	26.	E	46.	C
7.	D	27.	C	47.	E
8.	C	28.	C	48.	C
9.	C	29.	A	49.	E
10.	A	30.	E	50.	B
11.	C	31.	E	51.	D
12.	E	32.	D	52.	D
13.	D	33.	C	53.	C
14.	C	34.	E	54.	E
15.	C	35.	C	55.	B
16.	B	36.	B	56.	D
17.	E	37.	E	57.	E
18.	C	38.	A	58.	D
19.	E	39.	D	59.	C
20.	C	40.	C	60.	D

PRACTICE TEST 2: ASSESS YOUR STRENGTHS

The following tables show how Practice Test 2 is broken down by topic, the same as it would be on the official AP U.S. Government and Politics exam. If you need help with the free-response section, refer back to Chapter 2: Strategies for Success.

Topics	Question	If You Missed These Questions, Study:*
Constitutional Underpinnings of U.S. Government	6, 28, 35, 51, 52	Ch 3, 4, 5
Political Beliefs and Behaviors	26, 36, 37, 38, 46, 53	Ch 6, 7
Political Parties, Interest Groups, and Mass Media	11, 12, 27, 33, 34, 48	Ch 8, 9, 10, 11
Institutions of National Government: The Congress, the Presidency, the Bureaucracy, and the Federal Courts	1, 2, 3, 4, 8, 10, 13, 15, 18, 20, 22, 23, 25, 29, 31, 32, 39, 40, 41, 43, 47, 49, 56, 57, 58, 60	Ch 12, 13, 14, 15
Public Policy	5, 14, 21, 44, 45, 50, 54, 55, 59	Ch 16, 17
Civil Rights and Civil Liberties	7, 10, 16, 17, 19, 24, 30, 42	Ch 15

* Although topics do not exactly coincide with the chapters in this book, they should be used as a general guideline of where you need to focus your studies.

Topics	Number of Questions	Answered Correctly
Constitutional Underpinnings of U.S. Government	5	
Political Beliefs and Behaviors	6	
Political Parties, Interest Groups, and Mass Media	6	
Institutions of National Government: The Congress, the Presidency, the Bureaucracy, and the Federal Courts	25	
Public Policy	9	
Civil Rights and Civil Liberties	8	

ANSWERS AND EXPLANATIONS

SECTION I: MULTIPLE-CHOICE QUESTIONS

1. B

Reserved powers are guaranteed by the 10th Amendment. Reserved powers are any powers not given to the national government or prohibited to the states by the Constitution; these powers are reserved for the states.

2. C

Candidates for the presidency have been least likely to come from the Cabinet. Cabinet secretary is not a position that has been seen as a stepping stone position to the presidency. In recent years, many presidents have come from state governorships. Many feel that coming from a state governorship is an advantage because state governors are seen as having the required executive experience.

3. E

The Constitution grants Congress the power to create federal courts and to assign the number of judges who preside in them. If there were a call to increase the number of justices on the Supreme Court, that increase would have to be instituted by Congress.

4. D

The War Powers Resolution requires the president to bring troops home within 60 days unless Congress extends the time.

5. C

The belief that government should not meddle with the economy is called *laissez-faire*. The government for the better part of the country's history has practiced this approach.

6. C

To create a balance of power without harming presidential independence, the framers of the Constitution made sure to check presidential powers. Probably the best example of this is the power to declare war. Only Congress can declare war. The framers clearly did not want the power to declare war in one person's hands.

7. D

The Supreme Court decision in *Bakke v. California Board of Regents* dealt with a white man who had been denied entrance to the University of California. Because his scores exceeded those of some minority applicants, he argued that he was a victim of reverse discrimination. The Supreme Court ruled that a quota or preference system cannot be used unless its rules are addressing an actual past or present pattern of discrimination.

8. C

During the latter part of the 1800s, the primary mechanism for government employees to secure their jobs was the patronage system. Under the patronage system, which was sometimes referred to as the spoils system, government jobs were handed out as political favors. The controversy over changing from the patronage system to the presently used merit system was a bitter one.

9. C

Every 10 years, each state legislature redraws congressional districts based on population growth.

10. A

De facto segregation is segregation based on social patterns and forces. Although U.S. schools were legally desegregated in 1954, racial segregation continued into 1960s, an example of *de facto* segregation. *De jure* segregation is segregation enforced by law or governmental regulation.

11.   C
According to the table, cable TV news was viewed most favorably in 2001. It had an 88 percent approval rating that year. This was 5 percent higher than local TV news, which ranked second.

12.   E
The table shows that the approval rating of the Supreme Court dropped by 12 percent between 2001 and 2005.

13.   D
The framers left no doubts that their desire was that Congress would be the primary policy maker. Their concern over placing power in a single leader is well documented.

14.   C
Lyndon Johnson called his legislative program the "Great Society." The civil rights acts were central components of this program.

15.   C
The Department of Health and Human Services is the Cabinet department with the largest annual budget; because of Social Security and Medicaid, it outspends all other departments listed.

16.   B
The party that initiates a lawsuit is the plaintiff.

17.   E
The Supreme Court is most responsible for expanding the rights of accused criminals in the 1960s; it made numerous decision rulings in the 1960s that dramatically expanded the rights of accused criminals.

18.   C
The House Rules Committee establishes the legislative calendar and sets the rules for debating and amending a bill; it is a very powerful and important committee.

19.   E
None of the amendments listed were intended to overturn the Dred Scott decision.

20.   C
Veterans Affairs, Agriculture, and Transportation are all Cabinet-level departments. The White House counsel is a member of the White House staff, not a member of the Cabinet.

21.   B
The federal income tax brings in approximately half of the government's revenues, definitely not a small portion.

22.   E
"Full faith and credit" deals with each state recognizing documents and acts of other states.

23.   E
Representatives are elected every two years and must be at least 21 years of age. The Senate, not the House of Representatives, is a continuous body; only one-third of the membership of the Senate is up for election every two years. There are no term limits for representatives.

24.   D
Eminent domain is the right of the government to take private property for public use as long as the owner is fairly compensated.

25.   D
The Senate must ratify treaties with other nations negotiated by the president with a two-thirds vote. This is part of the system of checks and balances.

26.   E
It is not true that confidence in the Supreme Court declined from 1994 to 1996. Rather, the chart illustrates a sharp rise in confidence in the Supreme Court between 1994 and 1996.

27.   C

Most delegates to today's national party conventions are chosen during state presidential primaries.

28.   C

Under the Articles of Confederation, the bulk of the power rested with state legislatures.

29.   A

Bureaucratic agencies are originally created by Congress. Congress passes acts and then creates agencies to administer and enforce these acts.

30.   E

Gideon v. Wainwright guaranteed accused criminals the right to counsel during state trials.

31.   E

Appointments to the White House staff do not require Senate approval. The White House staff works for and advises the president.

32.   D

Conference committees work out the differences between the two houses of Congress on similar bills that both houses have passed with some differences. A bill must be passed by both chambers in an identical form before becoming a law.

33.   C

Federal money can be legally used to help fund presidential campaigns only.

34.   E

The Vietnam War and Watergate are seen as events that caused the relationship between the press and politicians to become more adversarial.

35.   C

The Establishment Clause is the part of the First Amendment that prohibits Congress from establishing a state religion.

36.   B

Initiative is the process by which voters can bring a proposed law to a vote of the people.

37.   E

According to the graph, the <15 group had the largest decline as a percentage of the population from 1900 to 2000. Their percentage dropped 13.1 percent over that period.

38.   A

According to the graph, the 45- to 64-year-olds and the 65+ age group each grew by 8.3 percent.

39.   D

The Speaker of the House is second in line for succession to the presidency, behind only the vice president.

40.   C

The War Powers Resolution was passed as a result of increasing numbers of U.S. troops being deployed to fight in Vietnam without Congress having formally declared war on this Southeast Asian nation.

41.   D

Bureaucracies are created by Congress. Many times, this is a result of Congress passing an act that is administered by an agency. This agency carries out the requirements of the act.

42.   C

A bill of attainder is a law that declares a person guilty of a crime without being tried. The bill of attainder is unconstitutional.

43.   E

It is not true that the U.S. Senate has strict rules and limitations concerning the debate of proposed bills because of its size; in fact, because of its relatively small size (compared to the House of Representatives), it has unlimited debate with very few rules and limitations.

44.   D

According to the graph, people from the South had the highest poverty rate in 1997 of the groups cited. (Be careful to only consider the groups that the question cites.)

45. C

Education level is not identified by this particular graph.

46. C

Conservatives seek to reduce the influence of the federal and other governments.

47. E

Marbury v. Madison is the landmark Supreme Court decision that established the Court's power of judicial review.

48. C

Blanket primaries allow voters to switch back and forth between parties to select the candidate they want for each office regardless of their political party.

49. E

Standing committees are permanently established committees designed to handle bills in specific policy areas.

50. B

Strict constructionists decide cases based upon the exact language of the Constitution. They do not make broad interpretations of the intentions of the Constitution.

51. D

The Constitution places the power to pardon federal criminals solely in the hands of the president.

52. D

The Connecticut Compromise, also known as the Great Compromise, combined aspects of both the New Jersey and Virginia Plans into one plan for congressional representation.

53. C

James Madison expressed his views on factions in the *Federalist Papers*, which were written to help the ratification process for the Constitution.

54. E

Native Americans have historically experienced the highest levels of poverty of any U.S. minority group.

55. B

Congressional subcommittees, interest groups, and government agencies form iron triangles.

56. D

The vice president does not serve as the chairperson of the Joint Chiefs of Staff. That position is filled by a high-ranking person from the military.

57. E

Dissenting opinions are written by justices voting in the minority. These written opinions sometimes become the basis for overturning or revisiting similar cases.

58. D

The party whip is responsible for making sure that members of his or her party are present for votes and that party members vote according to the party's wishes.

59. C

Block grants are preferred by states because the state has flexibility in spending the money.

60. D

Per curium is a term the Supreme Court uses when it issues a decision without any legal explanation.

SECTION II: FREE-RESPONSE QUESTIONS

RUBRIC FOR QUESTION 1: 6 POINTS TOTAL

Part (A): 2 Points

1 point for describing one of the two provisions listed. **1 point** for a specific historical example.

Description for the first provision would include discussion of the meaning of due process under the 5th and 14th Amendments. *Due process* is defined as protection against arbitrary deprivation of life, liberty, or property (**1 point**). The second point would come from citing the internment of Japanese Americans during World War II or defendants' rights during the 1960s, among others.

Description for the second provision would include discussion of the meaning of freedom of expression. *Freedom of expression* is defined as the constitutional rights of Americans to "freedom of speech, or of the press, or the right of the people peaceably to assemble, and to petition the Government for a redress of grievances" (**1 point**). The **second point** for freedom of expression would come from citing court cases involving burning the American flag or arguments over defining obscenity, among others.

Part (B): 4 Points

The key provision of Executive Order 9066–*Korematsu v. Japan* involved the internment of American citizens of Japanese descent during World War II (**1 point**). The **second point** would come from explaining that the U.S. government believed that the need to prevent these citizens from committing possible acts of espionage and sabotage outweighed their right to liberty.

A provision of the Espionage Act of 1917–*Schenck v. United States* was that it prevented a citizen from advocating lawless acts, such as refusing the call to military service during World War I (**1 point**). The **second point** would come from explaining that the U.S. government believed this order prevented chaos and military problems, despite limiting free speech.

RUBRIC FOR QUESTION 2: 6 POINTS TOTAL

Part (A): 4 points

Discussion of committee structure could include references to the composition of committees being dominated by the majority party (**1 point**). The majority party can prevent legislation it does not approve of from being sent to the floor for a vote (**1 point**).

Discussion of the Speaker of the House could include that the Speaker is the most powerful position in the House and that the Speaker comes from the majority party. The Speaker controls appointments of majority members to committees (**1 point**). The Speaker can control whether or not a motion is relevant and has a great deal of power over the debate of bills (**1 point**).

Part (B): 2 points

Discussion of a Senate's legislative process could include one of the following: filibuster, amendments not needing to be germane, or the fact that in the Senate legislation can bypass the committee hearing process altogether (**1 point**). Another point would be awarded for explaining how the minority party might use the filibuster, nongermane amendments, or bypassing committee hearings to influence legislation (**1 point**).

RUBRIC FOR QUESTION 3: 6 POINTS TOTAL

Part (A): 2 points for explaining that those who favor judicial activism believe that the Supreme Court should actively make public policy and that those who favor judicial restraint believe that the Court should not make public policy or redefine the Constitution.

Part (B): 1 point each (3 points total) for explaining the result of each ruling.

1. *Miranda v. Arizona*—An accused person must be read his or her constitutional rights at the time of arrest.

2. *Gideon v. Wainwright*—An accused person must be provided an attorney to represent him or her during a trial in state court.

3. *Mapp v. Ohio*—Established the exclusionary rule, which holds that illegally obtained evidence cannot be used in a trial.

Part (C): 1 point for explaining that Earl Warren was extremely unpopular among conservatives because of his judicial activism.

RUBRIC FOR QUESTION 4: 5 POINTS TOTAL

Part (A): 1 point each (3 points total) for identifying a federal agency, an interest group, and a congressional committee as comprising an iron triangle.

Part (B): 1 point for explaining that the three components develop a relationship that allows them to work together for the benefit of all three. The federal agency, the interest group, and the congressional committee are dependent upon each other, and all three benefit through their cooperation.

Part (C): 1 point for explaining that the iron triangle illustrates client politics in that the public at large bears the costs but the benefits are sometimes realized by a relatively small number of people.

Part Five

AP U.S. GOVERNMENT & POLITICS RESOURCES

APPENDIX 1: U.S. PRESIDENTS

#	President	Election Year(s)	Term of Office (Years in Office)		Party Affiliation
1	George Washington	1789, 1792	1789–1797	(8)	None
2	John Adams	1796	1797–1801	(4)	Federalist
3	Thomas Jefferson	1800, 1804	1801–1809	(8)	Democratic–Republican
4	James Madison	1808, 1812	1809–1817	(8)	Democratic–Republican
5	James Monroe	1816, 1820	1817–1825	(8)	Democratic–Republican
6	John Quincy Adams	1824	1825–1829	(4)	National–Republican
7	Andrew Jackson	1828, 1832	1829–1837	(8)	Democratic
8	Martin Van Buren	1836	1837–1841	(4)	Democratic
9	William H. Harrison	1840	1841	(1 month)	Whig
10	John Tyler		1841–1845	(4)	Whig
11	James K. Polk	1844	1845–1849	(4)	Democratic
12	Zachary Taylor	1848	1849–1850	(1+)	Whig
13	Millard Fillmore		1850–1853	(3)	Whig
14	Franklin Pierce	1852	1853–1857	(4)	Democratic
15	James Buchanan	1856	1857–1861	(4)	Democratic
16	Abraham Lincoln	1860, 1864	1861–1865	(4+)	Republican
17	Andrew Johnson		1865–1869	(4)	Republican/ National Union
18	Ulysses S. Grant	1868, 1872	1869–1877	(8)	Republican
19	Rutherford B. Hayes	1876	1877–1881	(4)	Republican
20	James A. Garfield	1880	1881	(7 months)	Republican
21	Chester A. Arthur		1881–1885	(3+)	Republican
22	Grover Cleveland	1884	1885–1889	(4)	Democratic
23	Benjamin Harrison	1888	1889–1893	(4)	Republican
24	Grover Cleveland	1892	1893–1897	(4)	Democratic

(continued on next page)

#	President	Election Year(s)	Term of Office (Years in Office)		Party Affiliation
25	William McKinley	1896, 1900	1891–1901	(4+)	Republican
26	Theodore Roosevelt	1904	1901–1909	(7+)	Republican
27	William H. Taft	1908	1909–1913	(4)	Republican
28	Woodrow Wilson	1912, 1916	1913–1921	(8)	Democratic
29	Warren G. Harding	1920	1921–1923	(2+)	Republican
30	Calvin Coolidge	1924	1923–1929	(6+)	Republican
31	Herbert Hoover	1928	1929–1933	(4)	Republican
32	Franklin D. Roosevelt	1932, 1936, 1940, 1944	1933–1945	(12+)	Democratic
33	Harry Truman	1948	1945–1953	(7+)	Democratic
34	Dwight Eisenhower	1952, 1956	1953–1961	(8)	Republican
35	John F. Kennedy	1960	1961–1963	(2+)	Democratic
36	Lyndon B. Johnson	1964	1963–1969	(6+)	Democratic
37	Richard M. Nixon	1968, 1972	1969–1974	(5+)	Republican
38	Gerald Ford		1974–1977	(2+)	Republican
39	Jimmy Carter	1976	1977–1981	(4)	Democratic
40	Ronald Reagan	1980, 1984	1981–1989	(8)	Republican
41	George H. W. Bush	1988	1989–1993	(4)	Republican
42	Bill Clinton	1992, 1996	1993–2001	(8)	Democratic
43	George W. Bush	2000, 2004	2001–2009	(8)	Republican
44	Barack Obama	2008, 2012	2009–		Democratic

NOTES ON PARTY LABELS FOR THE PRESIDENTS AND PARTY SYMBOLS

- Although the Federalist Party was formed under the leadership of Alexander Hamilton during the administration of George Washington and most of Washington's policies were aligned with that party's political beliefs and goals, Washington was never officially a party member.

- The label "Democratic-Republican" was attached to Thomas Jefferson's party after his presidency. They were first called the Anti-Federalists. The modern-day Democratic Party traces its roots back to the Democratic-Republicans as well as to the later Democratic Party of Andrew Jackson.

- The label "National Republican" was used during the campaign of 1824, when the party of Jefferson to Monroe began to splinter. All four candidates of that campaign were nominally from the Democratic-Republican party. However, J. Q. Adams ran a more "national" campaign, while his main opponent, Andrew Jackson, was forming the core of the new Western and Southern "Democratic" party.

- The Republican Party was originally an anti-slavery party. During the presidential campaign of 1864, the Republicans united with some Democrats of the border states. Together, they officially ran that campaign as the "National Union" party and included Democratic senator Andrew Johnson of Tennessee as their vice presidential candidate. Although many history books list Johnson as a Republican, he never thought of himself as one, nor was he welcome in the northern Republican circles.

- In the late 1800s, the Republican Party established itself as the conservative, pro-business party that it is today.

- The Republican Party symbol of an elephant and the Democratic symbol of a donkey both were created by the political cartoonist Thomas Nast. These symbols were originally used to make fun of both parties but soon became sources of pride.

APPENDIX 2: UNIQUE PRESIDENTIAL ELECTIONS

Year	Candidates (winner listed first)	Events
1796	J. Adams Jefferson	Electors ended up making Adams the president and Jefferson the vice president, even though they were from opposing parties.
1800	Jefferson J. Adams	Electors gave equal votes to Jefferson and his vice presidential candidate (Aaron Burr), which threw the decision to the House of Representatives. The 12th Amendment was passed to redesign electoral voting.
1824	J. Q. Adams Jackson Clay Crawford	Popular votes were publically reported for the first time. Jackson finished first with a plurality of popular and electoral votes, but the House had to decide the election. Adams was given the presidency with Clay's support.
1844	Polk Clay Birney	Third-party votes in two states gave Polk the election. This was the first time a third party made the difference. Also, this was the first time an incumbent (Tyler) was denied his party's nomination.
1860	Lincoln Breckinridge Douglas Bell	Lincoln received only 39.8 percent of the popular vote, yet he won the majority of the Electoral College votes. Douglas finished second in the popular vote but a distant third in the Electoral College.
1872	Grant Greeley	The weak Democratic party joined with "liberal" Republicans to nominate Greeley. Greeley died between the popular vote and the electoral vote. His 66 electors had no one to vote for, so they selected the names of leaders who were not on the November ballot.

(continued on next page)

Year	Candidates (winner listed first)	Events
1876	Hayes Tilden	Tilden won the popular vote, but allegations of voting fraud and disputed electoral votes sent the results to a commission to decide the election. The commission, which was comprised of five members each from the House, Senate, and the Supreme Court, voted along party lines and ended up awarding all of the disputed electoral votes to Hayes. Congress accepted their decision, which outraged Democrats. As a result of the negotiations that took place between leaders of both parties following the commission's decision, the Democrats agreed to accept the Hayes presidency in exchange for, among other conditions, the Republicans agreeing to remove the remaining federal troops from the South, which effectively ended Reconstruction.
1888	B. Harrison Cleveland	Cleveland won the popular vote but lost the electoral vote.
1892	Cleveland B. Harrison Weaver	Weaver's People's Party (Populist) won 1 million popular votes and pushed the two major parties into the beginnings of the Progressive Era.
1912	Wilson T. Roosevelt Taft	T. Roosevelt was rejected by the Republican Party. He finished second as a third-party candidate, and the Republican Taft finished third.
1948	Truman Dewey Thurmond H. Wallace	Dixiecrats in the form of the States' Rights Party started to split from the Democratic Party and won electoral votes in the South. The Progressive/Labor party candidacy of Henry Wallace further divided the Democratic vote, but Truman still emerged victorious.
1968	Nixon Humphrey G. Wallace	Further splits by Dixiecrats (American Independent Party) and the capture of Southern electoral votes signaled the gradual shift to Republican control of the South.
1992	Clinton G. H. W. Bush Perot	Perot captured nearly 19 percent of the popular vote but no electoral votes.
2000	G. W. Bush Gore Nader	Gore won the popular vote, but Bush won the electoral vote.

APPENDIX 3: MAJOR ELECTION SHIFTS

Year	Candidates (winner listed first)	Events
1800	Jefferson J. Adams	Jeffersonian Democratic-Republicans removed Federalists from power and would control politics for the next three decades.
1828	Jackson J. Q. Adams	The Jacksonian Democratic Party emerged and would dominate national politics until the Civil War.
1860	Lincoln Breckinridge Douglas Bell	Republicans replaced the fractured Whigs and Democrats and would dominate U.S. politics for the rest of the 19th century.
1892	Cleveland B. Harrison Weaver	The People's Party pushed the Republicans into ending the *laissez-faire* policies of the Gilded Age and both parties into addressing the needs of farmers and urban workers.
1912	Wilson T. Roosevelt Taft	A split in the Republican Party gave Democrats control until after WWI.
1920	Harding Cox	Republicans controlled the government until the Great Depression.
1932	F. Roosevelt Hoover	The rise of the New Deal coalition gave Democrats control of much of the political landscape until the late 1960s.
1964	L. Johnson Goldwater	The Republicans' conservative candidate backfired with one of the biggest losses in political history. Liberalism was at its political height.
1968	Nixon Humphrey Wallace	The assassinations of liberal leaders Robert Kennedy and M. L. King, plus anti-Vietnam violence, hurt the Democrats. Republicans began their reemergence.
1980	Reagan Carter	Reagan's emergence as an ultra-conservative began the dominance of the Republicans, especially in Southern states. Congress shifted to a Republican majority in 1994.

APPENDIX 4: CHIEF JUSTICES OF THE SUPREME COURT

	Chief Justice	Tenure	Notable Achievements
1.	John Jay	1789–1795 (6 years)	Few decisions, mostly "rode circuit"
2.	John Rutledge	1795 (Jul.–Dec.)	Interim service, turned down by Senate
3.	Oliver Ellsworth	1796–1800 (4)	President signature not necessary for constitutional amendment
4.	John Marshall	1801–1835 (34)	Established Supreme Court powers; the supremacy of the national government over the states
5.	Roger Taney	1836–1864 (28)	Usually backed states' rights; Dred Scott case
6.	Salmon Chase	1864–1873 (9)	Post-Civil War rulings
7.	Morrison Waite	1874–1888 (14)	
8.	Melville Fuller	1888–1910 (22)	
9.	Edward White	1910–1921 (11)	
10.	William Taft	1921–1930 (9)	Former president turned Chief Justice
11.	Charles Hughes	1930–1941 (11)	
12.	Harlan Stone	1941–1946 (5)	
13.	Frederick Vinson	1946–1953 (7)	
14.	Earl Warren	1953–1969 (16)	Major judicial activist
15.	Warren Burger	1969–1986 (17)	
16.	William Rehnquist	1986–2005 (19+)	Major advocate of judicial restraint
17.	John G. Roberts Jr.	2005–present	Extended First Amendment to corporations in the context of political donations

The original role of the Supreme Court was only briefly described in Article III of the Constitution. Supreme Court justices assumed that they would wait for rare challenges to federal laws, decide those, and then move back to their jobs of riding from one federal judicial district to another to give advice and hear circuit cases.

The *Marbury v. Madison* case was decided in 1803 and established the power of judicial review. This, and other rulings made during the Marshall era, dramatically increased the powers and workload of the Supreme Court.

APPENDIX 5: U.S. FEDERAL CONSTITUTION

WE THE PEOPLE of the United States, in Order to form a more perfect Union, establish justice, insure domestic Tranquility, provide for the common defence, promote the general Welfare, and secure the Blessings of Liberty to ourselves and our Posterity, do ordain and establish this Constitution for the United States of America.

ARTICLE I

Section 1. All legislative Powers herein granted shall be vested in a Congress of the United States, which shall consist of a Senate and House of Representatives.

Section 2. The House of Representatives shall be composed of Members chosen every second Year by the People of the several States, and the Electors in each State shall have the Qualifications requisite for Electors of the most numerous Branch of the State Legislature.

No Person shall be a Representative who shall not have attained to the Age of twenty five Years, and been seven Years a Citizen of the United States, and who shall not, when elected, be an Inhabitant of that State in which he shall be chosen.

[Representatives and [direct Taxes] shall be apportioned among the several States [which may be included within this Union,] according to their respective Numbers, which shall be determined by adding to the whole Number of free Persons, including those bound to Service for a Term of Years, and excluding Indians not taxed, three fifths of all other Persons. (This clause was changed by section 2 of the Fourteenth Amendment.)] The actual Enumeration shall be made within three Years after the first Meeting of the Congress of the United States, and within every subsequent Term of ten Years, in such Manner as they shall by Law direct. The Number of Representatives shall not exceed one for every thirty Thousand, but each State shall have at Least one Representative; and until such enumeration shall be made, the State of New Hampshire shall be entitled to chuse three, Massachusetts eight, Rhode Island and Providence Plantations one,

Connecticut five, New York six, New Jersey four, Pennsylvania eight, Delaware one, Maryland six, Virginia ten, North Carolina five, South Carolina five, and Georgia three.

When vacancies happen in the Representation from any State, the Executive Authority thereof shall issue Writs of Election to fill such Vacancies.

The House of Representatives shall chuse their Speaker and other Officers; and shall have the sole Power of Impeachment.

Section 3.   The Senate of the United States shall be composed of two Senators from each State, [chosen by the Legislature thereof, (This provision was changed by section 1 of the Seventeenth Amendment.)] for six Years; and each Senator shall have one Vote.

Immediately after they shall be assembled in Consequence of the first Election, they shall be divided as equally as may be into three Classes. The Seats of the Senators of the first Class shall be vacated at the Expiration of the second Year, of the second Class at the Expiration of the fourth Year, and of the third Class at the Expiration of the sixth Year, so that one third may be chosen every second Year; [and if Vacancies happen by Resignation, or otherwise, during the Recess of the Legislature of any State, the Executive thereof may make temporary Appointments until the next Meeting of the Legislature, which shall then fill such Vacancies. (This clause was changed by section 2 of the Seventeenth Amendment.)]

No Person shall be a Senator who shall not have attained to the Age of thirty Years, and been nine Years a Citizen of the United States, and who shall not, when elected, be an Inhabitant of that State for which he shall be chosen.

The Vice President of the United States shall be President of the Senate, but shall have no Vote, unless they be equally divided.

The Senate shall chuse their other Officers, and also a President *pro tempore*, in the Absence of the Vice President, or when he shall exercise the Office of President of the United States.

The Senate shall have the sole Power to try all Impeachments. When sitting for that Purpose, they shall be on Oath or Affirmation. When the President of the United States is tried, the Chief justice shall preside: And no Person shall be convicted without the Concurrence of two thirds of the Members present.

Judgment in Cases of Impeachment shall not extend further than to removal from Office, and disqualification to hold and enjoy any Office of honor, Trust or Profit under the United States: but the Party convicted shall nevertheless be liable and subject to Indictment, Trial, Judgment and Punishment, according to Law.

Section 4.   The Times, Places and Manner of holding Elections for Senators and Representatives, shall be prescribed in each State by the Legislature thereof; but the Congress may at any time by Law make or alter such Regulations, except as to the Places of chusing Senators.

The Congress shall assemble at least once in every Year, and such Meeting shall be [on the first Monday in December, (This provision was changed by section 2 of the Twentieth Amendment.)] unless they shall by Law appoint a different Day.

Section 5.   Each House shall be the judge of the Elections, Returns and Qualifications of its own Members, and a Majority of each shall constitute a Quorum to do Business; but a smaller Number may adjourn from day to day, and may be authorized to compel the Attendance of absent Members, in such Manner, and under such Penalties as each House may provide.

Each House may determine the Rules of its Proceedings, punish its Members for disorderly Behaviour, and, with the Concurrence of two thirds, expel a Member.

Each House shall keep a journal of its Proceedings, and from time to time publish the same, excepting such Parts as may in their judgment require Secrecy; and the Yeas and Nays of the Members of either House on any question shall, at the Desire of one fifth of those Present, be entered on the journal.

Neither House, during the Session of Congress, shall, without the Consent of the other, adjourn for more than three days, nor to any other Place than that in which the two Houses shall be sitting.

Section 6.   The Senators and Representatives shall receive a Compensation for their Services, to be ascertained by Law, and paid out of the Treasury of the United States. They shall in all Cases, except Treason, Felony and Breach of the Peace, be privileged from Arrest during their Attendance at the Session of their respective Houses, and in going to and returning from the same; and for any Speech or Debate in either House, they shall not be questioned in any other Place.

No Senator or Representative shall, during the Time for which he was elected, be appointed to any civil Office under the Authority of the United States, which shall have been created, or the Emoluments whereof shall have been encreased during such time; and no Person holding any Office under the United States, shall be a Member of either House during his Continuance in Office.

Section 7.   All Bills for raising Revenue shall originate in the House of Representatives; but the Senate may propose or concur with Amendments as on other Bills.

Every Bill which shall have passed the House of Representatives and the Senate, shall, before it become a Law, be presented to the President of the United States; If he approve he shall sign it, but if not he shall return it, with his Objections to that House in which it shall have originated, who shall enter the Objections at large on their Journal, and proceed to reconsider it. If after such Reconsideration two thirds of that House shall agree to pass the Bill, it shall be sent, together with the Objections, to the other House, by which it shall likewise be reconsidered, and if approved by two thirds of that House, it shall become a Law. But in all such Cases the Votes of both Houses shall be determined by yeas and Nays, and the Names of the Persons voting for and against the Bill shall be entered on the journal of each House respectively. If any bill shall not be returned by the President within ten Days (Sundays excepted) after it shall have been presented to him, the Same shall be a Law, in like Manner as if he had signed it, unless the Congress by their Adjournment prevent its Return, in which Case it shall not be a Law.

Every Order, Resolution, or Vote to which the Concurrence of the Senate and House of Representatives may be necessary (except on a question of Adjournment) shall be presented to the President of the United States; and before the Same shall take Effect, shall be approved by him, or being disapproved by him, shall be repassed by two thirds of the Senate and House of Representatives, according to the Rules and Limitations prescribed in the Case of a Bill.

Section 8. The Congress shall have Power To lay and collect Taxes, Duties, Imposts and Excises, to pay the Debts and provide for the common Defence and general Welfare of the United States; but all Duties, Imposts and Excises shall be uniform throughout the United States;

To borrow Money on the credit of the United States;

To regulate Commerce with Foreign Nations, and among the several States, and with the Indian tribes;

To establish an uniform Rule of Naturalization, and uniform Laws on the subject of Bankruptcies throughout the United States;

To coin Money, regulate the Value thereof, and of foreign Coin, and fix the Standard of Weights and Measures;

To provide for the Punishment of counterfeiting the Securities and current Coin of the United States;

To establish Post Offices and post Roads;

To promote the Progress of Science and useful Arts, by securing for limited Times to Authors and Inventors the exclusive Right to their respective Writings and Discoveries;

To constitute Tribunals inferior to the supreme Court;

To define and punish Piracies and Felonies committed on the high Seas, and Offences against the Law of Nations;

To declare War, grant Letters of Marque and Reprisal, and make Rules concerning Captures on Land and Water;

To raise and support Armies, but no Appropriation of Money to that Use shall be for a longer Term than two Years;

To provide and maintain a Navy;

To make Rules for the Government and Regulation of the land and naval Forces;

To provide for calling forth the Militia to execute the Laws of the Union, suppress Insurrections and repel Invasions;

To provide for organizing, arming, and disciplining, the Militia and for governing such Part of them as may be employed in the Service of the United States, reserving to the States respectively, the Appointment of the Officers, and the Authority of training the Militia according to the discipline prescribed by Congress;

To exercise exclusive Legislation in all Cases whatsoever, over such District (not exceeding ten Miles square) as may, by Cession of particular States, and the Acceptance of Congress, become the Seat of the Government of the United States, and to exercise like Authority over all Places purchased by the Consent of the Legislature of the State in which the Same shall be, for the Erection of Forts, Magazines, Arsenals, Dockyards, and other needful Buildings; And

To make all Laws which shall be necessary and proper for carrying into Execution the foregoing Powers, and all other Powers vested by this Constitution in the Government of the United States, or in any Department or Officer thereof.

Section 9.   The Migration or Importation of such Persons any of the States now existing shall think proper to admit, shall not be prohibited by the Congress prior to the Year one thousand eight hundred and eight, but a Tax or duty may be imposed on such Importation, not exceeding ten dollars for each Person.

The Privilege of the Writ of Habeas Corpus shall not be suspended, unless when in Cases of Rebellion or Invasion the public Safety may require it.

No Bill of Attainder or *ex post facto* Law shall be passed.

No Capitation, or other direct, Tax shall be laid, unless in Proportion to the Census or Enumeration herein before directed to be taken.

No Tax or Duty shall be laid on Articles exported from any State.

No Preference shall be given by any Regulation of Commerce or Revenue to the Ports of one State over those of another: nor shall Vessels bound to, or from, one State, be obliged to enter, clear, or pay Duties in another.

No Money shall be drawn from the Treasury, but in Consequence of Appropriations made by Law; and a regular Statement and Account of the Receipts and Expenditures of all public Money shall be published from time to time.

No Title of Nobility shall be granted by the United States: And no Person holding any Office of Profit or Trust under them, shall, without the Consent of the Congress, accept of any present, Emolument, Office, or Tide, of any kind whatever, from any King, Prince, or foreign State.

Section 10.   No State shall enter into any Treaty, Alliance, or Confederation; grant Letters of Marque and Reprisal; coin Money; emit Bills of Credit; make any Thing but gold and silver Coin a Tender in Payment of Debts; pass any Bill of Attainder, *ex post facto* Law, or Law impairing the Obligation of Contracts, or grant any Title of Nobility.

No State shall, without the Consent of the Congress, lay any Imposts or Duties on Imports or Exports, except what may be absolutely necessary for executing its inspection Laws: and the net Produce of all Duties and Imposts, laid by any State on Imports or Exports, shall be for the Use of the Treasury of the United States; and all such Laws shall be subject to the Revision and Controul of the Congress.

No State shall, without the Consent of Congress, lay any Duty of Tonnage, keep Troops, or Ships of War in time of Peace, enter into any Agreement or Compact with another State, or with a foreign Power, or engage in War, unless actually invaded, or in such imminent Danger as will not admit of delay.

ARTICLE II

Section 1.   The executive Power shall be vested in a President of the United States of America. He shall hold his Office during the Term of four Years, and, together with the Vice President, chosen for the same Term, be elected, as follows.

Each State shall appoint, in such Manner as the Legislature thereof may direct, a Number of Electors, equal to the whole Number of Senators and Representatives to which the State may be entitled in the Congress: but no Senator or Representative, or Person holding an Office of Trust or Profit under the United States, shall be appointed an Elector.

[The Electors shall meet in their respective States, and vote by Ballot for two Persons, of whom one at least shall not be an inhabitant of the same State with themselves. And they shall make a List of all the Persons voted for, and of the Number of Votes for each; which List they shall sign and certify, and transmit sealed to the Seat of the Government of the United States, directed to the President of the Senate. The President of the Senate shall, in the Presence of the Senate and House of Representatives, open all the Certificates, and the Votes shall then be counted. The Person having the greatest Number of Votes shall be the President, if such Number be a

Majority of the whole Number of Electors appointed; and if there be more than one who have such Majority, and have an equal Number of Votes, then the House of Representatives shall immediately chuse by Ballot one of them for President; and if no Person have a Majority, then from the five highest on the List the said House shall in like Manner chuse the President. But in chusing the President, the Votes shall be taken by States, the Representation from each State having one Vote; A quorum for this purpose shall consist of a Member or Members from two thirds of the States, and a Majority of all the States shall be necessary to a Choice. In every Case, after the Choice of the President, the Person having the greatest Number of Votes of the Electors shall be the Vice President. But if there should remain two or more who have equal Votes, the Senate shall chuse from them by Ballot the Vice President. (This clause was superseded by the Twelfth Amendment.)]

The Congress may determine the Time of chusing the Electors, and the Day on which they shall give their Votes; which Day shall be the same throughout the United States.

No Person except a natural born Citizen, or a Citizen of the United States, at the time of the Adoption of this Constitution, shall be eligible to the Office of President; neither shall any Person be eligible to that Office who shall not have attained to the Age of thirty five Years, and been fourteen Years a Resident within the United States.

[In Case of the Removal of the President from Office, or of his Death, Resignation, or Inability to discharge the Powers and Duties of the said Office, the Same shall devolve on the Vice President, and the Congress may by Law provide for the Case of Removal, Death, Resignation or Inability, both of the President and Vice President, declaring what Officer shall then act as President, and such Officer shall act accordingly, until the Disability be removed, or a President shall be elected. (This clause was modified by the Twenty-Fifth Amendment.)]

The President shall, at stated Times, receive for his Services, a Compensation, which shall neither be increased nor diminished during the Period for which he shall have been elected, and he shall not receive within that Period any other Emolument from the United States, or any of them.

Before he enter on the Execution of his Office, he shall take the following Oath or Affirmation: "I do solemnly swear (or affirm) that I will faithfully execute the Office of President of the United States, and will to the best of my Ability, preserve, protect and defend the Constitution of the United States."

Section 2. The President shall be Commander in Chief of the Army and Navy of the United States, and of the Militia of the several States, when called into the actual Service of the United States; he may require the Opinion, in writing, of the principal Officer in each of the executive Departments, upon any Subject relating to the Duties of their respective Offices, and he shall have Power to grant Reprieves and Pardons for Offences against the United States, except in Cases of Impeachment.

He shall have Power, by and with the Advice and Consent of the Senate, to make Treaties, provided two thirds of the Senators present concur; and he shall nominate, and by and with the Advice and Consent of the Senate, shall appoint Ambassadors, other public Ministers and Consuls, judges of the supreme Court, and all other Officers of the United States, whose Appointments are not herein otherwise provided for, and which shall be established by Law: but the Congress may by Law vest the Appointment of such inferior Officers, as they think proper, in the President alone, in the Courts of Law, or in the Heads of Departments.

The President shall have Power to fill up all Vacancies that may happen during the Recess of the Senate, by granting Commissions which shall expire at the End of their next Session.

Section 3.   He shall from time to time give to the Congress Information of the State of the Union, and recommend to their Consideration such Measures as he shall judge necessary and expedient; he may, on extraordinary Occasions, convene both Houses, or either of them, and in Case of Disagreement between them, with Respect to the Time of Adjournment, he may adjourn them to such Time as he shall think proper; he shall receive Ambassadors and other public Ministers; he shall take Care that the Laws be faithfully executed, and shall Commission all the Officers of the United States.

Section 4.   The President, Vice President and all civil Officers of the United States, shall be removed from Office on Impeachment for, and Conviction of, Treason, Bribery, or other high Crimes and Misdemeanors.

ARTICLE III

Section 1.

The judicial Power of the United States, shall be vested in one supreme Court, and in such inferior Courts as the Congress may from time to time ordain and establish. The judges, both of the supreme and inferior Courts, shall hold their Offices during good Behaviour, and shall, at stated Times receive for their Services, a Compensation, which shall not be diminished during their Continuance in Office.

Section 2.   The judicial Power shall extend to all Cases, in Law and Equity, arising under this Constitution, the Laws of the United States, and Treaties made, or which shall be made, under their Authority; to all Cases affecting Ambassadors, other public Ministers and Consuls; to all Cases of admiralty and maritime jurisdiction; to Controversies to which the United States shall be a Party; to Controversies between two or more States; between a State and Citizens of another State; between Citizens of different States, between Citizens of the same State claiming Lands under Grants of different States, and between a State, or the Citizens thereof, and foreign States, Citizens or Subjects.

In all Cases affecting Ambassadors, other public Ministers and Consuls, and those in which a State shall be Party, the supreme Court shall have original jurisdiction. In all the other Cases before mentioned, the supreme Court shall have appellate jurisdiction, both as to Law and Fact, with such Exceptions, and under such Regulations as the Congress shall make.

The Trial of all Crimes, except in Cases of Impeachment, shall be by jury; and such Trial shall be held in the State where the said Crimes shall have been committed; but when not committed within any State, the Trial shall be at such Place or Places as the Congress may by Law have directed.

Section 3.   Treason against the United States, shall consist only in levying War against them, or in adhering to their Enemies, giving them Aid and Comfort. No Person shall be convicted of Treason unless on the Testimony of two Witnesses to the same overt Act, or on Confession in open Court.

The Congress shall have Power to declare the Punishment of Treason, but no Attainder of Treason shall work Corruption of Blood, or Forfeiture except during the Life of the Person attainted.

ARTICLE IV

Section 1.   Full Faith and Credit shall be given in each State to the public Acts, Records, and judicial Proceedings of every other State; And the Congress may by general Laws prescribe the Manner in which such Acts, Records and Proceedings shall be proved, and the Effect thereof.

Section 2.   The Citizens of each State shall be entitled to all Privileges and Immunities of Citizens in the several States.

A Person charged in any State with Treason, Felony, or other Crime, who shall flee from justice, and be found in another State, shall on Demand of the executive Authority of the State from which he fled, be delivered up, to be removed to the State having jurisdiction of the Crime.

[No Person held to Service or Labour in one State, under the Laws thereof, escaping into another, shall, in Consequence of any Law or Regulation therein, be discharged from such Service or Labour, but shall be delivered up on Claim of the Party to whom such Service or Labour may be due. (This clause was superseded by the Thirteenth Amendment.)]

Section 3.   New States may be admitted by the Congress into this Union; but no new State shall be formed or erected within the jurisdiction of any other State; nor any State be formed by the junction of two or more States, or Parts of States, without the Consent of the Legislatures of the States concerned as well as of the Congress.

The Congress shall have Power to dispose of and make all needful Rules and Regulations respecting the Territory or other Property belonging to the United States; and nothing in this Constitution shall be so construed as to Prejudice any Claims of the United States, or of any particular State.

Section 4. The United States shall guarantee to every State in this Union a Republican Form of Government, and shall protect each of them against Invasion; and on Application of the Legislature, or of the Executive (when the Legislature cannot be convened) against domestic Violence.

ARTICLE V

The Congress, whenever two thirds of both Houses shall deem it necessary, shall propose Amendments to this Constitution, or, on the Application of the Legislatures of two thirds of the several States, shall call a Convention for proposing Amendments, which, in either Case, shall be valid to all Intents and Purposes, as Part of this Constitution, when ratified by the legislatures of three fourths of the several States, or by Conventions in three fourths thereof, as the one or the other Mode of Ratification may be proposed by the Congress; Provided that no Amendment which may be made prior to the Year One thousand eight hundred and eight shall in any Manner affect the first and fourth Clauses in the Ninth Section of the first Article; and that no State, without its Consent, shall be deprived of its equal Suffrage in the Senate.

ARTICLE VI

All Debts contracted and Engagements entered into, before the Adoption of this Constitution, shall be as valid against the United States under this Constitution, as under the Confederation.

This Constitution, and the Laws of the United States which shall be made in Pursuance thereof; and all Treaties made, or which shall be made, under the Authority of the United States, shall be the supreme Law of the Land; and the judges in every State shall be bound thereby, any Thing in the Constitution or Laws of any State to the Contrary notwithstanding.

The Senators and Representatives before mentioned, and the Members of the several State Legislatures, and all executive and judicial Officers, both of the United States and of the several States, shall be bound by Oath or Affirmation, to support this Constitution; but no religious Test shall ever be required as a Qualification to any Office or public Trust under the United States.

ARTICLE VII

The Ratification of the Conventions of nine States, shall be sufficient for the Establishment of this Constitution between the States so ratifying the Same.

DONE in Convention by the Unanimous Consent of the States present the Seventeenth Day of September in the Year of our Lord one thousand seven hundred and Eighty seven and of the Independance of the United States of America the Twelfth.

IN WITNESS whereof We have hereunto subscribed our Names.

[The first ten amendments (the Bill of Rights) were ratified December 15, 1791.]

AMENDMENT I

Congress shall make no law respecting an establishment of religion, or prohibiting the free exercise thereof; or abridging the freedom of speech, or of the press, or the right of the people peaceably to assemble, and to petition the Government for a redress of grievances.

AMENDMENT II

A well regulated Militia, being necessary to the security of a free State, the right of the people to keep and bear Arms, shall not be infringed.

AMENDMENT III

No Soldier shall, in time of peace be quartered in any house, without the consent of the Owner, nor in time of war, but in a manner to be prescribed by law.

AMENDMENT IV

The right of the people to be secure in their persons, houses, papers, and effects, against unreasonable searches and seizures, shall not be violated, and no Warrants shall issue, but upon probable cause, supported by Oath or affirmation, and particularly describing the place to be searched, and the persons or things to be seized.

AMENDMENT V

No person shall be held to answer for a capital, or otherwise infamous crime, unless on a present-ment or indictment of a Grand jury, except in cases arising in the land or naval forces, or in the Militia, when in actual service in time of War or public danger; nor shall any person be subject for the same offence to be twice put in jeopardy of life or limb, nor shall be compelled in any criminal case to be a witness against himself, nor be deprived of life, liberty, or property, without due process of law; nor shall private property be taken for public use, without just compensation.

AMENDMENT VI

In all criminal prosecutions, the accused shall enjoy the right to a speedy and public trial, by an impartial jury of the State and district wherein the crime shall have been committed; which district shall have been previously ascertained by law, and to be informed of the nature and cause of the accusation; to be confronted with the witnesses against him; to have compulsory process for obtaining witnesses in his favor, and to have the Assistance of Counsel for his defence.

AMENDMENT VII

In Suits at common law, where the value in controversy shall exceed twenty dollars, the right of trial by jury shall be preserved, and no fact tried by a jury, shall be otherwise reexamined in any Court of the United States, than according to the rules of the common law.

AMENDMENT VIII

Excessive bail shall not be required, nor excessive fines imposed, nor cruel and unusual punishments inflicted.

AMENDMENT IX

The enumeration in the Constitution, of certain rights, shall not be construed to deny or disparage others retained by the people.

AMENDMENT X

The powers not delegated to the United States by the Constitution, nor prohibited by it to the States, are reserved to the States respectively, or to the people.

AMENDMENT XI (RATIFIED FEBRUARY 7, 1795)

The judicial power of the United States shall not be construed to extend to any suit in law or equity, commenced or prosecuted against one of the United States by Citizens of another State, or by Citizens or Subjects of any Foreign State.

AMENDMENT XII (RATIFIED JUNE 15, 1804)

The Electors shall meet in their respective states, and vote by ballot for President and Vice President, one of whom, at least, shall not be an inhabitant of the same state with themselves; they shall name in their ballots the person voted for as President, and in distinct ballots the person voted for as Vice President, and they shall make distinct lists of all persons voted for as President, and of all persons voted for as Vice President, and of the number of votes for each, which lists they shall sign and certify, and transmit sealed to the seat of the government of the United States, directed to the President of the Senate; The President of the Senate shall, in the presence of the Senate and House of Representatives, open all the certificates and the votes shall then be counted; The person having the greatest number of votes for President, shall be the President, if such number be a majority of the whole number of Electors appointed; and if no person have such majority, then from the persons having the highest numbers not exceeding three on the list of those voted for as President, the House of Representatives shall choose immediately, by ballot, the President. But in choosing the President, the votes shall be taken by states, the representation from each state having one vote; a quorum for this purpose shall consist of a member or members from two-thirds of the states, and a majority of all the states shall be necessary to a choice. [And if the House of Representatives shall not choose a President whenever the right of choice shall devolve upon them, before the fourth day of March next following, then the Vice-President shall act as President, as in the case of the death or other constitutional disability of the President (This clause was superseded by section 3 of the Twentieth Amendment.)]. The person having the greatest number of votes as Vice-President, shall be the Vice-President, if such number be a majority of the whole number of Electors appointed, and if no person have a majority, then from the two highest numbers on the list, the Senate shall choose the Vice-President; a quorum for the purpose shall consist of two-thirds of the whole number of Senators, and a majority of the whole number shall be necessary to a choice. But no person constitutionally ineligible to the office of President shall be eligible to that of Vice President of the United States.

AMENDMENT XIII (RATIFIED DECEMBER 6, 1865)

Section 1.   Neither slavery nor involuntary servitude, except as a punishment for crime whereof the party shall have been duly convicted, shall exist within the United States, or any place subject to their jurisdiction.

Section 2.   Congress shall have power to enforce this article by appropriate legislation.

AMENDMENT XIV (RATIFIED JULY 9, 1868)

Section 1.   All persons born or naturalized in the United States, and subject to the jurisdiction thereof, are citizens of the United States and of the State wherein they reside. No State shall make or enforce any law which shall abridge the privileges or immunities of citizens of the United States; nor shall any State deprive any person of life, liberty, or property, without due process of law; nor deny to any person within its jurisdiction the equal protection of the laws.

Section 2.   Representatives shall be apportioned among the several States according to their respective numbers, counting the whole number of persons in each State, excluding Indians not taxed. But when the right to vote at any election for the choice of electors for President and Vice President of the United States, Representatives in Congress, the Executive and judicial officers of a State, or the members of the Legislature thereof, is denied to any of the male inhabitants of such State, being twenty-one years of age, and citizens of the United States, or in any way abridged, except for participation in rebellion, or other crime, the basis of representation therein shall be reduced in the proportion which the number of such male citizens shall bear to the whole number of male citizens twenty-one years of age in such State.

Section 3.   No person shall be a Senator or Representative in Congress, or elector of President and Vice President, or hold any office, civil or military, under the United States, or under any State, who, having previously taken an oath, as a member of Congress, or as an officer of the United States, or as a member of any State legislature, or as an executive or judicial officer of any State, to support the Constitution of the United States, shall have engaged in insurrection or rebellion against the same, or given aid or comfort to the enemies thereof. But Congress may by a vote of two-thirds of each House, remove such disability.

Section 4. The validity of the public debt of the United States, authorized by law, including debts incurred for payment of pensions and bounties for services in suppressing insurrection or rebellion, shall not be questioned. But neither the United States nor any State shall assume or pay any debt or obligation incurred in aid of insurrection or rebellion against the United States, or any claim for the loss of emancipation of any slave; but all such debts, obligations and claims shall be held illegal and void.

Section 5. The Congress shall have power to enforce, by appropriate legislation, the provisions of this article.

AMENDMENT XV (RATIFIED FEBRUARY 3, 1870)

Section 1. The right of citizens of the United States to vote shall not be denied or abridged by the United States or by any State on account of race, color, or previous condition of servitude.

Section 2. The Congress shall have power to enforce this article by appropriate legislation.

AMENDMENT XVI (RATIFIED FEBRUARY 3, 1913)

The Congress shall have power to lay and collect taxes on incomes, from whatever source derived, without apportionment among the several States, and without regard to any census or enumeration.

AMENDMENT XVII (RATIFIED APRIL 8, 1913)

The Senate of the United States shall be composed of two Senators from each State, elected by the people thereof, for six years; and each Senator shall have one vote. The electors in each State shall have the qualifications requisite for electors of the most numerous branch of the State legislatures.

When vacancies happen in the representation of any State in the Senate, the executive authority of such State shall issue writs of election to fill such vacancies: Provided, That the legislature of any State may empower the executive thereof to make temporary appointments until the people fill the vacancies by election as the legislature may direct.

This amendment shall not be so construed as to affect the election or term of any Senator chosen before it becomes valid as part of the Constitution.

AMENDMENT XVIII (RATIFIED JANUARY 16, 1919)

Section 1.   After one year from the ratification of this article the manufacture, sale, or transportation of intoxicating liquors within, the importation thereof into, or the exportation thereof from the United States and all territory subject to the jurisdiction thereof for beverage purposes is hereby prohibited.

Section 2.   The Congress and the several States shall have concurrent power to enforce this article by appropriate legislation.

Section 3.   This article shall be inoperative unless it shall have been ratified as an amendment to the Constitution by the legislatures of the several States, as provided in the Constitution, within seven years from the date of the submission hereof to the States by the Congress.

AMENDMENT XIX (RATIFIED AUGUST 18, 1920)

The right of citizens of the United States to vote shall not be denied or abridged by the United States or by any State on account of sex.

Congress shall have power to enforce this article by appropriate legislation.

AMENDMENT XX (RATIFIED JANUARY 23, 1933)

Section 1.   The terms of the President and Vice President shall end at noon on the 20th day of January, and the terms of Senators and Representatives at noon on the 3d day of January, of the years in which such terms would have ended if this article had not been ratified; and the terms of their successors shall then begin.

Section 2.   The Congress shall assemble at least once in every year, and such meeting shall begin at noon on the 3d day of January, unless they shall by law appoint a different day.

Section 3.   If, at the time fixed for the beginning of the term of the President, the President elect shall have died, the Vice President elect shall become President. If a President shall not have been chosen before the time fixed for the beginning of his term, or if the President elect shall have failed to qualify, then the Vice President elect shall act as President until a President shall have qualified; and the Congress may by law provide for the case wherein neither a President elect nor a Vice President elect shall have qualified, declaring who shall then act as President, or the manner in which one who is to act shall be selected, and such person shall act accordingly until a President or Vice President shall have qualified.

Section 4.   The Congress may by law provide for the case of the death of any of the persons from whom the House of Representatives may choose a President whenever the right of choice shall have devolved upon them, and for the case of the death of any of the persons from whom the Senate may choose a Vice President whenever the right of choice shall have devolved upon them.

Section 5.   Sections 1 and 2 shall take effect on the 15th day of October following the ratification of this article.

Section 6.   This article shall be inoperative unless it shall have been ratified as an amendment to the Constitution by the legislatures of three-fourths of the several States within seven years from the date of its submission.

AMENDMENT XXI (RATIFIED DECEMBER 3, 1933)

Section 1.   The eighteenth article of amendment to the Constitution of the United States is hereby repealed.

Section 2.   The transportation or importation into any State, Territory, or possession of the United States for delivery or use therein of intoxicating liquors, in violation of the laws thereof, is hereby prohibited.

Section 3.   This article shall be inoperative unless it shall have been ratified as an amendment to the Constitution by conventions in the several States, as provided in the Constitution, within seven years from the date of the submission hereof to the States by the Congress.

AMENDMENT XXII (RATIFIED FEBRUARY 27, 1951)

Section 1.   No person shall be elected to the office of the President more than twice, and no person who has held the office of President, or acted as President, for more than two years of a term to which some other person was elected President shall be elected to the office of the President more than once. But this Article shall not apply to any person holding the office of President when this Article was proposed by the Congress, and shall not prevent any person who may be holding the office of President, or acting as President, during the term within which this Article becomes operative from holding the office of President or acting as President during the remainder of such term.

Section 2.   This article shall be inoperative unless it shall have been ratified as an amendment to the Constitution by the legislatures of three-fourths of the several States within seven years from the date of its submission to the States by the Congress.

AMENDMENT XXIII (RATIFIED MARCH 29, 1961)

Section 1.   The District constituting the seat of Government of the United States shall appoint in such manner as the Congress may direct:

A number of electors of President and Vice President equal to the whole number of Senators and Representatives in Congress to which the District would be entitled if it were a State, but in no event more than the least populous State; they shall be in addition to those appointed by the States, but they shall be considered, for the purposes of the election of President and Vice President, to be electors appointed by a State; and they shall meet in the District and perform such duties as provided by the twelfth article of amendment.

Section 2.   The Congress shall have power to enforce this article by appropriate legislation.

AMENDMENT XXIV (RATIFIED JANUARY 23, 1964)

Section 1.   The right of citizens of the United States to vote in any primary or other election for President or Vice President, for electors for President or Vice President, or for Senator or Representatives in Congress, shall not be denied or abridged by the United States or any State by reason of failure to pay any poll tax or other tax.

Section 2.   The Congress shall have power to enforce this article by appropriate legislation.

AMENDMENT XXV (RATIFIED FEBRUARY 10, 1967)

Section 1.   In case of the removal of the President from office or of his death or resignation, the Vice President shall become President.

Section 2.   Whenever there is a vacancy in the office of the Vice President, the President shall nominate a Vice President who shall take office upon confirmation by a majority vote of both Houses of Congress.

Section 3.   Whenever the President transmits to the President *pro tempore* of the Senate and the Speaker of the House of Representatives his written declaration that he is unable to discharge the powers and duties of his office, and until he transmits to them a written declaration to the contrary, such powers and duties shall be discharged by the Vice President as Acting President.

Section 4.   Whenever the Vice President and a majority of either the principal officers of the executive departments or of such other body as Congress may by law provide, transmit to the President *pro tempore* of the Senate and the Speaker of the House of Representatives their written declaration that the President is unable to discharge the powers and duties of his office, the Vice President shall immediately assume the powers and duties of the office as Acting President.

Thereafter, when the President transmits to the President *pro tempore* of the Senate and the Speaker of the House of Representatives his written declaration that no inability exists, he shall resume the powers and duties of his office unless the Vice President and a majority of either the principal officers of the executive department or of such other body as Congress may by law provide, transmit within four days to the President *pro tempore* of the Senate and the Speaker of the House of Representatives their written declaration that the President is unable to discharge the powers and duties of his office. Thereupon Congress shall decide the issue, assembling within forty-eight hours for that purpose if not in session. If the Congress, within twenty-one days after receipt of the latter written declaration, or, if Congress is not in session, within twenty-one days after Congress is required to assemble, determines by two-thirds vote of both Houses that the President is unable to discharge the powers and duties of his office, the Vice President shall continue to discharge the same as Acting President; otherwise, the President shall resume the powers and duties of his office.

AMENDMENT XXVI (RATIFIED JULY 1, 1971)

Section 1.   The right of citizens of the United States, who are eighteen years of age or older, to vote shall not be denied or abridged by the United States or by any State on account of age.

Section 2.   The Congress shall have power to enforce this article by appropriate legislation.

AMENDMENT XXVII (RATIFIED MAY 7, 1992)

No law varying the compensation for the services of Senators and Representatives shall take effect until an election of Representatives shall have intervened.

APPENDIX 6: A GUIDE FOR TEACHERS

HOW CAN A REVIEW GUIDE HELP?

At least two major challenges face a high school teacher when presenting a university-level curriculum. The first is the issue of time management. The second is mastering the higher level of analysis and vocabulary. In both of these areas, a well-designed guide can be of significant help. Use Kaplan's guide for creating an efficient calendar, monitoring your course's pace, and focusing on the most important pieces of the course.

The goal of this guide was to give a comprehensive overview without requiring the reading of another full text. Students already have that kind of resource, and they likely will not have the time or initiative to read the course text twice. The emphasis has been on making usable tables, notes, outlines, and definitions that will strengthen review and learning. These also are the kind of materials that can help a teacher present information succinctly and easily. The glossary selections have been chosen to reflect the kinds of issues likely to appear on the exam. They should be a central component of the materials students should master.

USING THIS GUIDE AND BUILDING YOUR CALENDAR

The key to establishing priorities is the course outline given by the College Board. It is summarized in Chapter 1. The following table takes that information and matches the guide's chapters to the College Board's. In addition, a blank column allows the teacher to estimate the number of days to commit to each of the major topics. Whether you have a semester of one-hour-a-day classes, a block schedule of classes every other day, or even a full year, the building of a realistic timeline is essential. Don't forget to account for school days lost to state/district testing and schoolwide activities such as pep rallies, etc.

Various texts and guides use slightly different sets of scope and sequence; therefore, the chapters of this work do not match the College Board outline exactly. However, they follow the sequence found in most college texts and are valuable for setting up a rough calendar.

PLANNING YOUR TIME

College Board Topics	Kaplan Guide Chapters	Percent of the Exam (approximate number of questions)	Total number of days you have to teach this course = _____. Take this number and multiply it by the % in column 3 to estimate the number of days you should target for each topic.
Constitutional Underpinnings of U.S. Government	Ch 3, 4, 5	5% to 15% (3 to 9)	
Political Beliefs and Behaviors	Ch 6, 7	10% to 20% (6 to 12)	
Political Parties, Interest Groups, and Mass Media	Ch 8, 9, 10, 11	10% to 20% (6 to 12)	
Institutions of National Government: The Congress, the Presidency, the Bureaucracy, and the Federal Courts	Ch 12, 13, 14, 15	35% to 45% (21 to 27)	
Public Policy	Ch 16, 17	5% to 15% (3 to 9)	
Civil Rights and Civil Liberties	Ch 15	5% to 15% (3 to 9)	

BE SURE TO...

- Spend a class period reviewing the test structure information given in this guide, the hints for success, and the ways to set up a study schedule.

- Allow time in class to discuss the practice questions; use them for quizzes and measures of student progress.

- Help students practice free-response rubric construction. (See Chapters 1 and 2.)

- Use diagnostic test questions as a pretest or in-class practice test.

- Be sure to fully discuss the ways to identify the logic of correct answers.

- Focus on the chapter notes and charts as summative guides to materials given in class.

- Have students study the vocabulary provided in the glossary.

- Have students take the practice tests in structured settings and with the appropriate time limits, giving them more opportunities to get comfortable with the pace of the exam.

- Use the College Board's scoring rubric when scoring student exams.

PRACTICE TEST QUESTIONS AND TEACHER'S USES

The materials presented in this volume have been specifically designed to reflect the style used by the College Board. Also, use the the materials found in released tests and on the College Board website for in-class practice. The more students get used to questions with five choices, multiple variants of choices, and the kinds of language required to score well, the actual AP exam will be less of a challenge for them.

GLOSSARY

527 group
A tax-exempt organization, named after a section of the U.S. tax code, that can engage in election activities on behalf of causes or issues. 527s are not regulated by the Federal Election Commission (FEC).

advice and consent
The power of Congress to confirm or deny presidential appointments to executive and judicial posts and to approve international treaties.

affirmative action
A policy aimed at helping minority groups previously discriminated against to receive equal opportunities. Recent challenges have been based on the idea that affirmative action creates reverse discrimination against majority-group citizens.

Aid to Families with Dependent Children (AFDC)
The main form of individual welfare payments until the mid-1990s, when the program was reformed by the Clinton administration in an effort to promote individual responsibility and reduce government spending on social service programs.

American Bar Association (ABA)
This professional association of attorneys ranks judicial nominees as well qualified, qualified, or not qualified. These rankings are used to assess nominees prior to their Senate confirmation hearings.

amicus curiae brief
Case arguments given by parties who may be affected by the outcome of a case. This "friend of the court" brief is supposed to sway a judge's rulings.

Anti-Federalists
Members of the opposition to the Constitution; their objections to the centralized government authority established by the Constitution led to the creation of the Bill of Rights.

apportionment
The distribution of the number of members of the House of Representatives based on the population of each state.

appropriation
A grant of money by Congress to be used for a specific purpose.

appropriation bill
A bill that provides the legal authority to spend government revenues.

approval rating
A measurement of how popular, or unpopular, a government leader or program is among the public.

balanced budget
When the federal government spends only the amount of money collected from tax revenues. Previous efforts to legislate such spending limits or to create an amendment requiring this have failed.

ballot initiative
A form of direct democracy that allows citizens to propose a law or state constitutional amendment that will be voted on in an election.

beltway ("inside the beltway")
A term referring to the highway loop that surrounds the greater Washington, D.C. area and is perceived by some to represent national leaders' isolation. If leaders concern themselves only with power and are not concerned with the interests of the people, they are said to be thinking "inside the beltway."

bicameral
Consisting of "two chambers."

bilateral agreement
The resulting agreement when two nations create a joint foreign policy.

bill
A proposed law presented to Congress.

bipartisan
Involving members of two parties.

bloc
A voting group that tends to include those with common beliefs and goals.

block grants
Monies given to states for general purposes, such as improving education.

blog
A source of political news and opinion available on the Internet. Blogs tend to be highly partisan and are frequently criticized for misrepresenting facts. This usually independent media source, however, often investigates issues not covered by the mainstream media.

blue states
The label given to states where the Democratic Party expects to win electoral votes.

Boll Weevils
Southern Democratic members of Congress who supported the liberal economic policies of president's F. Roosevelt and Truman but who opposed desegregation and the Civil Rights Movement.

brief
A summary of case arguments to be made that is given to the judges and justices before a hearing.

budget resolution
A congressional resolution binding the legislature to a specific budget for the fiscal year.

bully pulpit
A term that comes from President Theodore Roosevelt's reference to the White House as a "bully pulpit," meaning an effective platform from which to advocate a legislative agenda.

categorical grants
Grants given to states for specific purposes.

caucus
The arena in which some states select delegates as party candidate representatives through meetings where only party members are allowed to participate.

charter school programs

Public schools that receive tax money, but are not subject to some of the rules and regulations that apply to other public schools, in exchange for producing certain results that are established in each school's charter.

checks and balances

The system that allows the three branches of government to "check" the power of the other two and limit that power, if necessary, to maintain a balance.

civil liberties

Constitutionally based individual freedoms.

class action suits

A lawsuit involving numerous defendants affected by the same law or action who are represented as a group.

clear and present danger test

The standard for limiting the rights of free speech if the government deems certain forms of speech as a clear and present danger to the public. These limits were first defined in the case *Schenk v. U.S.*, 1919.

client politics

Policies developed to help specific, smaller groups, where the costs of the actions will be paid by the general public.

closed primary system

A type of primary in which only registered party members may vote.

closed rule

A procedure used by the House of Representatives to prohibit amendments from being added to speed consideration of the bill.

cloture

Procedure in the Senate to end a filibuster through the approval of 60 senators.

coattail effect

The favorable influence that a popular candidate has on the other candidates from his or her party during an election.

Code of Federal Regulations (CFR)

The rules for the various executive departments and agencies.

commercial speech

A form of speech regulated and restricted to uphold "truth in advertising." Deception for the sake of money gains is not legal. The Federal Trade Commission (FTC) is in charge of such regulations.

community standards

Local norms defining acceptable conduct. Sometimes these standards are invoked in legal situations to resolve disputes.

comparable worth

A reform concerning equal pay for employees of different genders.

concurring opinion

A Supreme Court opinion written by one or more justices who agree with the majority opinion but who reached their conclusion for different reasons.

constant campaign

The situation in which presidential candidates and members of the House, who face reelection every other year, continually campaign to maintain their positions.

constituent

A person represented by a government official. Government officials are accountable to their constituents.

containment

The policy of attempting to limit the spread of communism.

continuing resolution

An action allowing the government to continue to be funded temporarily if Congress is unable to complete the new federal budget by the October 1 deadline.

"Contract with America"

A document used during the congressional elections of 1994 by conservatives led by Newt Gingrich. The document defined the basic goals of a Republican majority if, and when, they gained control of the House of Representatives. The contract included a balanced budget amendment, and other conservative reforms.

cooperative federalism

The concept of federal and state governmental units working together equally to make policy.

cost-benefit analysis

Comparing the cost of a policy or project with the potential benefits.

C-SPAN

This cable television network shows the activities and debates of Congress.

de facto segregation

The segregation that takes place without the backing of laws or governmental actions.

deficit

The economic condition created when the federal government spends more than it collects in revenues.

de jure segregation

A form of segregation that occurs through laws.

delegates

Members of a political party selected by party caucuses, primary votes, or other mechanisms. The party nominee is the candidate who receives the majority of the delegates' votes at the convention.

democracy

A form of government where people exercise political power either directly or through elected representatives.

détente

The policy of working with opposing nations in an attempt to avoid open conflicts.

Discharge petition

A process in the House that can allow a bill to be released from committee without committee approval.

discretionary spending

The expenditures that Congress can choose to make.

divided government

When one party controls the one or both chambers of Congress, and the other party controls the presidency.

domino theory

The idea that allowing one country to fall under the influence of communism would topple nearby democracies. This was a leading cause of U.S. involvement in Korea, Cuba, and Vietnam.

dual federalismis

This interpretation of the Constitution has the federal government exercising limited powers, with most power being held by the states.

earmarks

Funds for specific government projects.

Earned Income Tax Credit

A refundable federal income tax credit for low to moderate income working individuals and families.

Elastic Clause

A statement in Article I of the U.S. Constitution giving Congress considerable leeway to expand the scope of its enumerated powers.

Electoral College
The process by which electors are selected by states and are "directed" by the popular vote to select the president.

elitist theory of government
The belief that the government is ruled by those with elite status, usually determined by wealth and education level.

Emily's List
A national organization dedicated to electing pro-choice, Democratic women to office.

eminent domain
The power of the government to seize private property for the public good. Property owner must be given "just compensation" for their loss.

entitlement
A government payment required by law that is given to people who meet specific eligibility requirements. Social Security is an example of an entitlement.

environmental impact statement
A statement showing the possible effects of work by government agencies or private industry receiving government funding on the air, land, or water.

espionage
The practice of using spies or secret agents to obtain government information.

Establishment Clause
The part of the First Amendment section prohibiting establishment of a government religion.

exclusionary rule
The rule that evidence obtained in an illegal manner cannot be used in court against a defendant.

exclusive jurisdiction
The authority of federal courts alone to hear and decide certain types of cases.

exit poll
Polls taken immediately after voters are finished to develop an early prediction of the outcome.

ex post facto
A law barring the government from inflicting punishment for actions that were legal when they occurred.

fast-track authority
Presidents are sometimes given this authority when beginning talks concerning treaties so that the Senate must take them or leave them.

federalism
The distribution of power between the federal government and the 50 states.

Federalist
One who supported a strong federal government.

***Federalist* Number 10**
Madison's essay on "factions" or the influence of political parties and interest groups.

***Federalist* Number 51**
Madison's essay on the balance of powers.

***Federalist* Number 78**
Hamilton's discussion of the federal judiciary and the powers of these courts.

Federalist Papers (The Federalist)
A series of essays by Federalists that explain their support of the Constitution.

Federal Register
The official publication of executive orders and the rules and regulations of various federal agencies. These are codified in the "Code of Federal Regulations" (CFR) volumes.

filibuster
A tactic used in the Senate to delay voting on a bill.

flat tax
A tax rate that would be the same for all income levels.

"fourth branch"
An informal name sometimes given to the U.S. bureaucracy because many of its agencies have the power to make and enforce rules. This label is also sometimes applied to the media to describe its influence.

franking
A traditional privilege allowing members of Congress to send mail to their constituents for free.

Freedom of Information Act, 1966
A law created by Congress that allows for the full or partial disclosure of previously unreleased government documents.

frontloading
The process of scheduling presidential primaries earlier to increase their impact.

Full Faith and Credit Clause
The clause in the Constitution that requires states to honor the documents and acts of other states.

gender gap
A trend in U.S. voting where women have given more support to Democrats and men to Republicans.

General Schedule Rating (GS Rating)
The salaries of members of the civil service are set in levels, ranging from GS1 to GS18.

gerrymandering
The division of voting districts with the goal of giving an advantage to one party.

glass ceiling
The institutional and societal barriers faced by women and minorities in their pursuit of economic advancement.

good faith exception
The doctrine that evidence collected by police can still be used in court, even if it violates the exclusionary rule.

graduated income tax
The progressive ideal that people with higher levels of income should pay higher percentages of tax.

grassroots
Local citizens' political efforts.

Great Compromise (Connecticut Plan, Sherman Plan)
The plan that created the bicameral Congress.

gridlock
A conflict between Congress and the president or within Congress that results in inaction.

government corporations
The U.S. Postal Service is the most famous example of a governmental agency that runs like a business.

hold
A request for a delay in the discussion of a bill in the Senate. If the leadership agrees, this hold can be a permanent block to the bill.

House Un-American Activities Committee
The investigative committee that gained infamy during the late 1940s for its hunts for communists in the United States.

hyper-pluralist theory
The contention that strong groups within societies will weaken the power of governments.

impeach
The act of charging a public official (often the president) with criminal acts or misconduct while in office. The House can impeach, and the Senate must decide whether to remove a person as a result of an impeachment.

inalienable rights
Rights that are not contingent upon laws or customs and that are often referred to as natural rights.

incorporation
The process of applying the Bill of Rights to the states.

incumbent
A person already holding an office, often seeking reelection.

indictment
A grand jury's determination that sufficient evidence has been presented to charge a person with a crime or other offense.

inflation
The overall rising of price levels in the economy. Inflation is caused by excessive consumer demand or increases in the costs of producing goods.

informal amendments
A change to the Constitution without change to the document.

interest group
Organization of people supporting a cause or political interests.

interest payments on the debt
The payments required each budget year for interest owed on the public debt.

Jim Crow Laws
The various laws and practices that supported segregation in the South, after Reconstruction ended.

judicial review
The power of the Supreme Court to evaluate the constitutional status of laws and lower court rulings, established as a result of the case *Marbury v. Madison*, 1803.

jurisdiction
Powers of a court to interpret and apply the law.

lame duck
A person who has been defeated in a recent election or has announced that he or she is retiring and has not yet been replaced. His or her power usually becomes severely limited.

leaks (news leaks)
Intentional slipping of key pieces of information to supportive members of the press.

Lemon Test
A test for the level of financial involvement of government agencies in religious schools based on *Lemon v. Kurtzman*, 1971. The government might assist religious entities if (1) there is a legitimate secular purpose for the help, (2) the help does not have the primary effect of advancing or prohibiting religion, and (3) the help does not create "excessive entanglement" between the government and the religion.

libel
Any malicious or false content written about a person with the intention of causing ridicule and public derision.

limited government
A political system in which the powers of government are limited and individual rights are guaranteed.

linkage institutions
The groups and agencies that connect citizens with the government.

litigating
Presenting a lawsuit in court.

litmus test
Issues such as abortion, gay rights, and gun control that help determine whom voters will give their support to.

lobbyists
Registered professionals who work on behalf of interest groups.

majority opinion
The decision written by the majority of the justices of the Supreme Court describing the reasons for their ruling.

mandatory spending
Budget items that Congress is required to fund.

margin of error
A positive or negative percentage attached to all polls to identify their levels of accuracy. If a candidate's support is 45 percent with a margin of error of 2 percent, then the prediction is that the support is between 43 percent and 47 percent.

markup
The actions made when revising a bill.

means testing
The proof of individual need for government services.

midterm elections
The elections for members of Congress when the presidency is not up for election.

minority opinion
When the one to four justices who did not vote with the majority give their reasons for opposing the majority opinion. The legal community uses minority opinions as a guide to future challenges to that decision.

Miranda warning
An advisement of rights that must take place before police can question a suspect.

muckraking
The practice of journalists exposing the inappropriate actions of public officials, government organizations, or corporations.

narrowcasting
Mail and email campaigning toward certain demographic groups to gain support in Congress for specific issues.

NASCAR dads
Conservative male voters, often from the South, named after the race car organization because of its popularity among that group.

national chairperson
The director of the national party organization. The leader can be critical in the development of party platforms and other party actions.

national committee
The committee group for a political party that focuses on elections, money-raising activities, party building, and the development of party platforms.

naturalization
The process of becoming a citizen for someone born outside of the country.

New Federalism
A conservative movement designed to return more power to the states. The term was coined during the Nixon presidency, and the movement was promoted by the Reagan administration.

New Hampshire primary
Traditionally, the first presidential primary. In 2008, it was held January 8.

New Jersey Plan (Paterson Plan)
The smaller states' counter to the Virginia Plan. It called for a unicameral (one chamber) Congress with equal representation for all states.

Nuclear Test Ban Treaty
A document signed to limit the above-ground testing of nuclear weapons. The United States, the United Kingdom, and the Soviet Union were the main signers.

"off the record"
Information given to journalists with the understanding that the source is not to be attributed. This condition must be stated before a source divulges the information.

omnibus legislation
Legislation that covers many different measures in one bill.

open primary system
A primary that allows a voter to decide on election day which party's candidates to vote for.

open seat
The relatively rare event when no incumbent is running for a congressional seat.

original jurisdiction
A court's authority to hear and decide a case for the first time.

patronage (or the "spoils system")
The act of doling out political positions to supporters of a party and its candidates, often used as incentive to gain that support. This system was so corrupt that it was ended.

penumbra rights
Rights not clearly defined but existing in the "shadow" of formal constitutional rights.

per curium decisions
Supreme Court decisions that are announced without legal explanation or without a majority opinion.

petition for redress
The right to complain to the government without fear of punishment.

platform
A formal statement national parties draw up, outlining how they would address specific issues if voted into office.

Plum Book
The list of federal civil service positions.

pluralism
The guiding principle that access to government should be open and widespread. Interest group proliferation is evidence of this in action.

plurality
Winning an election by finishing first, without having won a majority of votes.

political action committee (PAC)
The political arm of an interest group that raises funds for candidates and campaigns.

poll
A sampling of opinions, political affiliations, or voting patterns used to predict outcomes or trends.

pork barrel
A government project that only benefits a specific locality or a legislator's district and constituents.

poverty line
The level of income, based on the size of a household, that a family must be under to be eligible for many government assistance programs.

press corps/White House press corps
The journalists invited to cover the executive branch.

price controls
Freezing prices of products to keep inflation to a minimum.

probable cause
The requirement that police must have sufficient reason before searching a suspect's personal property or possessions.

pure speech
Spoken communication of ideas and opinions.

quorum
The number of members needed to hold an official meeting or conduct binding votes. The traditional number in the U.S. Congress is half of its members plus one.

realignment
The major regrouping of support within political parties. The New Deal was a source of realignment for Democrat support, and the Reagan election did the same for Republicans.

reapportionment
The law created by Congress in 1929 that banned the addition of new seats to Congress, establising a cap at 435 seats. After the census, seats would be redistributed instead. Faster-growing states would gain seats from declining states or less rapidly growing states.

recess appointments
The ability of the president to fill vacant federal positions, such as federal court judgeships, without senatorial approval if the Senate is in recess. These appointees can serve for almost a year before approval must be given.

reciprocity
The practice of collecting vote promises from other members of Congress in exchange for vote support for their bills and projects.

red states
States where the Republican Party won the electoral votes during a presidential election and those that have a tendency to support conservative candidates.

red tape
The critical label for the paperwork and procedures often required for actions to be completed by government agencies.

republic
A form of democratic government in which supreme power rests with citizens who vote for the government leaders responsible to them.

revolving door
The practice of major lobby groups hiring recently retired members of Congress for high-paying positions. The advantage of having a person who knows all about making policy and has relationships with the key power brokers is seen as a major advantage for those lobby groups.

rider
An amendment to a bill that has nothing to do with the bill's subject.

safe seat
A term used when a representative appears to have an overwhelming level of support in his or her home district. With greater uses of gerrymandering to ensure party domination, safe seats have become more common, thus allowing representatives to be more partisan and less willing to compromise.

safety net
A term that describes the idea of giving those in need some financial assistance.

target polling
Polls that target specific groups that have certain ethnic, economic, or voting characteristics to see how these groups react toward issues or candidates.

search warrant
An element of the Fourth Amendment requiring that citizens be given a court-ordered document telling them what the police are searching for and the area to be searched.

self-incrimination
An element of the Fifth Amendment giving citizens protection from testifying against themselves.

senatorial courtesy

The tradition that the president is expected to get approval for nominees from the senators of the states involved. This term also is used to refer to the tradition that the senior senator of the state of that nominee can block the approval of that person.

seniority system

Those with the longest amount of service in Congress get the committee chairperson positions. Reforms in the seniority system allow some chair positions to be given to those with less seniority, but this is rare.

separations of powers

The division of the government power among legislative, executive, and judicial branches.

school voucher programs

A reform initiative by conservative groups to reallocate tax funds normally given to public school systems to parents in the form of vouchers. This tax voucher allows parents to use the money to send their children to private schools.

shield laws

Laws giving the press protection from revealing confidential sources of information.

slander

Spoken words that are intended to injure a party and are knowingly false.

spin

The manner in which a news story is emphasized or explained, often by administrative representatives, to try to ensure a certain interpretation of information.

split-ticket voting

A trend where voters select candidates of different parties for various offices from the same ballot.

soccer moms

A label given to stay-at-home moms who tend to vote more conservatively.

social contract/social contract theory

An idea from Rousseau and Locke stating that people develop government and agree to follow its rules in exchange for order and protection.

stare decisis

Using Supreme Court decisions to make rulings on similar cases.

straight-ticket voting

When voters choose all of the candidates of the same party.

Strategic Arms Limitations Talks treaties (SALT treaties)

A set of agreements that began the process of reducing the number of missile and nuclear weapons held by the United States and the Soviet Union.

Strategic Defense Initiative (SDI) or "Star Wars weapons"

A proposal of the Reagan administration to place an antimissile weapon system in space.

subsidies

Financial assistance given to businesses aimed at promoting stability.

suffrage

The constitutional term for the right to vote.

summit diplomacy

A series of efforts made in the Cold War period to have the leaders of the major world powers sit down together to work on issues and resolve conflicts.

Superfund

Environmental program to clean up toxic waste sites around the country.

super majority

A conservative proposal that any legislation to increase taxes would need a vote percentage of two-thirds, or 66 percent, to pass, considered a "super" majority.

surplus

The amount of money left over when the government spends less than it collects in taxes.

swing voters

Key voters who tend to be independent, or less loyal to the party system, and have a significant influence on close elections.

symbolic speech

Nonverbal actions that have political meaning, such as flag burning.

term

The amount of time an elected official serves in that position.

think tank

A group whose main purpose is to research, develop, propose, and lobby for types of policies that favor specific political causes.

transfer payment

The economic term used to describe the redistribution of income.

trial balloons

A tactic of giving information about possible policy decisions and checking the reaction of the public and other governmental groups. If the reaction is extremely positive or negative, then further plans can be developed.

unilateral policies

A term defining the efforts of a single country to change policies and align those changes with their relations with other countries.

Virginia Plan (Randolph Plan, Madison Plan)

An outline of a constitution drafted by Madison before the formal meetings began. Governor Randolph presented the plan. It proposed a bicameral legislature (two chambers) but gave populated states the most representation in both houses. The general outline was used by the convention delegates to build the basic framework of the Constitution, thus giving Madison the nickname "Father of the Constitution."

watchdog function

The idea that it is a duty of the media to keep the public informed of political events and to ensure that the rules of government are being followed.

whip

Name of the assistants to the House majority and minority leaders.

whistleblowers

A name given to government employees who reveal waste or fraud within their own agencies. They are sometimes attacked by superiors, the press, and the general public for their actions.

white-collar

A term denoting careers and jobs in business and office management. These positions usually do not involve any manual labor.

workfare

A proposed reform of the welfare system to require recipients to find employment in order to receive governmental assistance.

writ of mandamus

A court order requiring action by government.

writ of habeas corpus

A court order that requires a judge to determine whether there is enough cause to keep a person in jail.

INDEX

NOTES

NOTES

NOTES

DEVELOPMENT OF FEDERAL SYSTEM OF GOVERNMENT

DECLARATION OF INDEPENDENCE

> List of freedoms > Rights of citizens

ARTICLES OF CONFEDERATION

> Initial road map for union > Participation voluntary
> Local and state governments dominant
> No mechanisms for foreign threats
> Disagreements among states
> Financial chaos > No executive branch
> No tax collection > No judiciary

CONSTITUTION

> Designed to correct flaws in Articles of Confederation, including **amendment** procedure
> **Preamble**—sets out six basic goals of new government
> Seven articles
> **Article I** is most detailed. Describes Congress; legislative powers:
  - Commerce Clause - Elastic Clause
> **Article II** lays out executive powers:
  - purposely vague
  - powers were to be checked by Congress
  - Judicial and State powers less detailed
> **Bill of Rights**—first 10 amendments that came out of ratification process; ratified in 1791; 17 additions since
> Constitutional themes include:
  - Representative govt. - Separation of powers
  - Indirect democracy - Checks and balances
  - Federalism - Civil liberties limit govt.

FEDERALIST PAPERS

> Essays explaining U.S. system of government
> Central versus regional power
> Political parties took shape around this issue:
> Alexander Hamilton—Federalist
> Thomas Jefferson—Democratic-Republican (anti-federalist)
> Focus of debate throughout history—still important today

FEDERALISM AND U.S. GOVERNMENT

> Powers not in Constitution are reserved for States
> Concept of **federalism** has changed dramatically since inception. Major points of change:
  - Civil War - Great Depression - World War II
> Shift over time from relative isolation between federal and state authority to domination of federal standards.
> Major shifts in federal power since the Great Depression include creation of:
  - Social Security - Voting Rights Act
  - Medicare/Medicaid - Civil Rights Act

> Separation of powers and **checks and balances** continue to limit government
> **Judicial review** not in Constitution
> **Federal government controls money;** extends its powers

BRANCHES OF GOVERNMENT

LEGISLATIVE BRANCH

> Constitution is mostly about Congress:
  - How each house is structured - How laws are made
  - Role of conference committees
  - Role of presidential veto in lawmaking
> **Lawmaking** is complex—hard to pass new laws or amend existing laws
> Creation of **federal budget**—major duty of Congress
> Party leaders central to control of issues, budgets
> Federal laws in 20th century expanded **influence of federal government**
> **Incumbents** usually win re-election

EXECUTIVE BRANCH

> **Executive authority** expanded throughout history:
  - Expressed/Implied powers - Changes over time
> Presidential image shifts often based on events, media
> Executive branch large and powerful; high-level political executives have significant power
> When president makes unpopular decisions, Americans usually willing to accept them despite backlash
> Citizens expect members of government to behave/use influence appropriately
> History of power shifts between Congress and president

Federal Bureaucracy

> Most dramatic change in structure of government is growth of **bureaucracy**
> Powers similar to constitutional branches of government
> Controlled by interlocking groups that benefit from existence of federal programs
> Agencies have major role in policy-making and governing
> Plays key role in filling public needs
> 15 Cabinet departments work closely with president

JUDICIAL BRANCH

> Structure of federal court system:
  - Circuit courts - Appeals courts - Supreme Court
> **Judicial review** began with *Marbury v. Madison* (1803)
> **14th Amendment** created legal shifts
> **Supreme Court** hears small minority of cases sent to it

BRANCHES OF GOV'T (CONT'D)

- 1960s and '70s—many famous Supreme Court decisions
- Structured methods exist to decide cases, define rights, etc.
- Tension between **judicial activism** and **judicial restraint**

POLITICAL BELIEFS & BEHAVIORS

- Overall—free participation, limited government controls
- Meaning/policy impact of **liberal** versus **conservative** has shifted throughout U.S. history
- Voter turnout low; voters tend toward moderate viewpoint
- Political spectrum relatively **centrist**
- Family and other factors influence political beliefs
- **Voting access** has often been restricted

PUBLIC OPINION/POLLING

- **Public opinion data** has become important to leaders in pursuing agendas
- Most citizens focus on jobs and self-interests
- Polls—statistical samples, carefully crafted questions

POLITICAL PARTIES

- U.S. system dominated by two parties: **Democratic** and **Republican**
- Policy positions of parties have switched from days of Founding Fathers, particularly regarding role of federal government
- Democrats tend to dominate in Northeast and West; Republicans have majorities in South and rural states
- Some typical **voting patterns** are changing
- **Money** for parties is increasing
- Current parties diverging, more **polarized**
- History of third parties and independent voters; role of independents in 2008 election

CAMPAIGNS AND ELECTIONS

- **Elections** are frequent, time consuming, expensive
- Money is part of controversy, but few restrictions made or followed
- **Political Action Committees (PACs), lobbyists,** and **special interests** can be major influencers
- Changes in way presidential candidates are nominated, leading to rise of the **primary system**
- Functioning and history of **Electoral College**
- Since 1896, significant political realignments have occurred

MEDIA AND FREE SPEECH

- **Bias** in media coverage
  - Perceived bias
  - Role of Watergate

POLITICAL BELIEFS (CONT'D)

- Role of government in setting national/news agenda
- Recent legal cases and court rulings have shown limits on freedom of speech for journalists
- Most media outlets owned by big corporations.
- Candidates and parties use media to get ideas out
- **Technological advances** have changed role of media and the way facts are presented/shared:
  - Radio
  - Television
  - Internet

POLICY DEVELOPMENT

FEDERAL BUDGET/ECONOMIC POLICY

- Central task of federal government is to create **budget**
- **Office of Management and Budget** (federal agency) drafts budget, but Congress prepares final version
- Large mandatory spending limits discretionary spending
- Tension exists between open competition and government guidance for economy
- Twentieth century has seen expanded government role
- **Unfunded mandates** are rules Congress makes without allocating money for enforcement, creating conflict between federal and local/state governments

DOMESTIC POLICY

- Public demands large-scale domestic policy to address retirement needs, bank and stock stability, needs of poor
- Federal policies:
  - Assist business and individuals directly
  - Create rules to encourage certain behaviors
  - Help those unable to help themselves
- Many federal priorities set through financial assistance to states and local governments in form of **grants.**
- Federal government often sets policy priorities based on cost-benefit analysis
- Domestic policy changes often brought about by responses to industrial developments, monopolies, abuses, economic crises, and civil rights

FOREIGN POLICY: MILITARY/ECONOMIC

- Vast majority of military conflicts conducted without congressional declaration of war
- President plays role in foreign and military policy; relies on large staff/network
- Various agencies and entities involved in decision making
- Treaties often replaced by executive agreements that don't require Senate approval
- U.S. leader in United Nations/World Trade Organization

OH, WHAT A TANGLED WEB WE WEAVE...

SPINDOC

...is the electrifying new thriller by Steve Perry, a stunning vision of future shock and techno-intrigue. Many readers have already discovered Perry's mastery of alternative futures in the exciting *Matador* series. Now, in this powerful novel of suspense, Steve Perry takes the act of murder one step further...to the high-tech world of tomorrow.

PRAISE FOR STEVE PERRY'S *MATADOR* NOVELS...

"A crackling good story. I enjoyed it immensely!"
—Chris Claremont, author of *FirstFlight*

"Action and adventure flow cleanly from Perry's pen."
—*Pulp and Celluloid*

"Heroic...Perry builds his protagonist into a mythical figure without losing his human dimension. It's refreshing."
—*Newsday*

"Another sci-fi winner...accelerates smoothly at an adventurous clip, bristling with martial arts feats and as many pop-out weapons as a Swiss Army knife!"
—*The Oregonian*

"Effective and logical...recommended highly for all who enjoy intelligent, thoughtful outer-space adventure!"
—*Science Fiction Review*

"Noteworthy!"
—*Fantasy and Science Fiction*

"Perry writes thrilling, action-packed, compelling science fiction. His *Matador* series has become a classic...Pick up one of Perry's novels. You won't be disappointed."
—*VOYA*